SELECTED
SERMONS

Theodore Parker Ferris

SELECTED
SERMONS

TRINITY CHURCH 1976

Frontispiece from a painting by William F. Draper

A Prayer on the Thirtieth Anniversary of Theodore Parker Ferris as Rector of Trinity Church

ALMIGHTY GOD, our heavenly Father, we give thanks for thy Church, not only throughout the world but as it has been gathered in this place. We give thanks for the men you have called to serve here, and in particular for the continual ministry of Theodore Ferris. We thank you for the clarity with which he represents your Gospel, your Good News, not just to us gathered here, but to the far reaches of the earth. We thank you for this loyalty and devotion to us and to You. We thank you for his vision and strength that continually lead us from those dimly lit corners of our own lives to the bright ray of light that only comes with such faithfulness to your Son, Jesus Christ.

We give thanks for this ministry on this anniversary not being proud or boastful, but because such honesty and truth always demand our attention.

As you have called us to follow such examples, O God, may we be true to the new life which demands such sacrifice, even the Cross.

As we humbly thank you for our blessings may we make this place an even greater witness to your truth in the future, sending us from strength to strength in the life of perfect service. In Christ's name we pray. *Amen.*

THOMAS B. KENNEDY

Contents

Acknowledgments

T HIS SELECTION of sermons of The Reverend Theodore Parker Ferris is published by the Wardens and Vestry of Trinity Church, Boston, Massachusetts, where Dr. Ferris was Rector from 1942 to 1972.

The book was undertaken as a project of the Trinity Church family in memory of their beloved Rector. Thus, it is appropriate that many have had a hand in its publication. The project was under the direction of a Committee of the Vestry, of which Peter R. B. Hemery was Chairman. Members of the staff of Trinity Church, close friends of Dr. Ferris, including The Right Reverend Henry Knox Sherrill, and countless parishioners who responded generously to the Vestry's request for suggestions, have participated in the selection of the fifty-two sermons. To all of these the Vestry expresses its warm thanks. And to Bishop Sherrill and The Reverend John Bell, who together prepared the foreword to this volume, a special word of thanks and appreciation is extended.

Our final expression of thanks is to Dr. Ferris himself for the thirty-one years of devoted service he gave to our parish and for the ministry which deeply affected the lives of all who were privileged to know and love him.

THE VESTRY
Trinity Church
Boston, Massachusetts

Foreword

THEODORE PARKER FERRIS died in the Rectory of Trinity Church, Boston, on Sunday, November 26, 1972. He was born in Port Chester, New York, on December 23, 1908, the son of Walter Andrew Ferris and Eva Parker Ferris. His father was District Attorney of Westchester County, New York, for many years. Dr. Ferris went to high school in Port Chester. He was graduated from Harvard in 1929 and from the General Theological Seminary in 1933. From 1933 to 1937 he was Fellow and Tutor at the General Theological Seminary and Assistant to the Rector at Grace Church in New York City.

It was at Grace Church that his career as a preacher began. From the beginning he was the regular preacher at the Sunday evening services. From 1937 to 1942 he was the Rector of Emmanuel Church, Baltimore. Here, week by week, a one-page précis of the previous Sunday's sermon was printed in the *Pelican*, as the service leaflet was called. Almost immediately these précis began to have a wide circulation, far beyond the parish he was serving. In 1942 he became the Rector of Trinity Church in Boston. Now the sermons were printed in full. Within a few years the mailing list included every state in the country and many foreign lands. He was greatly sought after as a preacher by other churches, colleges, and preparatory schools. For many years he was an instructor of homiletics at the Episcopal Theological School.

The sermons at Trinity Church were recorded live at the Sunday services. After they were transcribed, they were edited for printing by Dr. Ferris himself. In addition to the preaching at the weekly services, he conducted some thirty-five Three Hour Services on Good Fridays.

This enormous accumulation formed the basis for his many books and the *Exposition* of *The Acts of the Apostles* in *The Interpreter's Bible*.

Dr. Ferris was a literary artist in the most basic meaning of the words. His experience of the presence of God in everyday life, his sensitivity to the joys and woes of human life, his awareness of the majesty of nature, his appreciation of music, sculpture, and painting, all these lived in his mind and soul. As he perceived great and invisible truths in all these dimensions, being an artist he was empowered to give them outward and visible expression in words, both spoken and written. This was done in the most simple and straightforward vocabulary, with no use of high-flown phrases or unusual words. The result was a clarity of statement and an inevitable progression of thought from opening sentence to ultimate conclusion. In fact how often after hearing or reading him, one said, "Why, I knew that all the time!" Yet the fact is one did *not* know it, but needed his help to give utterance to realities only dimly felt and to become aware of truths never before realized. He had the artist's power to communicate and evoke.

It is not that he thought of himself as an artist, but that he used his artistic talents to reveal truths about God and the human heart. His gifts served the church to illuminate the Divine Presence and Activity in history and to reveal their relevance to society and the individual alike. Above all in his sermons and books the Person of Jesus always was of central concern. His fascination with the historic life of our Lord in time and place was unbounded. His ability to see this life as the very entrance of God himself into our earthly situation revealed to all who heard him and read (and still read) him the awesome mystery of the Word made flesh. The sermons in this book are abiding evidence of Dr. Ferris' power to illuminate and reveal.

Dr. Ferris was also an outstanding pastor and administrator. As the Rector of two great parishes he entered into the lives of many, many people, sharing their problems and joys, illnesses and strengths. His personal knowledge of physical illness and the ways in which the love of God can convert such liabilities into assets was of significant help to those in troubled confusion and even despair. So, also, the administration of churches set in the midst of the complexities of the city was his constant concern. His sense of order and his ability to form a loyal and competent staff were important themes in his ministry. This pastoral insight and administrative talent are further expressions of that art which the sermons express.

During his rectorship Trinity Church continued, deepened, and broadened its involvement in the life of the larger church and the community. He always found skilled people to provide a wide variety of service in the city as well as in the Diocese and worldwide church. His great devotion was to Trinity Church and its people; yet how wide was his span of interest and activity! Conductor of a weekly radio program for many years; delegate to the World Council of Churches; many times a deputy to the General Convention; a member of various diocesan committees and organizations; a prime mover in the construction of the new Sherrill House, a residence and nursing home for older people; both an accomplished pianist and a Trustee of the Boston Symphony Orchestra for many years; all this reveals the breadth of his ministry. Though he be remembered primarily as a preacher, let it not be forgotten that his life was many-faceted and that the pulpit, though the outstanding focus of his great gifts, was not an exclusive concern.

It is, of course, most appropriate that this book be one fitting memorial to Dr. Ferris' ministry. Yet, surely it is only a memorial in the sense that memory is the power to make the past be present and alive. While here and there a paragraph or two may be dated because of some reference to a then-contemporary matter, these words carry an abiding and immediate revelation of the nature and action of God and his involvement in, and concern for, the life of us all. Whether or not heard or read during his life, to read these sermons now is the better to understand and know God, our fellow-man, and ourselves.

JOHN A. BELL
HENRY KNOX SHERRILL

An Invitation to Joy

I SEE PEOPLE almost every day who have no joy in their lives. They may have the substitutes for joy, innumerable amusements, expensive entertainments, transient pleasures and dissipations, but there is no real joy in their lives. They look like the streams in California in the summertime. The river bed is there but there is no water, no life, no movement, nothing but dryness and dust and the rocks which reflect only the heat and none of the sparkling brilliance of the sun. And to make matters worse, they live in an age that has been described as the age of anxiety, the chief symptom of which is a deep-seated melancholy which all the superficial frivolities of life never successfully hide.

For those people I have an invitation. It is an invitation from Jesus Christ to enter into the joy of the Lord, and I am proud to extend that invitation in his name to all of you who have lost the joy of life.

Before some people will be able even to listen to that invitation, let alone accept it, there are two questions which must be dealt with. The first one is, How can there by any joy in a life like mine? One woman says, I have three children; my husband has left me; I have no means of support; one of the children is a chronic invalid; I have lost my job; how can there be any joy in a life like mine? Another person says, I live in a small family in which there is constant friction and irritation. Each one of us rubs the other the wrong way continually. I dread to go home. How can there be any joy in a life like mine? Another person says, I have had five major operations and I am living on borrowed time; I never know whether I will wake up tomorrow morning or not. How can there be any joy in a life like mine? Or an elderly lady says, I have lost the last person in the world who was related to me. I live in one room

1

and there is not one human being in the world who is akin to me. How can there be any joy in a life like mine?

And on top of it all, of course, these joyless people are living in a world which is threatened continually by political and economic storm clouds which are gathering with a deepening and frightening intensity. We all have the feeling that we are sitting on a keg of dynamite, that the world is in a major crisis and that it may be gradually going to pieces. How, then, can there be any real joy in anyone's life in a world like that?

The answer to that question is to be found in the difference between pleasure and joy. Pleasure is by its nature a sensation in response to an external stimulus. Good food, for instance, produces a pleasant sensation on the palate and when you remove the stimulus, the pleasure suddenly ceases. Joy, however, is deeper than that. Joy is more like the undertow of life than the waves that the wind can whip up on the surface. Joy is the total disposition of a man's spirit, the posture and the bearing of his soul. It lies away down below the levels of physical sensation and stimuli and, as the storms and disappointments and discouragements of life pass over it, like the tides in a man's life, those deep undercurrents of joy may still abide.

Paul the Apostle must have had a joy like that. His life was not an easy one. It was full of trials and tribulations, physical sufferings, spiritual disappointments. One day he was up and the next day he was down, and yet in one of his letters he writes these unforgettable words: "We are troubled on every side, yet not distressed; we are perplexed, but not in despair; persecuted, but not forsaken; cast down, but not destroyed." The joy that I am speaking of, therefore, every one of you can have regardless of what is happening in your lives at the present time for it is something that lies way down beneath the level of circumstance in the very disposition of your soul and spirit, not on the surface where the seasonal disturbances are to be found.

The second question is, How can religion be the source of joy? A great many people have the idea that religion is all sackcloth and ashes. Religion at once suggests to them something that is full of gloom and darkness, something that people turn to only when they are in a solemn mood. Religion at once suggests to them the sinfulness of man, the wrath of an angry God. There is no wonder that they have that idea for some people have made religion a matter of darkness and shadow. They have taken one aspect of religion and made it the total picture. They have taken the somber, sober note of man's miserable failures and made that the total interpretation of religion from which every drop of joy has been extracted. There are always people who do that, but that emphasis prevails more at one period than it does in another.

For instance, Mary Ellen Chase has given us the fascinating story of a Maine parson named Jonathan Fisher. He had a long pastorate of almost fifty years in the little town of Blue Hill, Maine, way up near Bar Harbor. When he was twenty-two years old, when most young men are full of the joy of life, he wrote a letter to his brother in which he said, "I have too little sense of the Redeemer's dying love, which ought to melt my soul to tears." And when he got to Blue Hill and ministered to the little flock in the Congregational meetinghouse, the principal themes of his preaching for fifty years were the Divine Election and the total depravity of the human soul, and some of his favorite subjects for sermons were these: he preached against carrying the mails on Sunday, against slavery, against intemperance, against the proposed separation of Maine from Massachusetts, against the inroads of sin in high places! It is not likely that these sermons made the congregation leap for joy. Far more likely is it that they made the people cringe in fear. So there is an excuse, you see, for some people who are surprised when they get an invitation to joy from Jesus; they have been led to think of religion as a matter of sackcloth and ashes from which they want to flee.

But if you look at the New Testament you don't get that picture of religion at all. To be sure, Jesus has been called the Man of Sorrows, and his life does reveal a pattern in which joy is mingled with great sadness. His life is often filled with tears. But you cannot read the story of that life without being conscious of the fact that underneath the sadness there is a deep, abiding, reassuring joy like the joy of a child who is at home in his father's house. Every page of the New Testament either directly or indirectly reflects the radiance of that life. "There is more joy in heaven over one sinner that repenteth than over ninety-nine just persons who need no repentance." When the seventy men whom Jesus had sent out to do his work in the world, to heal the sick and preach the gospel, came back, they came leaping with joy because of the tremendous success they had. The very devils, they said, were subject unto them.

When you get into the book of the Acts of the Apostles and see the beginning of that small Christian fellowship in Jerusalem, it is a story that is pulsating with a kind of enthusiasm and exuberance, and a perpetual gladness surrounds that group from beginning to end. When you turn to Paul, in spite of all the hardships of his life, in spite of the fact that he spent a good deal of his time in prison, the word that recurs more often than almost any other word in the letters of Paul is the word *rejoice*. There is in Christianity an overwhelming joy so that one might say that the theme of the entire New Testament is the sentence "Your sorrow shall be turned into joy." I am prepared to say this, that a person who does not have some measure of that joy in his life does not know the meaning of Christ or of his religion.

Having dealt with those two questions which might hinder a person from accepting this invitation, we are ready to look at the invitation itself. "Enter thou into the joy of the Lord."

The joy of the Lord is, in the first place, the joy that we find in Jesus himself. One of the greatest joys in life is the joy we find in people. There are always a few people in everyone's life in whom there is incomparable joy. Just to be with them is enough to fill life with gladness, the way they look, the way they move, the inflection of their voice, the sort of things they do, the way they think and feel is something that makes them happy through and through. We find that kind of joy in Jesus. Perhaps in an instance like this I may be permitted to speak for myself and you may find in what I say a reflection of what you would like to feel, if you do not already feel it.

I enjoy, for instance, what Jesus said and the way he said it; that cleanness of speech by which he could put into words the most profound truths of life, and that exquisite form in which he expressed the truth. Listen to it. "Blessed are the pure in heart; for they shall see God." I enjoy that. I enjoy what Jesus did and the way he did it; the way he could be waked up during a storm at sea and get up quietly, with perfect composure, rising to an almost titanic height as though in a position to rebuke the sea and to calm the waves, and say, "Be still. Why are you afraid?" I enjoy that magnificent gesture of faith. I enjoy the way he treated people who made mistakes, always with infinite discernment of the inside of a person's life, discriminating between the thing he had done which might be desperately wrong and the living, tender, human, feeble, frail spirit inside him which had led him to do the thing that was wrong. I enjoy the way Jesus dealt with sinners; I enjoy the compassion with which he dealt with the multitude. I enjoy that quiet, yet absolute decisiveness with which he faced the ultimate issue of his life and went straight toward Jerusalem with his face set like a flint. And I can say also that I even enjoy the way he died, so free, so fine, without any quibbling, peevishness, or pettiness, in a kind of superb offering of his life for the life of humanity. I enjoy that. And I, for one, believe that you may admire Jesus, you may even worship him, you may obey him, you may follow him, you may fear him, but if you do not enjoy him, you do not really know him, for the joy of the Lord is, in the first place, the joy that we find in Jesus himself.

But the joy of the Lord goes deeper than that. It is the joy that you find in participating in the life and work of Jesus. There is a greater joy in our ordinary daily lives than the joy we find in people. It is the joy of creative action, of making something, or repairing something, of setting something right, putting somebody on his feet. There is in that activity of creation one of man's most superb enjoyments. And it is that joy that we find in Jesus, the joy of participating in his life and work.

Sometimes I think that a Christian might be simply defined as a person who communicates life, and the life is the life that was incarnate in Jesus. It is the person who has the ability and the will, and I expect that the will is more important than the ability, to transmit that life, to let it flow from him and through him to those who are limp and lagging behind in the race of life. There is not anything more wonderful in the world than to see a person who is continually, in every kind of circumstance, communicating life. Whenever he touches a life, that life becomes more alive. I think that there is no joy in this life greater than that joy of communicating life to those who need it.

5

You do it, of course, very simply by loving people, and by loving them I mean not merely a sentimental attachment for them. I mean the patience which makes it possible for you to listen to them hour after hour. I mean the willingness to give your intelligence and your skill to help them solve some insoluble problem, the willingness to bear in your sympathy the burdens which they are trying bravely to bear. I say this to you in as direct a way as possible: if your life is one of those joyless lives, one way you can find joy is to begin to communicate life, and the best place to start is in your family. Start right now in your own family, perhaps at the most difficult point in the family, the person who never quite understands you, or the friction that is between your mother and some other member of the family, or two brothers who don't get along, or a brother and a grandmother who are always quarreling, or with your relationship to the family as a whole. Start right there. It may be almost a mechanical move at the beginning, but begin by saying to yourself, I love those people and I am going to communicate life to them. You will be surprised how quickly the situation will change, how vastly different the people will be and how much more joy there will be in your own life.

There is, however, a still deeper level than that. It is the joy you find in the whole universe when you see it in the light of Jesus. A man's outlook depends largely on the people in the light of whom he sees life. You know very well what happens to a man when he falls in love. The whole world looks different for he sees it in the light of his beloved. And even if you don't happen to be in that fortunate position at the moment, you know what it is like when out of the disquietude of the world you go into the presence of a great person, perhaps a great artist, perhaps a great husband or wife, or father or mother. When you come out into the world again the whole picture looks different in the light of that one fine person.

That is what happens when a man comes close to Jesus. It is hard to explain, but it certainly is one of the deepest things in a Christian's life. You might put it in words like these, that life looks different in the light of Jesus. Certainly people look different. Instead of being miserable wrecks of humanity that are drifting on their dreary way toward death, they become potential sons of the living God, responding to love, with hidden and undreamed of capacities waiting to be revealed. Suffering looks different. Instead of being a calamity that you shrink from when you contemplate the pain of it and the agony of it, it becomes an opportunity to bear a part of the burdens of the suffering of the world. It becomes your part and your share in the cross of Christ. The good life looks different in the light of Jesus. Instead of being something to strain for, it becomes something which you take up gladly because you are drawn to it by his inimitable, good life. God looks different. Instead of being a kind of cold, abstract principle that you never get anywhere near, God becomes a reality that is warm and intimate and closely tied up with your own life, nearer than breathing, nearer than hands and feet, a power that dwells in you, that knows you, that loves you. Death looks different. Instead of being the end and final curtain of a man's life it becomes the last great adventure on this side of the unknown.

I don't know how to describe it in any other words, but I can promise you who may be sincerely reaching out for this joy which you know you do not have and which you want, that once you begin looking at life in the light of Jesus the whole world, its valleys and its heights, its pains and its joys, will look different.

This, then, is my invitation. It is extended to all of you in the name of Christ. "Enter thou into the joy of the Lord." I bid you as you leave this place leave here behind you your sadness and your grimness, your anxiety and all that makes your life inflexible and mute, and go out with the unconquerable gladness dwelling in you, the gladness that man has when he knows Jesus, when he sees life in the light of Jesus, and when he is willing to go out into the world to serve mankind in the name of Jesus.

Deepen our joy, O God, that we may go out to meet the difficulties and perplexities of life with untroubled spirits and quiet minds; take away our vain pleasures and superficial frivolities, and give us that deep, abiding joy that comes to all those who know thee. Amen.

(This sermon was preached by the Reverend Theodore P. Ferris, Rector, in Trinity Church, Boston, February 13, 1949. It was reprinted and was in the pews on Sunday, November 26, 1972, the day on which he died.)

Depending on God

⁊

O~NE OF THE THINGS~ that religious people talk a lot about is dependence upon God. We sing hymns about it, we imply it in our
prayers, we preach sermons about it constantly. I was speaking about it
myself last February to a group of students in the University of Ohio,
and in the question period one of the students asked me this question,
"Isn't it possible to be too dependent upon God?" That was a question,
of course, that you would expect to come from a student because students are at the point in their lives when they are both discovering and
asserting their independence. And you would also expect it particularly from an American group of students because Americans above
everything else like to be independent. They like to stand on their own
feet and fight their own battles and pay their own way, and if they are
New Englanders, they don't like to be beholden to anybody, human
or divine!

As a matter of fact, Americans in an adult congregation like this, if
they spoke what was really on their minds, might be a little suspicious
of the psalmist who wrote in the 91st Psalm, "I will say of the Lord, He
is my refuge and my fortress: my God; in Him will I trust." They
might say it, or read it in concert as part of the service but make the
mental reservation to themselves that the psalmist might have done better if he had trusted less in God and done something about it himself.
So this question, Isn't it possible to be too dependent upon God? is one
that deserves serious consideration.

I

The answer, of course, is Yes *and* No. If you depend on God, for in-

8

stance, to get you through an examination (if you happen to be a student) the following day and have not opened any of the books through the preceding year that have to do with the subject in hand, you are depending upon God altogether too much. Or, if you depend on God to save a man who has been struck down by a truck and is bleeding to death, and do nothing whatsoever to stop the bleeding, you are depending on Him far too much. If you depend on God to clean up a slum and lift not a finger to change the legislation or condition of sanitation in the slum, then you are depending, of course, too much on God, and I think all of us would agree to that and see that perfectly clearly. But, if *after* and *while* you do everything you can in a situation, you depend on God, you cannot depend upon Him too much because everything you are and everything you have or can ever hope to be comes ultimately from God. From Him your life, your thoughts, your imagination is derived, and upon His energies you are completely and utterly dependent.

It is as if a man were sailing a boat. If he depended upon the wind to such an extent that he didn't do one thing to raise a sail, you would say that he was depending upon the wind too much. But if, after and while he is raising his sail and adjusting it to the wind, he depends on the wind in the sense that he knows he is dependent on it and that, therefore, to the degree to which he understands the ways of the wind and co-operates with its ways will he sail forward, then he cannot depend on the wind too much.

II

This raises another question which the students in this particular instance did not raise, namely, where does this whole idea of depending upon God come from? I think sometimes young people think when they hear us older people talk about it that it is something that we thought up, as it were, something to impose upon them to make life more difficult for them, one more restraint to take the joy out of living. Of course, when you stop to think about it and look into your selves and into what you know about life, you realize at once that it comes right out of our human situation, just as spontaneously as the grass

9

comes out of the earth. No one thought it up; it came up all by itself as soon as man had the wits to take it in.

We are born completely helpless; I think no one would question that. A baby can do nothing for himself; he is dependent entirely upon his parents or upon some older person to take care of his needs. As we grow up we learn in a marvelous way, and very quickly, to do a great many things for ourselves, and if we grow up in America, as I have already intimated, we learn to think right from the beginning that there is virtue in doing for ourselves, and that God helps those who help themselves, all of which is true. And we get to the point, after about fifteen or sixteen years, when we can do so much to help ourselves that we are sometimes misled into believing that we are not dependent upon anything, that we can do everything that is required under any emergency, and we do not need to acknowledge any dependence upon anyone or anything outside ourselves. If a person does come to that point of view, and I think many of us have gone through that stage in varying degrees, we then, of course, have to learn all over again that while we can help ourselves in many of the daily tasks of life, we never become completely independent, and the older we grow, I think, the more we realize how dependent we really are.

A few weeks ago there was an article in one of the New York papers by an anonymous columnist celebrating the anniversary—I forget which one it is, perhaps the twentieth or twenty-fifth—of the first transatlantic broadcast, the first time that someone in Paris or London spoke across the ocean without wires and was heard on this side. In rather an amusing, yet serious article, he reminded us of that line we heard so many times, much to our annoyance, in those days which were before tape-recording, the line, "Due to atmospheric conditions, our commentator from Paris will not be heard at this time." And then he went on and described that as a "graceful submission to larger forces," and I thought to myself, It's good to know that even in this day and age, when we have done so much to conquer even the weather, that there are men writing columns in newspapers who are sensitive to the fact that there are still larger forces in life to which we had best make a graceful submission in order to live life most creatively and fruitfully. The people, when you really think of it, who have made the most of life are the people, aren't they, who have made the most graceful submission to the larger forces which mysteriously press upon them from all sides, which they never completely understand, at least they never presume to understand them, but with which they make some satisfactory, secret terms.

You find this, this dependence upon God, this sense of depending upon the larger forces outside oneself, not only in pious people. That, I think, is worth pointing out to some of the younger people who may think of this as something that is peculiar to people who go to church all the time and are pious in the framework of their thoughts and behavior. That is not true. I turn as far away from the category of the pious as I can think, to D. H. Lawrence. Not T. E. Lawrence of Arabia, but the English novelist, and poet, and essayist, D. H. Lawrence. He certainly was not in any conventional sense of the word pious; he had a great many things that were unpleasant to say about Christianity, and yet in this regard, he was very much aware of the fact that he was dependent upon outside forces. In one place he says, "I often think that one ought to pray before one works and then leave it to the Lord. I always feel as though I stood naked for the fire of Almighty God to go through me."

And if you think of all the creative artists that you have ever known or heard about or read about, and the evidence they have left of the process by which they work, I think you would agree that there is one thing that they have in common, one thing that they all agree to, and that is, that they are in the very nature of their lives agents of communication. They are not imitators of anything, they are channels through which something greater is communicated to the world and, therefore, they are constantly aware of the fact that they are dependent upon this source outside themselves. One of them calls his own mind and imagination a tenement which the best he can do is to keep prepared for a visitation.

No, it is not by any means only the pious who know they are dependent upon God. And another thing we might notice about it is that you don't grow out of this sense of dependence upon God; you grow up into it, and the older you get the more you are aware of it.

One of the most interesting people, to my way of thinking, in American history, one of the most cosmopolitan, sophisticated, urbane, wise people that we have ever produced is Benjamin Franklin. His friends all thought of him as a free-thinker; he belonged to no church and subscribed to no creed, and as far as they knew did not practice any of the ordinary religious techniques of life. When the Convention was meeting to draw up the Constitution of the United States, they were amazed when he stood up in the Convention and made a resolution that each one of its sessions begin with prayer, after which he said, "The longer I live, the more convincing proofs I see of this truth; that God governs in the affairs of men." And I think most of the people here would be willing to agree with him that it is the longer you live that the more convincing proofs become that there are forces outside yourself which in the long run govern the world, and the men who have been prominent in the world's affairs grow up into the realization of this fact.

Lincoln talked more and more about his dependence upon God as he grew into the pressures of the presidency, and it troubles me when I hear people criticize our present President and say that he never used to go to church until he became President; perhaps he didn't. I know nothing about his habits in those days. But it would be the most natural thing in the world for him now to be growing up into this sense of his own inadequacy to cope with the things that he has to cope with, apart from the powers that can come to him from outside. Rather than criticize him, it would be more appropriate to congratulate him, and to sympathize with him in his effort to draw on the power and wisdom of the Almighty.

III

There is still one other question that I should like to raise and that is, What sort of help can we expect from God? Granted that we are aware of our dependence upon Him, and that we express it, and try to put it into action in our lives, what kind of help can we expect as the result? The man who wrote the 91st Psalm, if you remember the psalm, had very definite expectations. He expected immunity against all disaster. He said that the kind of man who puts his trust in God walks through a forest and if there are traps laid there by the hunters, they will not spring if he touches them; and if the plague strikes the village where he lives, it will not strike his house; and if he is out fighting in the wars, men will fall around him by the thousands, but he will not fall. He even goes so far as to say that "There shall no evil happen unto him, neither shall any plague come nigh his dwelling."

I don't know how you feel when you read that, but I have always wondered about it, and I used to be suspicious of it because I have known too many people who trusted in God and who had a wonderful sense of the way that they depended upon God, but whose house has been struck by the plague; people who have fallen in the battle, and who, when they walk through the woods of the world, the traps laid by the hunters have sprung most cruelly upon them! I used to think that this was all the result of the author's imagination and an exaggerated statement brought about by his enthusiasm but, again, as I grow older, I think there is something in it, and it is this. It is true, isn't it, that the man who loses himself in something great and significant has a greater power of resistance than other people. At least, doesn't it seem that way from your observations? You can't make a general principle out of it, but it happens so many times. I was interested in reading the new short life of Gandhi that Vincent Sheean has written, and in the description of those very crucial years that Gandhi spent in South Africa where the whole pattern of his life took shape, he describes one of the plagues that came to that area, a pneumonic plague, which Vincent Sheean says is infinitely more destructive than the bubonic plague. Gandhi, with his characteristic impulse to be of help, gathered around him four other young Indians who nursed African Negroes through the plague for the weeks that it lasted and not one of them caught the deadly disease. He, in his modesty, attributed his immunity to the fact that he didn't eat very much, but I wonder whether there isn't something to be said for the fact that the more you submerge yourself in some great interest the greater your resistance is to the things that are likely to strike you down. The more you trust in God, the more you stave off the inroads of disaster.

The reason for it, I suppose, is that it eliminates fear. A person who

13

really trusts in God is not a fearful person, and fear is something like a lightning rod, it draws disaster to itself but, unlike a lightning rod, it does not drain the disaster off into the harmless soil of the earth, but concentrates it, and magnifies it at the place where it can do the most damage.

There is another kind of help we need even more, and this we can speak of with greater assurance. It is not so much immunity against disaster, which I think we cannot guarantee people, rather I cannot honestly do it, but rather the enlargements of our powers to meet the demands of life when they come. That I can speak of with absolute confidence. Once in a while I use illustrations from my own life; not often because I think it is not in order but, in this case, perhaps it is. When I am beginning to prepare a sermon, I know perfectly well that I have to work on it. If I do nothing about it, nothing will happen. But I also know that all I can do will not make a sermon, that the sermon has to come from beyond, that in the last analysis something has to come through me, and when the times come when everything inside me is tight and nothing will come into any form or shape, and there is nothing there to say and I am in a state of complete frustration, I know always that the reason is that I am pressing too hard, and that once I can find the secret that will relax the strings of my nervous system and let the spirit of God upon which I know I depend function through me, then the chances are that something will begin to happen. Not always, but often. In other words, depending on my own efforts, nothing happens; depending on God, anything may happen.

I know that there are people here in this congregation who could say the same thing about themselves. Placed in other situations in life where they were facing circumstances for which they had not at all adequate resources, they realized that by themselves alone they could not do it, and yet when they recognized that fact and acknowledged that they depended ultimately upon a God who could help them, somehow from somewhere through them came the energies that they themselves could not have dreamed possible.

The psalm, interestingly and I think encouragingly to us, ends on that note, and I end on that note. It begins with man speaking to God in all confidence, "In God is my hope and my strength, my refuge, my fortress, in Him will I trust and He will deliver me from all the disasters of life." But it ends with God speaking, curiously enough in much more modest terms than the man speaks. God says, "He shall call upon me," that is the man, "He shall call upon me, and I will hear him; yea, I am with him in trouble and I will deliver him and bring him to honor." And in my own case, the most that I can hope for, and the best that God can give me when I am in trouble and pray to Him as my fortress is that He will be with me in trouble to enlarge whatever resources I might have so that I can meet that trouble well. It is not always the will of God to get us *out* of trouble; there are times when it is His will to see us *through* trouble.

We know, O God, that everything we are and have, and everything that we can ever hope to be, ultimately comes from thee. Keep alive in us that sense of dependence upon thee, and give us the grace and the wisdom so to cooperate with thy laws that we may work together with thee to do things which by our-selves we could never accomplish at all. Amen.

15

This Is the Day

"This is the day which the Lord hath made; we will rejoice and be glad in it." Psalm 118:24

THE WORLD is filled with people who wake up in the morning dreading the day. They may not actually dread it, but they do not look forward to it, they take no delight in it, and they secretly wish it were over before it has begun. It is needless to say that they begin the day with ten strikes against them, for if they have no enthusiasm for the day and no capacity for delight in the day, the chances are that they will not live that day fully. If you should ask them why it is that they meet a new day with such a negative response, they would probably point to certain external conditions in their lives which they find difficult to face. It might be a thing as unimportant and trivial as the weather which does not happen to please them that day. Or it might be the state of their health, or their nerves. It might be something to do with their job or their family; it might be some obligation from which they shrink or a responsibility which they do not want to undertake. But whatever it is, it would be an external condition in their lives which the day brings them and upon that they place the blame for their negative response. It is the experience of all religious people, I think, and especially Christians, that such a negative response to life does not come really from any external condition which cannot be changed. Rather it comes from an internal religious attitude which can be changed.

It is fair to say, I am sure, that all of us wake up some days dreading the day that is to come, and some of us find that it has become a chronic habit. Therefore, it is part of our religious duty and obligation to see if we can so alter our religious attitude toward life that we will meet the day that God gives us with gladness. One of the psalmists will help us in the affirmation which he makes and which has been repeated so many times through the centuries. "This is the day which the Lord hath made; we will rejoice and be glad in it." We begin with that ancient affirmation and we follow it, as we have followed so many lines from the Old Testament, letting it lead us whithersoever it will into a more positive acceptance of our lives.

I

One of the first things that the psalmist's words suggest is that there is no time like the present. "*This* is the day." Yesterday is gone and it cannot be recalled. Tomorrow is not yet here and it cannot be anticipated, neither can its way toward us be hastened by any day-dreaming that we may indulge in. But today—it is here, with all its infinite possibilities. We can live it, we can explore it, we can enjoy it. And yet scores of people let the day go by strangely unlived as though it were unwanted, like a good book lying unopened on the library table, its riches not even grazed, let alone devoured.

Some people live in the past and they wrap themselves up in memories which they have enjoyed so that the day through which they live never brushes them. We should like to be explicit but it is hard to do so in such a large group of people as this. But take one example. You know the type of person who looks back upon his college days with so much delight and thinks so well of the relationships then that he never seems to make any adult, mature relationships as life goes on from year to year. Other people miss the day by living in the past because they worry about mistakes that they have made and they see the consequences of those mistakes accumulate and pile up until they feel themselves under a mountain of regrets and remorse. No wonder, then, that their day is overshadowed before the dawn has a chance to lighten it, and they dread it. They shrink from it back into the days that are past.

Other people live in the future. Their minds are set on some far distant time that may someday exist. They may see the future with anxiety or they may see it with a certain kind of anticipation, but however they

17

see it, they concentrate so entirely upon it that they miss the day that now passes. For example, one couple is spending so much time preparing for their old age so that they can have the kind of a house they want, in the place where they want to live, that they are now living in a place they loathe, under conditions which they can hardly tolerate, in the hope that in the future their life will be the way they want it to be. Hence they might well take no delight in this day that is now passing. They remind us of the Spanish proverb: The path of presently and the road of tomorrow lead to the castle of nothing at all.

Not so with Jesus, our Lord and Master. Certainly no one ever appreciated the past any more than he did. He drew upon the reserves of the past constantly. He was always turning back to the spiritual insights of his forefathers and drawing from them the strength and inspiration to live his own life. And certainly he did not ignore the future. His prayer was "Thy kingdom come," in the future, in its fullness. But certainly we cannot observe the life of Jesus carefully at all and not recognize the fact that while he appreciated the past and looked to the future, he lived in the present. *This* day was for him the important day. Listen to his prayer, "Give us *this* day our daily bread." Not enough bread for the years to come, but this day our daily bread. And when people were anxious about the future, he pointed out to them in very brief terms, "Sufficient unto the day is the evil thereof." When a man was looking forward to the future and preparing for it with such activity that he had to sacrifice the present, he said, "This night thy soul shall be required of thee." And when his friends were fearful about the future and imagined themselves under persecution and not knowing what to say, he said to them, "Words will be given you when the time comes." And at the very last hour of his life when the penitent thief was beside him on the cross and turned to him with a sign of hope, he said, "Today shalt thou be with me."

We have to do some readjusting of our religious attitudes, and the first thing to do is to say over and over again to ourselves, There is no time like the present. If you have made mistakes, do what you can *today* to correct them. If you are not prepared for the future, do what you reasonably can *today* to make those preparations and then let the past go

18

and let the future take care of itself and live today. Enjoy it, that is what God wants you to do, not endure it, enjoy it, as a gift filled with manifold blessings. That is the first thing.

II

Another thing that these words suggest, and this perhaps you will not be quite so ready to receive, is that there is no such thing as good days and bad days, for they are all God's days. "This is the day which *the Lord* hath made." You did not make it. This is not your day even though sometimes you presume to think of it in such terms. It is His day. He made it and filled it with all its divine possibilities. And if that is true, it is true as a corollary that there is no such thing as good days and bad days.

Perhaps we ought to explain a little more carefully what we mean by that for some of you are saying, Oh, well, he doesn't know me! I have my good days and my bad days. There are days when I feel well and days when I feel like a limp rag. There are days when I am full of energy and days when I have none, days when things go well and days when nothing goes well, days when I seem to live fully and days when I feel like a lake that has been drained dry. We all know that, and yet in a deeper sense we can say that all our days are good days because they are God's days. Remember that God makes the fog as well as the sunshine. I was disciplined myself once on a summer vacation when I was in more or less of a complaining mood because of the persistent fog. One person, more alert to the possibilities of life came along, and before I had a chance, I am glad to say, to display my complaint, he said, "I love the fog." That is a parable of an attitude toward life. God makes the fog and he makes the sunshine. Is it not true that God works in shadow as well as in light? God is in the darkness as well as in the blazing of the sunlight. Is it not true that God uses the sorrows of life as well as the joys? While we are not saying that everything that comes to us in life comes directly from God—it does not always; it comes sometimes from our stupidity and folly and the sin of our fellowmen—nevertheless, the day comes from God and in that sense it is good, and in that sense every-

19

thing that happens to us in the day has its divine possibilities because God is in it.

One of the great literary figures whom I think has been neglected in our time is Nathaniel Hawthorne. (Parenthetically, I recommend that you reread him. He is way ahead of most of the nineteenth century literary people in his understanding of life.) In middle life, Hawthorne took his family back to Salem where he had spent some of the darkest years of his early life. He went there because he had been given a job in the customs house and he had to have a job because he could not earn enough money by writing. The author of the biography says this: "Hawthorne was going back to the town he had never thought he liked. He was to be there five years, and they were not to be happy years. But for all their grimness they were to be his great years." They were the years of the *Scarlet Letter* in which Hawthorne reached one of the peaks of American creative, artistic achievement. They were his grimmest years and his greatest years. It was as though the author were trying to say that all our days are from God. They are all God's days and even in their grimness, there is the possibility that the pattern may be worked out gradually, provided the individual responds to it and meets it with enthusiasm. There are people in life who cultivate consciously an attitude which habitually accepts whatever comes as having divine possibilities. One of the greatest of these and one to whom I turn over and over again is the Dutch painter Van Gogh. He is as great in his letters as he is in his paintings, and in one of his letters, he wrote this, which ought to humiliate some of us. "How beautiful it is outside when everything is wet from the rain! I ought not to let a single shower pass." The eagerness with which he went out to meet everything that God's day brought him, not merely the sunlight which he adored as perhaps no man ever did, and put on canvas certainly as no one ever did, but the showers! "I ought not to let a single shower pass!" He found in the showers the same vitality, the same wonder and the same potential beauty. Dread not the day for it is indeed God's day, and if as you meet it you see dark shadows casting themselves across the day, say to yourself, The shadows, too, are in God's hands and even though this day be a grim one, I am approaching it as one who expects the possibility, at least, that it may be a great one because it is God's day, not my day.

This sentence from the psalmist leads us to one final thought, that a man can be better than he feels. Notice the English grammar of the last line. "This is the day which the Lord hath made. We *will* rejoice and be glad in it." I am afraid some young people in the congregation do not appreciate the meaning of that because grammar is not often stressed now in school and they do not know what the difference is between *will* and *shall*. If the sentence read, We *shall* be glad in it, it would mean that just as a matter of course we shall be glad. But we *will* be glad means that we are going to be glad, we are determined to rejoice. We may not feel like it at all but we are going to do it because we have a share in the control of our emotions and we are not entirely the victim of the way we feel at the moment.

I do not presume to speak as anyone trained in psychology and I am speaking only out of my own personal experience. I know enough, and you certainly know enough also, to know that a man, in his interior makeup, is something like a house that has an attic and a cellar. In the attic of a man are his thoughts, his intentions, his conscious activities, and in the cellar of his nature are what the psychologists call the autonomic nerves, the nerves over which a man has no control, like the nerve in his eye that twitches and which he cannot stop by telling it to stop. Down there are the instinctive emotions, the fears which rise up when you least expect them and over which you have no apparent control. A great many people are tempted to believe these days that they are the victim of what is down in the cellar of their lives. It is true, I think, to the experience of a great many people that while there are things down in those lower levels over which we have not the same kind of control that we have over our hands, nevertheless, the attic can send messages down to the cellar and the cellar heeds the messages. Just as a man can send messages to his muscles and make them relax by telling them to relax, a man can send messages to his emotions and feelings and change them. Therefore, when you wake up in the morning and say to yourself, Well, I certainly don't feel good today; I wish I could stay in bed all day, leave the curtains down, the blinds shut, let the day pass, I don't want to have anything to do with it, that is the time for you to begin to send messages from the attic down to the cellar. You can do it by making simple affirmations which at first may come only from the lips, but if you try, you will be surprised to find how they do get down there and do change your feelings. For instance, you can get up in the morning and say to yourself, This is the day which the Lord hath made; I will rejoice and be glad in it, regardless. You can find other affirmations which give the same implication in their message to your emotions. One of the ones that I say over and over again is, "O be joyful in the Lord all ye lands. Serve the Lord with gladness and come before his presence with a song." Sometimes it will be a simple verse or a hymn that may not represent the highest of your intellectual achievements but which does something to change the emotional tides of your day.

> Glad that I live am I,
> That the sky is blue;
> Glad for the country lanes
> And the fall of dew.
>
> After the sun the rain.
> After the rain the sun;
> This is the way of life,
> Till the work be done.
>
> All that we need to do,
> Be we low or high,
> Is to see that we grow
> Nearer the sky.

As you make these affirmations and these suggestions which go out as messages to your feelings, you realize that you are no longer the victim of your feelings and you are better than you feel. Take, then, these suggestions as they apply to your own lives and begin experimentally tomorrow morning to dread not the day. It is God's day and miraculous to say, you can be better than you feel.

THIS IS THE DAY

O God, we thank thee for this day. Open our eyes that we may let none of its wonders pass unseen. Give us a courageous positive interest in everything that happens around us. Help us to lay hold upon every opportunity to be of use this day, and then take from our hearts all vain regrets and all empty dreams of the future that we may follow him who went about day by day doing the good of that day, Jesus Christ, our Lord. Amen.

Love in Power

As you go in the door on the north side of St. Paul's Cathedral in London, you are likely to see a brief inscription—four Latin words: *Si monumentum requiris, circumspice.* Those four words, translated into ten English words, mean, "If you would see the man's monument, look around you." The man was Sir Christopher Wren, and the inscription was written by his son.

Christopher Wren was that extraordinary astronomer who early in life became an architect, and when a large part of the City of London, including St. Paul's Cathedral, was destroyed by the fire of 1666, he was engaged to design and build a new cathedral. The work began in 1675 and was finished in 1716, and during those years he designed and built fifty-two other churches in London, in addition to Marlborough House and many other secular buildings! You can see what his son meant by the inscription, for even today, if you go to London, almost anywhere you look you will see Christopher Wren.

Paraphrasing that inscription, we might say today, *If you would see Christ, look around you.* Look at the building, surely, because there are many things in it that suggest him and bring him close to you. But look far beyond the building; look through the building. Look at the people. And not only at the people in the building. Look at the healers, the people who are resisting the plague, the plague of disease, of ignorance, of violence, of mistrust and sin. Look at the reconcilers, the people who are giving their lives to mend, to put together again, the broken pieces of human life. Look at the burden-bearers, who carry their load without a word of complaint, and even with joy on their faces. See the undefeated, and the undiminished greatness of the failures. Also, see the sufferers and the oppressed; the neglected and the forgotten; the people you don't feel at ease with, that you don't like, that you don't understand.

If you are looking for Christ, look around you, look at the people; look in their eyes.

Today we are reminded by the church that there is more to it than that. That's one side of the story, to be sure, and an essential side, the side that has been receiving most attention during the last ten years. But there is another side to the story and it, too, is essential.

The church is saying to us today, If you would see Christ, look not only around you, but look up; look up in the sky. And where is the sky? The sky is everywhere. He is with God; and who is God? God is the unchangeable background of life without whom there would be no life. Before Him things come and go, people, men and women; nations and empires rise and fall. But He does not come and go; He remains.

The church is saying to us in this season of the Ascension, Christ is the unchanging love of God which neither time nor tide can take away. That is what the church is reminding us of on Ascension Day. To put it in another way, it is saying, The story of Jesus did not begin in Bethlehem, and it did not end on Calvary. It began and ended in the mind of God. To say this, it uses picture language. It says that "he was conceived by the Holy Ghost, born of the Virgin Mary." That's the way it began. And when it comes to the end, it says that "he ascended into heaven and sitteth on the right hand of God the Father Almighty."

That is picture language. God does not have a right hand or a left hand, and there is no chair beside him upon which Jesus is sitting through all eternity. This is a perfect example of picture language.

The church is saying to us, If you want to see Jesus, look around you, but also look up above you, and the church says it because it believes that the love that was once alive in Jesus, once so alive and alert, so active, so sensitive to all the innuendoes of evil and of goodness, that love is alive now. And not only alive, but in power; not like a king in exile, but like a king in power on his throne. That is what the church is saying to us: Love is in power.

You listen to it politely. You would like to believe it, you are inclined to believe it because so many of you were brought up to believe it, but many of you are wondering: Can it be true? For instance, you look around you. You see a person, a good person, completely incapable of understanding another person. It may be a parent who has absolutely no idea of what his child is all about. Or, it may be a child, not an infant, but a child of eighteen, nineteen, or twenty, who has no understanding, not the slightest comprehension of the anxieties of his parents, their intentions, why they are the way they are, and what makes them think and say the things they do. There is no understanding of him in them, as there is none of them in him.

It may be a student who with all the impatient idealism of a young person has no understanding of a college president or his administration; or it may be the college president and the administration that is incapable of understanding what it is that makes the young people do the things they do and what the legitimate concerns on their minds and in their hearts may be.

Or, it may be a black man who has no understanding of what the white man's problem is now, how he is trying to correct the mistakes of the past, but is moving slowly. Or, it may be a white man who has absolutely no understanding of what it is that is going on in the black man and what it is that makes him feel the way he does. So each withdraws from the other. They never come together. Fright is mixed with scorn. They try to love in many cases, they really try. They try to care; but they do not know, and when you do not know and are not known or understood, you cannot love.

You see this kind of thing every day and you say, If love is in power (which is what the church is saying today), if love is really in power, why doesn't it smash these infernal barriers that keep people apart when they should be together? By way of an answer—love doesn't smash, love doesn't shatter. It draws, but it never drives. Love in power is the love that knows how to wait. Love in power is the love that lets the loved one go his own "unremembering way," sometimes to his own destruction, if it need be.

Or, you look around and you see the old order changing, changing more rapidly than at any other time in our existence. The city looks different, it is different; the people look different, and many of them are different, quite different—especially, in this part of the city. The shops are different; prices are higher, service is almost an unknown quantity. The balance of power in the world is shifting rapidly; we are not quite sure where or how, from West to East, or from white to black. The standards of behavior are different; many of the guidelines have disappeared. Old manners have been dropped and new ones are being born. Then you come to church and you find that the church is different!

How you feel about this kind of change depends partly on how old you are. Not altogether, because there are some people older than I am who are completely flexible and can meet change; they may not like it, but they meet it with grace and confidence better than some of the young do. And there are young people who blunder through changes like this, and miss their opportunity. So it is only partly a matter of age. It depends partly on how much you have invested in the old order; how much it means to you; how much this building means to you; how much this way of worship means to you; how much this order of society means to you. And it also depends upon how much you are involved in the new order.

But however you feel, the change that we are now going through, whether you are old or young, whether you like it or whether you don't, rips and tears the fabric of life, and it isn't easy for anyone.

Once again you wonder how love can be in power; how we can say that the love that was in Christ is in power, "on the throne," if this kind of ripping, tearing, agonizing change is allowed to take place.

Again, by the way of beginning an answer—love in power is love that knows "where true joys are to be found." It knows that they are never to be found in the vessels that contain life, no matter how important those vessels may be, but always in the life itself, and sometimes the vessels have to go. It knows that the true joys are never in the things we possess. I love many of the things I possess. I have things that mean a great deal to me and that I should hate to lose by fire or theft, but I must be reminded over and over again that the real life that I am talking about and that I am supposed to be the servant of is not in the things we

27

possess but in the dreams, ideas, principles and spirit that possess us.

Two specific things that happened to me have helped me see Christ above us, Love in Power. I am not now talking about the story of the Ascension in the New Testament, because I do not think that the church is primarily concerned about the movement of Jesus from one place to another. That again is picture language. It is concerned with the expansion of man's understanding of the love of God; with his seeing and knowing that it reaches to the depths of the sea and to the highest point of heaven. That's what it is about, and it is sometimes very hard to feel it. Two things have happened to me and I am going to tell you about them because they will indicate to you at least how I as a person understand these things and how things like these help me. They might not help you at all.

On one of the strange holidays that we had in April that was moved to some other day so that I didn't realize that it was a holiday, I went into a drugstore that I didn't know and I saw some paperback books. Right away I saw one that had the name of a painter on the cover, a famous painter, and I wanted to know more about him. I picked it up, I saw that it cost only seventy-five cents, and that in the middle of it were fifty good reproductions. I bought it. Then I opened it and read quickly the first paragraph. I am going to read the paragraph to you now, but I shall leave out one or two key words because I would like to see as I read it if you have any idea who the painter was, what the time was, and if it makes the same impression on you that it did upon me. This is what the author wrote:

> In the towns and cities a new class was taking shape, while the traditional religious culture was undergoing a transformation in response to new needs. Theological dogmatism had to face continuous attack from the movements of renovation and from society's profound, though not yet fully conscious, search for new values, worldly as well as religious. Heresies and outbreaks of rebellion were springing up everywhere and the traditional authorities were unable to find a point of contact between the demands of the old order and the new popular longings. Then,

suddenly appeared a man who understood the ardor and the truth of the heresies while retaining his respect for authority. Faith was renewed around him. . . . Christ's message of love was steeped in reality and the problems arising from ascetic theories were related to everyday life. That message of love was given new meaning for the citizens of the new industrious bourgeois society.

Now, the description of the situation might almost be a description of the situation today. Actually, the century was the thirteenth, the man was St. Francis of Assisi, and the painter was Giotto. It is a description of the transition from the other-world of the Middle Ages to the secular world of the Renaissance, and St. Francis was the man who was able to see the validity in the claims of the secular world and Giotto was the painter who caught the message and put it on the walls of the great church in Assisi.

You may not see that this has anything to do with the Ascension at all, but somehow it made me realize that we were not quite so contemporary, not quite so time-bound, as we thought, and that whatever happens to save us, it will be the same love coming down, as it were; not in another Francis, but in someone else, in a different way. It will be the love of Jesus made relevant to the needs of a new society. It will be the Love in Power acting to seek and to save.

The other thing that happened to me is quite different and much more personal. On Friday morning a letter came from France. I recognized the handwriting, and when I opened it, inside was a postcard. It was an aerial view of the mountains in southern France, in the foothills of the Pyrenees. On the back of it was this message: "My dear friend, From this place of silence and peace (here are the Benedictine monasteries) my thoughts go to you with affection and gratefulness. It is hard in this atmosphere to believe our poor world is so troubled, but one feels strongly that some essential values cannot be defeated. And one is guided by an inner certitude and love. Believe me to be with respect and faithfulness, Your Nadia B."

Nadia Boulanger has been described over and over again as the greatest musical mind in the world. She will be eighty-two in September. This message from her seemed to me to come down, if you know what I mean. It came out of her serenity in the midst of all the turmoil of which she is acutely aware, and spoke to me of things that are above us, things that the Ascension tries to tell us and which we find it difficult sometimes to understand. It lifted my mind above the horizon of the twentieth century to the things that are timeless.

One final word. I remember the Prophet of the Exile. He was one of the most shrewd observers of the current scene anywhere around. But at one point he changed his tune and said, "Lift up your eyes and see." See what? See the stars. "Who created them? He who brings out their host by number, calling them all by name; by the greatness of his might, and because he is strong in power, not one is missing."

I should like to say to you quietly, Lift up your eyes and see. Who recreated you? He who by his love and care enables you to do and to face anything and everything that may befall you. Lift up your eyes and see love in power.

In the midst of confusion, O God, grant that we may go steadily on our way, neither censuring our journey by the weather we meet, nor turning aside for anything that befalls us, knowing that the love that was once incarnate in Jesus is now in power forever. Amen.

Our Text Just Now

&

A MAN NAMED JOSHUA SPEED was one of Abraham Lincoln's closest friends. They met on a day in 1837 when the young, penniless lawyer arrived in Springfield, Illinois, to practice law. Mr. Speed had a store and Lincoln went there to see if he could buy a bed. The available bed cost more than he could afford to pay for it. He said that if Mr. Speed would sell it to him on credit until Christmas, and if his experiment there as a lawyer were a success, he would pay him then. If he failed, he continued, he would probably never pay him at all.

Something about the melancholy face of Mr. Lincoln impressed Joshua Speed. He offered to share his own large double room with the young lawyer. Lincoln asked where the room was. It was upstairs. He put his saddlebags over his shoulders and went upstairs. In a few minutes he came down with a smile on his face and said, "Well, Speed, I've moved."

They continued to share the same room for four years, and their friendship continued until Lincoln died. One of the things that drew them together was that they both suffered from a kind of nervous debility, and by helping Speed through one of his bad spells, Lincoln unwittingly began to get himself out of the doldrums. In one of the letters that Lincoln wrote to Speed, he says this: "Whatever he designs he will do for me yet. 'Stand still and see the salvation of the Lord,' is my text just now." He who designs, of course, is God; the words *me* and *still* are underlined. The letter was not written from the White House when Mr. Lincoln was grief-stricken by the death of his son, or pacing the floor through the long dark hours of the night when the Civil War was at its most crucial and agonizing point. The letter was written from his room in Springfield where he was agonizing over his broken engagement to Mary Todd. He was thirty-two. The engagement had been broken on January 1, 1841, and shortly after that Speed moved back to his hometown in Louisville, Kentucky. That is when the correspondence begins.

After the breaking of the engagement, whether caused by it or occasioned by it—and there is a difference—a long spell of what was then called *hypochondria*, what we would call now *melancholia* or *depression* or *neurasthenia*, set in. Lincoln moved through dark days of low spirits and indecision. When he turned to the Bible he was drawn to the text that told him to calm down, to do nothing at the present time while he was in a state of turbulent anxiety and indecision, to give the hand of the Lord a chance to work behind the scenes. "Stand still, and see the salvation of the Lord." That was his text then and many times thereafter.

About ten months later he and Mary Todd were married. The salvation promised by the text was not always apparent in the years ahead. The marriage had its sunny side, there is no doubt about that; but it also had its dark side. William Wolf, professor of theology at the Episcopal Theological School, in his book *The Religion of Abraham Lincoln*, has this to say: "Mary had a towering rage, was unduly concerned over little things, and seemed unable to achieve a satisfactory relationship with the children." There were times when Mr. Lincoln would simply leave the house when that towering rage descended upon him. This looks to us more like damnation than salvation. Look a little deeper. Mr. Wolf goes on to say, "Lincoln learned forbearance and forgiveness, not as doctrines but in practice." He worked out his salvation on the anvil of the Lord. He hammered out a character in which there was no room for malice.

II

Before we ask whether this is the text for us now, we must look at the text itself. You will find it in Exodus, the second book of the Old Testament; and Exodus is a story of salvation, the salvation of a people. The Hebrews were saved from slavery in Egypt by what seemed to them a miraculous escape from the country of their masters. One man dominates the scene, Moses; massive, titanic in stature and in character, and how amazing it is and how worth stopping to think it is, that a man who lived twelve or thirteen hundred years ago can stand before a congregation now with so much vividness and power.

He had the two essential requirements of every great leader. First, he was committed to his course, and never had the slightest doubt that he was right. Second, he was able to keep the people with him. He never found himself in the position of the general who got so far ahead of his troops that when he met the enemy he looked around and there was no one to be seen! Like all leaders, Moses had his difficulties. The enemy was stubborn. Pharaoh, the King of Egypt, was not about to let his best slave labor get away, and it was a long time before they were able to make the break. After many false moves, Moses was able to get his people out of Pharaoh's immediate grasp. Also, the people were not always easy to deal with. When the going was hard they grumbled, and they never grumbled more loudly than when they were at the Red Sea.

As a human being, you can see why; I think I can. There ahead of them was the sea, an unknown quantity, an unseen shore they knew not where. They didn't know what was on the other side. And behind them were the enemy's armies pursuing them. They were trapped between the sea and the slave masters; and they turned against Moses. They said, Why didn't you leave us in Egypt? As slaves there we were better off than we are as free men in this terrible place. They grumbled, and it must have been hard for Moses. Moses did not scold them, and apparently from the records, he did not lose his temper. He stood before the people quite calmly and said, "Fear ye not, stand still, and see the salvation of the Lord" (Exodus 14:13). As we might say in our current, vernacular English, "Cool it!" Apparently, they did just that, and the record goes on to say that the "Lord caused the sea to go back by a strong east wind all that night, and made the sea dry land. And the people of Israel passed through the sea as on dry ground."

The cynic might easily say, A lucky break for Moses! What if the wind hadn't come up and the sea hadn't been driven back. Nature is not always on the side of the righteous, we know that. A more temperate man might say, Without Moses there would have been no exodus; without God there would have been no Moses; without his vision of God he would have made no attempt to set his people free. That same temperate man, given the insight and perception, might go on to say, Great things come to pass when men join forces with the stars. History is the joint effort of man and God. When man acts properly in response to what God does, a noble page is written in the history of man. That is the text; the text for the Hebrews then; the text for Lincoln later on.

III

The question is, Is this our text now? Can we afford at a time like this to stand still, to keep still, to say nothing, do nothing? Must we not say something, do something, start something? Is this the text for us now?

I say it is. Not for all of us, and not for us all the time. There are many people who are saying and doing many things, many of them right things. Protests and pronouncements are being turned out by every dedicated group I know. I have one from the students and faculty of the Episcopal Theological School, and one from the Boston University School of Theology, and others from students of other schools. There is a time and place for these; and there is a time for you and for me to add our names to this kind of statement if we so desire. But I say that this is the text for us *now*, here in this particular place, at this particular moment. The old strategy of Moses is now for us—here, where we are, engaged in the worship of God. Stand still and see. See what?

See first, as clearly as you can, the dark, ominous facts in the foreground. The country is divided by a difference of opinion about a particular war. Good people are on both sides for reasons that seem good to them. I have no way of knowing what the division is, how many are on one side or the other. Most of the people I know are on the same side that I am on, but that does not concern me at the moment. What does concern me is that from a point of view of pure strategy no war can be won by a divided nation. Nothing of any account can be done by a divided people. Nothing can be done by an individual who is of a

34

double mind. There will always be objectors to everything that the country attempts, but nothing great will ever be done when the country is split down the middle. "If a house be divided against itself, that house cannot stand." Whichever side we are on we see that fact clearly.

We also see that the country is disturbed, deeply disturbed. Young and old are disenchanted. They are losing confidence in the powers that be, not only in the government but in every institution that exists. They have been disappointed too many times, turned away too many times, unheard too many times. And looking at the facts in the foreground from this place of quiet we can see that the war in Asia is breeding a more serious war in America.

If we look, we can also see some of the dangers ahead. One is the danger of overreacting. People on both sides have already been guilty of it. Leaders under attack have said unwise things and called people names. People who feel powerless and frustrated have thrown rocks. Both were wrong. Calling names and throwing rocks accomplishes nothing and destroys much. And yet here, in this moment of detachment, most of us can see how easy it is for any person who is in a position of authority to be so worn and wearied by the burdens, and so irritated by the opposition that he might well say things which he wished he hadn't said. And also, we can see how the young can feel so frustrated and so left out of the picture of things that they too will do things in a moment of anger and impatience that they may wish later on they had never done.

We also see the danger of a cure that is worse than the disease. Schools and universities are closed, and I assume that in some instances their closing is a necessity for the safety of individuals. But certainly none of us can fail to see that never did the schools need to be open more than now; never was there greater need for places where young people can learn the lessons of the past, train themselves in the disciplines of thought and action, places where they can be heard, places where they can investigate what has happened and predict what may happen in the future without the intrusion of outside affairs. The police and the National Guard are on call. They should be on call to protect the people, but they should not be needed to keep order in a civilized community.

These are dangers of a cure that may be far worse than the disease.

Again, to go back to Mr. Lincoln, a guide for every American at any time, he said on one occasion, "By general law, a limb must be amputated to save a life, but a life is never wisely given to save a limb." You don't give away the institutions of learning to save a political situation if you can possibly help it.

We can also see some of the possibilities for good, the possibility of change from within. The moderate students are working for this. You see them on the sidewalks offering you statements of their position and suggested letters to write to your representatives. They are intelligent; they are courteous; they are dedicated. You hear them on television where they are presenting their cause to the leaders of the nation. And there are leaders who are listening, listening more than they have in the past. I realize that many will say that if something extreme hadn't been done perhaps they would still be deaf. Once in a while, it is inevitable that something extraordinary must be done, something that shocks and shatters, something that goes against every fiber of our being, in order to get the attention of people. In the long run, however, it is not the bolt of lightning that makes things grow; it is the spring rains, the fresh winds, and the shining sun.

We see these things in the foreground, these facts, these dangers, these possibilities, and we see them against the background of history. Sometimes we get so preoccupied with what is going on now that we miss the perspective of time. Barbara Ward is one of the most articulate Christians in the modern world. She once wrote this: "Mankind as a going concern has been operating now for about a hundred thousand years. Our experiments in advanced civilization, which go back no more than four or five thousand years, are relatively brief." See that perspective of history. Five thousand years of civilization; ninety-five thousand years of human life before civilization began! As a nation we have existed slightly less than two hundred years, and as a world power on the political front line of action, twenty-five years. It is little wonder that we are groping our way, making mistakes, sometimes succeeding, to find out how to use that power and how to behave on the front line of political history. Up to this point in time, nations have been predatory, the strong preying on the weak. Whether we can change this pattern of history remains to be seen.

We see the facts before us against this background of history, and against the greater background of God. "Before the mountains were brought forth, or ever the earth and the world were made, thou art God from everlasting world without end." "All nations before him are as nothing; behold the nations are as a drop in a bucket." That doesn't relieve anyone from his responsibility to take action as a citizen, but it does give him the broad background of eternity against which he takes that action and it saves him from acting in a fit of hot temper, or the depths of despair, doing something which he will wish for the rest of his life that he had never done, or saying something he wished he had never said.

And we see Jesus on this Sunday after his ascension. In a letter circulated among the early Christians, written by a man whose name we will never know, something like this comes at the very beginning of the letter. We see not yet all things put under man. In other words we see man the victim of war, injustice, death, disease, all these things we see. "*But*," he writes, "we see Jesus, crowned with glory and honor; it became him to make the captain of our salvation perfect through suffering" (Hebrews 2:9, 10). Will there ever be any salvation in any society, no matter how much improved it is upon our own, without suffering?

An epilogue. In the *Boston Herald*, in the summer of 1954, there was a series of articles on What To Do If You Get Lost in the Woods. In one of them this paragraph occurs, and I hope that you will see it in the light of what I have been saying. "Your toughest job would be to persuade yourself that you really are lost and then the whole thing is out of your hands, except for minor housekeeping functions. Forces you wouldn't be aware of would be set in motion. Your job is to make yourself as available as a politician in an election year. You'd look for a clearing where you would be the most visible from the ground or the air."

That is what I hope you will do now. Look for a clearing where you will be visible from the ground or the air, and make yourself available as an instrument of him whose design He will carry out yet. Do not hesitate from time to time to stand still, and see the salvation of the Lord, the forces already set in motion.

Let each one of us, privately and in silence, offer his own prayer for guidance, direction, support, and for the guidance of those upon whose leadership we depend.

We ask everything that we have in our hearts and minds, in the name and in the spirit of him who was made perfect through suffering. Amen.

The Man Called Jesus

T HE SERMON TODAY begins with a simple statement of fact, and this is the fact: The Christian religion begins, continues, and ends in a Man called Jesus. To my way of thinking it is an undeniable fact; it is also a fact that is often forgotten. Therefore, in the first part of this sermon I shall dwell on the fact itself, first by looking at the church at the very beginning of its life, and then twelve hundred years later.

It all began when a small group of young men were drawn to a man about their own age about whom they knew virtually nothing. He asked them to follow him. He didn't ask them to believe in him, or even to believe him, or to worship him; he asked them simply to follow him, to join him, to watch him the way an apprentice watches a master-craftsman, to listen to him, to share his life. And they did! If you had asked them why they did it, they couldn't possibly have told you. They had no theories about him whatsoever at that time. They didn't know exactly who he was except that he was the son of a carpenter, and that he came from Nazareth. They didn't know what he was going to do. He promised them little or nothing, except "the pleasure of his company" (if we may use a phrase that has been used in a quite different context) and to share in his mission and life by way of suffering.

They didn't always understand him. In fact, they often misunderstood him. They loved his stories because they were good stories, but they also often missed the point of the stories, as many people do now when they listen to a sermon and hear an illustration which intrigues them and then can't tell you for the life of them the point that the illustration was meant to illustrate.

They were impressed by the wonderful things that he did, by the extraordinary way in which he could make sick people well; by the way he could make a little go a long, long way; by the way he could change a man's attitude and outlook on life.

They often disappointed him. Sometimes they let him down, and at the crucial moment they left him utterly alone. But they came back. His death shook them, and his resurrection renewed them. They came back changed, sobered, and above everything else, cheered.

They lived in a new world. The old one was still there with all its problems and questions and insoluble difficulties. The Roman troops were still marching through the cities; the taxes were unbearable, the evil was still rampant in every city, town, and village. The old world was still there, but they went on their way rejoicing. They didn't try to destroy that old world, they just ignored it. They could go on their way rejoicing because in that Man called Jesus they found God, the mystery of life, the ground of their being; and what's more, in them he found a habitation for his spirit.

They never equalled him, they never really successfully explained him, although they tried to in generations to come, and are still trying to, but they were never able to put into words exactly what he meant to them. But they had a way of treating each other, and above all else, a way of meeting life; life when it is harsh and cruel, that was unique. And that way they caught from him, and this eventually caught the attention of the civilized world. That's the way it began: a small group of people were drawn to a Man called Jesus and took him seriously. It's as simple as that.

Now skip twelve hundred years and see how it continued. The small group had grown into an enormous institution. The church had a great deal of property, power, and prestige; its leaders, especially its bishops, and above all, the Pope, were political leaders as well as spiritual guides. To be sure, they inspired artists and made it possible for them to work. They encouraged educators and in the Dark Ages were largely responsible for keeping alive the learning of the past, when it might have been lost; and above all, they inspired architects to send up buildings that seemed to touch the skies.

What happened to the Man called Jesus in all this? He was there; he was glorified, theologized, painted, pictured, worshipped, but I am sorry to say, not always followed. He was too far away, too remote, too much apart from the life of the people who belonged to the church. This I suppose was inevitable and a natural development. A movement, any movement, that starts rather simply is likely to become complicated if it grows to any great extent, and the church did become more and more complicated as it grew in power, in majesty, prestige and wealth. By the twelfth century, it was overgrown, top-heavy, and the Man Christ Jesus was almost lost in the shuffle.

Then something unexpected happened. A young man appeared on the scene. He was not a Jew, he was Italian; the eldest son of a rich family. In his young days he was the playboy of the town, the leader of the dandies of his village. His name was Giovanni Francesco Bernadone. Things began to happen to him. First, he was taken seriously ill; he recovered. He tried to do something useful to make up for the time that he had wasted, and he made many clumsy attempts to do it. For one thing, he stole from his own father to do the work that he thought he was called upon to do in the little chapel that he wanted to restore. The result was that he was completely alienated from his family. His father even went to law against him, and the two were never reconciled.

Then on February 24, 1209 (it was St. Matthias Day as it is now), he went to mass in the little chapel and he listened to the Gospel. The Gospel for that day was from the tenth chapter of St. Matthew, and this is a part of it. "Go rather to the lost sheep of the house of Israel. And as ye go, preach, saying, The Kingdom of heaven is at hand. Heal the sick, cleanse the lepers, raise the dead, cast out devils: freely ye have received, freely give. Provide neither gold nor silver, nor brass in your purses. Nor scrip for your journey, neither two coats, neither shoes, nor yet staves: for the workman is worthy of his meat."

He had already separated from his family, he was already living on what people would give him for what work he could do, but at that moment something happened. His biographer says that Francis' mind took a swift plunge into the literal. Right there, before the little altar, he threw away his stick and his bag, his purse and every cent of money that

41

he had, and went out to do what he had never done before, to preach. He wasn't a learned man, he had very little formal education; but he went, if you can believe it, to his own home town, to Assisi. There were no pulpits in the churches because preaching was not often done in those days except in an informal way, so he stood outside, jeered by the crowd because he looked like a madman, a beggar.

Every biographer has pointed out that he was not handsome, nor robust; he was slight. But there was a grace in his movement and something unforgettable about his voice. It was his voice that first made the people listen. He stood there in the street and talked to people about the love of God. What he said had none of a sermon's artistry. He simply talked out of what had happened to him, without ever mentioning himself.

When he finished and started to go away, three men asked if they could join him; two of them had very little, and one was a well-to-do man. They went with him. Later, more and more sought him until thousands began to look for him and ask what they must do to join his group. He required no training period; he required only two things. First he asked them to give away everything that they owned. Do you know what the other one was? He required that they be cheerful, that they could mourn their sins in private, but as they went about their way, they must sing.

He never attacked the institution. He went his own way within it, but somehow a breath of fresh air swept across the western world, and if we try to say what it was that made the difference, it was the cheerfulness, the gaiety of Francis and his followers that spread like wildfire. The world was no longer "a vale of tears"; it was "a wondrous world, and neither vice nor iniquity was strong enough to destroy its loveliness." He didn't change the institution, not its structure, but he changed the lives of people in a way that is hard to describe.

So much for the statement that the Christian faith begins, continues and ends in the Man called Jesus. Now a question, and not an easy question to ask. Is it conceivable to you that anything like that can happen today in a world like ours? Is it possible that a small group of people, people like us, can take Jesus seriously, and by doing so, change the world, make some difference to it? At first, you say it is unthinkable. The world is entirely different, we don't think in the way people did in St. Francis' day, and our problems are so colossal that to think that a group of people taking a Man called Jesus seriously can do anything to change it is ridiculous. I think we can.

I now speak for myself simply because I can't speak for anyone else, though I am reasonably sure that I will include some of you. In speaking for myself, I could not take him literally the way St. Francis did. For instance, I couldn't cut off my right hand or pluck out my right eye, even though in St. Matthew's Gospel Jesus says, "If thine eye offend thee, pluck it out, and if thy right hand offend thee, cut it off." I couldn't do that. I couldn't hate my father and mother, even though in one place in the Gospels Jesus is said to have told us to do it. I couldn't do it. I couldn't give away everything I have and live on welfare, not in this day and age. I couldn't believe that I could get everything that I prayed for even though in one place Jesus said, "Ask and ye shall receive."

But there are other things that I can do. You may think that they are unimportant when compared with the great advance toward the secular world that has been made by our church at the General Convention, but they are things that I know I can do. I am going to mention only three of them. I can *simplify* my life. Every once in a while I hear that word spoken to me: Simplify, Simplify! You live such a cluttered life. Your life is so filled with so many things that you never do anything thoroughly. Cut out some of the nonessentials. Drop every unnecessary committee, forget the polls and the surveys. Give up trying to be everywhere at one time, even though now because you have the means of transportation you can be almost everywhere at the same time. You can't be everywhere; and what's more, you don't need to be everywhere. Don't try to do everything; leave some things to other people; and some things to God. Simplify, not in order to have more leisure, but more intensity. In other words, to simplify means to concentrate your energy on some one great thing. Every person who has burned with any great brightness has been concentrated on some one supreme thing. They may have done a lot of other things, but some one thing has been at the center of their life. Simplify!

43

I also think that as the leader of this church one of the things I can do is to simplify the life of the church, not multiply its organizations, not add to its machinery, but concentrate on the great thing and let the lesser things be taken care of in other ways.

Second. I can keep an eye on my *style* of life. That is a word that is used a great deal now to describe what used to be called Christian ethics, My *style* of life; it has to do with many things. First, how I dress. That is what you think of when you hear the word *style* first. I can dress not to conform, even though the instinct to conformity is very strong in all of us; and not to rebel, though there is a rebel slumbering in the mildest of us all, neither to attract or offend. I can dress in a way that will not hide the person that I really am. In my vocation, I usually wear a uniform, and I can see to it that I wear that uniform not to protect myself, or to be sure that I have all the perquisites that are granted to clergy to make life easy for them. I hate that. Nor to promote myself if anyone thinks that it brings him any esteem to be seen in the company of clergy! I wear it only to let people know who I work for. I can keep myself well, look as well as I can, because I respect myself, and also because I do not wish to be one more eyesore on the scene.

Style also has to do with the way I speak. Every three or four hundred years we go through what you might call a "bawdy" period: Chaucer and then the Restoration, and now we are going through another one with a vengeance. The language of the barnyard has become the language of the theater, the novel, the poet, and the home. I am not prepared to speak for anyone else. All I can say is that the way I speak is one indication of the level on which I live. Because I take Jesus seriously, I will not willingly add to the polluted air we breathe by language that is either profane or obscene. To my mind it is a commentary on our people that they can accept without any reservation books in which the leading characters, even though they may be Harvard and Radcliffe graduates—that is, educated people—use habitually language that is both profane and obscene. They may be good people, many of them are. Yet eventually the kind of language they habitually speak will determine the kind of people they eventually become.

My style of life, in the long run, declares itself not only in the way I

44

dress, and in the way I speak, but primarily in the way I treat other people, the ones I don't like or agree with. On a hot, clear day I come into Copley Square, and I don't like everyone I see. I see people having their lunch and leaving the litter behind. I see other people in the fountain. I see others doing things that I don't like. But on the whole I am glad that people are there. Many of them come into the church, and when I get to the point of thinking that they are beyond the pale, I speak to one of the most unlikely looking ones. I never have been rejected. They are polite, they are interested. We don't talk about religion always, but we talk; and I find that they are human beings and that they are looking for something. I ask them if they have been in the church. Most of them have. If they do come into it, they know more about the building than most of the people who are here Sunday after Sunday.

How I treat the people I don't like will not always be the same because they are not always the same, but I will always approach them as human beings. Some of them need me; they are waiting for me, not only because I am a minister, but because I am a man and I represent something more than myself. There are people waiting for you, people who need you. Sometimes I hold back, and I don't go, I don't get there. When I do go, I realize that not because of anything that I am but because of what I represent, what I take to them, something happens to them. And there are other people that I need, the ones who reassure me, and in whom I see and feel the spirit of the Man called Jesus.

And if I am going to take him seriously, I must get to know him better than I do. Sometimes I begin with the Gospels, trace the figure as well as I can, and then recognize him in some person, shattered, bruised, yet brave, dauntless, in one of the wards of the White Building. At other times I begin out there with some manifestation of the risen Christ, and then I go back to see how it all began, and trace the features of Jesus in the Gospels.

If you and I did all these things and more besides, would the world be any different, do you think? I don't really know. To be quite honest, I don't know. All I know is that when a man takes Jesus seriously, the world around him is brighter, the burdens are lighter, and the future, strangely enough, is full of hope!

O God, who hast revealed to us thy love, care and justice in the Man Christ Jesus, help us to take him seriously. Give him a habitation in us that he may radiate life and light through us into a world that is dark, and sometimes seems to be going to pieces. It is thy world and in it we cannot be hopeless. Amen.

A Door into Faith

PROPERLY SPEAKING, this sermon has no text but it begins with a line from the Acts of the Apostles which may serve as a springboard for our thought. When Paul and Barnabas returned to Antioch after their first missionary journey into Asia Minor, they called the church together to make their report on the results of their journey. The sum and substance of the report was this; they told the people how God had been with them, what He had done and "how He had opened a door into faith for the Gentiles." Surely, you recognize the phrase from which our thought will spring: "how God had opened a door into faith for the Gentiles."

Notice that Paul and Barnabas did not presume to say that *they* opened the door. Rather, they went ahead to clear away the clouds of doubt and ignorance, to remove all unnecessary obstacles and to set forth the truth as they had seen it revealed in Jesus. *God* opened the door, a door into new life, wider horizons, broader vistas, larger visions, and greater liberty, a promise fulfilled. There is in that phrase all the suggestiveness of the infinite possibilities of the future. The prayer of this sermon is that by means of it God may open a door into faith for those of you who sincerely want to know Him as He made Himself known in the Christian revelation and in the Christian movement through history.

I

We had best begin with something concrete and there is nothing more concrete or more familiar than a book. In 1879, Phillips Brooks was invited to give the Bohlen Lectures. It was a course of lectures estab-

47

lished in the interests of Christian theology. There was in the world at that time, surprisingly as it may seem to us, the growing mood of skepticism of which we are now reaping the terrible harvest. The household of faith had already been shaken from without by the development of modern science, and it had been shaken from within by the discoveries of modern biblical critics and scholars, and Christians were not exactly sure where they stood or what they believed or what they were going to do, and the atmosphere was a prevailing atmosphere of uncertainty, and skepticism, and doubt. Matching the growing skepticism of the time was the growing stature of Phillips Brooks. He had been preaching in this church for ten years, and as he preached he lived, and as he lived he grew. And in the process of his growth he tried to find that in the Christian religion which could match the disintegrating forces in the society around him and bring to his people the reassuring good news of the Gospel.

As you follow his preaching through those years, you see that one idea is becoming increasingly preeminent. It is the idea of the personal influence of Jesus upon the individual lives of men and women. So, with that idea in mind he sat down, right after Christmas, of all times, to write the Bohlen Lectures, four of them in all, on the influence of Jesus on the moral, social, intellectual, and emotional life of men. They were written rapidly in a few months and finally delivered. The theme of those lectures, as you might guess from what we have already said, is this: "I have been led," wrote Phillips Brooks, "to think of Christianity and to speak of it not as a system of doctrine, but as a personal force." And the personal force that he was speaking of was the power and personality of the living Christ. People listened to the lectures with great interest and many more read them after they were printed. They were reassured by them; the truth that he set forth with such clarity and power became a part of their own inner lives and convictions. They were infused with the idea which he had set forth in the lectures. Sixty-six years later I happened to be preaching in the chapel of Harvard University on Sunday, the thirteenth of December, the birthday of Phillips Brooks. Before we went into the chapel, the Dean of the chapel said to me, "When I was a young student, going through the travail of doubt and skepticism and uncertainty, not knowing exactly what I believed, if anything, my father put into my hands a little book. No book outside the Bible," he said, "has influenced my life, my thought, my prayers, my belief more than that book." The book was *The Influence of Jesus* by Phillips Brooks.

Now, there is the whole story beginning, you see, with an invisible idea conceived in the mind of a man, something purely abstract, no form or substance at all. But it germinates in that mind, is encouraged by forces from without, it spins round and round, it grows and develops until finally it presses itself out into the actual form and substance of a book that you can pick up, handle, see and read. You might think that that idea becoming tangible, visible, physical would be reduced in its power and lose something of its wonder. Not at all, for once the idea became visible, it then began to have influence and infuse itself into the lives and minds and hearts of other people so that they too were made alive by the great idea, influenced by it, strengthened by it, reassured by it.

There, you see, we have three separate things—an idea, a book and the influence of the book, and yet, they are not separate at all. They are inseparable. You cannot divorce the book from the idea which the book expresses. You cannot divorce the influence of the book from either the idea or the book. The three are all tied up in one thing, all part and parcel of one reality, and once you start with the invisible idea conceived in the mind of the author, you cannot stop until you come to the influence of that idea as it dwells in and empowers the life of some other person. So that, if you wanted to give this reality a name, it would be idea-book-influence, all three. You might try to evaluate the individual items in the triumvirate and say that one is more important than the other. Chronologically, of course, the idea comes first; but strategically the book comes first in importance, for the book is the thing that both reveals and releases the idea. Without the book the idea would never have been known. Consequentially, the influence comes first since that is what bears fruit in the world; that is the net result of the idea having become expressed in the substance of a book. But in reality, they all come together at one and the same time, the idea, the book and its influence, with no difference or distinction among them. Three separate things, yet everlastingly one and inseparable.

I hope that the door is just a little ajar and that you are beginning to see what we are moving toward.

II

Enlarge now the circle of your thought and take in the idea that what happens in the case of this book or any other book happens over and over again in every realm of life, so that this incident that we have turned to is a sample of the very nature of existence. The creative power of life is always an invisible, intangible thing. Even the physical power of life is invisible. You cannot see electricity; you cannot see the wind that sails a ship; you cannot see the current that makes the river run to the sea. They are unseen things, yet they are the driving power of life. When you ask what makes the great things in life go, what are the answers? Dreams, hopes, loyalties, love, vision, ideas, ideals. One man said this about dreams; "Dreams that men dream in sleep are mists and shadow. The dreams men dream while waking can become the substance of a world." Those invisible, untouchable things are the creative powers that make the great things in life move, the dreams, the hopes, the love and the ideals; they are the things that become the substance of a world.

But the invisible power always moves toward visibility, just as the idea stirs in the mind of a man and will not let him rest until it is put down on paper so that it can be communicated to other minds. So, these invisible creative powers in life will not rest until they are made concrete, until they have substance, until they are expressed in bodily form. A young man and woman dream of a home, for example, and that dream will not let them rest until they have a house and a family. So, some people have a vision of beauty, and that vision will not let them remain idle until they have given it substance on canvas, in marble, in stained glass, on paper. Men and women from the beginning of time have had a hope for a better world, and yet that invisible, abstract thing has always moved toward concretion, toward visibility—Plato's Republic, More's Utopia, St. Augustine's City of God, and the United

Nations. The love of a person, that deep, sincere admiration which is certainly more than simply approval of someone whom we recognize to be preeminently great, never gives us peace until it takes shape in some bodily form, and the adoration of a people for a leader like Lincoln becomes the dignified grandeur of the Lincoln Memorial. An ideal in life, as it develops in a person's mind, becomes a character that you can see, have confidence in and trust, something that has body and substance, that gives it reality. So, the compassion that people have in their hearts for children takes flesh and blood in the Children's Hospital. Always, you see, the invisible moves toward visibility and as in the case of the idea in the mind of the author taking substance in a book, far from reducing its power, its power is then released and it has influence in the lives of people, everywhere.

I looked up for my own interest the meaning of the word "influence." It means in its literal derivation "in-flow" and it was originally used to describe the radiation of an ethereal fluid from the stars. Remember that when you speak of the influence of a man's life upon a boy, or the influence of a good home upon a family, or the influence of a great book like the Bible upon the character and language of Abraham Lincoln. It is these concrete things that have influence, that radiate something like the ethereal radiation from the stars. Far from reducing the power of the original invisible thing, that power is increased, enhanced as it is communicated from this point of concrete reality and in-flowing into the lives and minds of everyone. So much for our experience in general.

III

Go one step further now, and see a vision of God. The creative power of God is invisible. What is it that makes you go? What is it that gives you the power to stand upon your feet and draw a deep breath and throw your shoulders back and take in the glory and the beauty and the wonder of life? It is an invisible, intangible dynamic energy. *Deus rerum tenax vigor.* Personally, I am not academically minded and do not often use Latin quotations, but I use that one because the sound of it helps to translate the meaning of it. God, the persistent energy of things! But it is energy that is invisible. You cannot put your finger on it. Here it is expressed in the stride of a man. Somewhere else it is made visible in the thrust of a tree or in the shining of the sun. Whatever else may be said of that creative power of God by which all things live and move and have their being, it is invisible, and yet that invisible power moves toward visibility and as Christians we believe that it was made manifest in the personality of Jesus Christ.

According to Christian belief, we do not hold that Jesus as a man was deified into a god. We do not believe that a human being grew to such supreme stature that finally he arrived at the dignity of the divine. There is a sign of that in the early Epistles, but Christianity outgrew that mistaken notion. No, we do not believe in the deification of a man; we believe in the incarnation of God; that is, that urge to go out, that thrust of the divine life to make itself visible and concretely real, so that what had been intangible and only vaguely guessed at was finally warmed into the personal relationship that men and women have with Jesus. So, the love of God which was originally something that men only thought about as an abstract and theoretical thing took shape in the touch of a hand and the throb of a heart.

Some theologians and philosophers would be inclined to say that by believing that about God we therefore reduce the omniscience and the omnipresence of God and bring Him down to the small stature of a human being. Not at all! For once the invisible was made visible, it then had infinite consequences for it went out from that point of visibility to influence the lives of men and women down through two thousand years all around the globe. And that spirit rests today upon men and women to give them the strength that they need to overcome obstacles, to meet handicaps and to face the hard, blunt realities of life. It sits like fire upon them and is like a wind behind their sails to give them motion.

That is the God we worship. That is the God we try to see through the doctrine of the Trinity, the Creative Power, the Created Substance, the Everlasting Influence, three separate realities, and yet inseparable; all three together tell the whole story about God. He is a God who is related to the life we know. I hope from what we have said that you have begun to grasp the fact that this doctrine about God is not some unrelated, theoretical thing, but that it grows out of the very nature of existence in which the invisible always moves toward visibility that thereby it may have infinite consequences in human life. Our knowledge of God comes, at least to begin with, from that panorama of human experience. He is not a static God like the moon, but a living God like the sun, not standing off there, apart from His creation, dead, merely reflecting the light of another, to be gazed at but never giving His life to anyone, but shining so that His life can come into us and be a part of the very texture of our skin and the fiber of our thought and the structure of our character.

We worship, therefore, not only the invisible God, mighty and great as He is, but we worship the concreteness of God and we worship the God who in Himself has all the precious relationships, all that urgency to go out of Himself to create and to love, to redeem and to dwell in the lives of people. Some people think this is intellectually difficult. Perhaps it is. Let's forget that for the moment. Certainly from a total point of view how much richer is a God like that than a cold theoretical principle out there, far off in the heavens of the universe who never took one step outside His own supreme serenity to make Himself visible or concrete in any living human being; and how unlike anything that we know about the ways of creative power. Such a God would be a sterile God, and sterility has no place in the structure of the universe as we know it.

We ourselves, of course, are fulfilled only as those things which are invisible in us are made concrete, and if you are looking for practical results and applications to this sermon, and you have a right to look for them, this is it; you and I who worship the God of the Trinity recognize that our own lives will never be fulfilled until the dreams and the hopes and the loyalties and the loves and the ideals cease to be abstract and are translated into concrete reality of action, until the desire becomes the deed, and the deed becomes the fulfillment. In the deed will be the consequences that may make life richer for other people. This, then, is no unrelated doctrine about God. It is a part of the very stuff of life and where men follow it carefully and believe it sincerely it enriches the life of multitudes.

God opened a door into faith. That is about all God can do. He never

53

forces anybody to go through the door. If perchance He has opened a door to faith by this sermon, some of the obstacles perhaps having been removed, some of the misunderstandings been cleared up, I pray with you that you and I may have the grace and the wisdom and the courage to go through the door into a larger, broader, freer life than otherwise we would ever know.

We thank thee, O God, for the doors that thou hast opened into faith; for the new and wide horizons which thou hast set before us, leading to ever-increasing lives of usefulness. Give us the courage to go through the door, setting aside our prejudices and our fears that we may walk the broad highway of thy truth. Amen.

When the Well Is Dry

❧

Y OU MAY REMEMBER that last summer was an unusually dry one. As a matter of fact, beginning in the early spring, continuing through the summer and into the late autumn there was virtually no rain at all. It was one of the driest seasons in the history of the weather bureau. One natural result was that many wells went dry. Some of them were low, others were completely dry, and many people, therefore, were without water. Some managed reasonably well by restricting their use of water to the absolute necessities, some went to the trouble of carrying water from other wells that were fed by springs, and some had to move temporarily to another place.

This season of drought makes us think of the dry spells that people go through in more serious ways. They have no shortage of water, especially if they live in the city, but they are short of energy, vitality, ideas, courage, faith. They are limp, and in their own vernacular they feel like a dishrag. Just as there is from time to time a recession in the national economy, there is in every individual life from time to time a recession of vital energy.

Sometimes the reason is obvious. A person has been through a long period of stress and strain, has carried the burden of many anxieties and responsibilities and during that time he has overdrawn his supply of spiritual energy. After the strain is over, he slumps. Or, after a series of shocks and blows, he feels shrunken.

Or another person may have lived in a dry, arid land of pleasure and comfort in which he thinks little about the necessities of life, the things that he will need when the days are dark. Few demands are made upon him and, when he comes to a crisis, he finds that his reserves are gone

55

because he has been living all those years on the superficial wells that are easily dried up.

Once in a while the reason is not obvious. It may be hidden in the secret mysteries of the body's chemistry, or in the delicate adjustment of the nervous system. But whether or not the reason is obvious, the *fact* is that the well is dry; and the question is, What can I do when my well is dry?

You cannot do anything until you get it out of your head that there is something peculiar about you, until you are perfectly clear in your own mind that you are not the only one who goes through this particular kind of experience. All you have to do is to look at the people you know. Is there any one of them that has a steady level of spiritual energy, a level that never drops, that is always at its highest? I have never known such a person, either among the few great people that I have known, or among ordinary people like myself. I have never known anyone who had a steady level of spiritual energy.

To be sure, some show it more than others. Some have an amazing ability to hide their empty wells but, if you know them well enough, you know that there are times when their water level is alarmingly low.

If that does not convince you that you are not the only person who experiences this particular kind of lethargy, look at the people you know about. William James, for example. You know how often I turn to him. Of all the people who abounded in energy and vitality, and who communicated it constantly to everyone who met him and heard his lectures, William James is perhaps one of the greatest. And yet, in 1895, only fifteen years before he died, he wrote to one of his friends, "I am a victim of neurasthenia and of the sense of the hollowness and unreality that goes with it."

Woodrow Wilson, President of the United States, the one who fought so doggedly for the League of Nations, was in the law school after he finished his college course. One of his biographers writes, "In the winter of his second term his digestive system began to act up alarmingly, and he had to leave school. There followed a period of intense depression and discouragement."

Coming closer to this place, I think of Phillips Brooks and, from everything I read about him and everything I know about him, I think of a man who was everlastingly buoyant, who was always on the crest of the wave, who always had more than enough to give to anyone who needed strength and vitality. After serving this parish for twenty-two years, he was elected Bishop of Massachusetts in 1891. On the last Sunday before his consecration he preached twice in this church, once in the morning on "Let your Light so shine before men," and again in the afternoon on "Let him that is athirst come," and a third time in the evening at St. Andrew's on "He that overcometh shall inherit all things." Each time he seemed full of the same vitality and buoyancy. Each time the church was crowded with people waiting to be fed. When he wrote to one of his closest friends, this is what he wrote: "I resigned the rectorship of Trinity Church and it seemed like dying."

The more you realize that this experience is a common, natural thing, not something peculiar to you, the better you can handle it, the more calmly you can face it.

After you have done that, learn to do nothing. I may say in advance that for one who shares my temperament it is one of the hardest of all lessons to learn.

Many years ago when I was in Baltimore, a friend of mine was a very successful businesswoman. She said that the only time she really rested was when she was taking a trip on a train, and I asked her to explain that in a little more detail, for a long train trip often tires me if only from boredom. She said, "When I am on the train, I know that I don't have to run it." The trouble is, you see, with many of us (I hesitate to tell you that I am one of them) that we try to run the train from our seat in the coach, just as we try to drive the automobile from the back seat, and make all the decisions and share all the ones that are made, even if we resist the temptation to criticize them and put on the brake even though someone else is running the car. We cannot sit back and let him run it.

Some people have to learn how to drop the things about which they can do nothing. You see a family in trouble, you want to help, but there is nothing you can do; but you continue to do it in the long night watches. You have to learn to drop it, to do nothing.

John Keats, the poet, was one of the wisest men, even though he lived so brief a life, and he expounded from time to time the principle of what he called "diligent Indolence—the power of mere passive existence, of receptive pleasure." In a letter to his friend John Hamilton Reynolds, written on the 19th of February, 1818, almost a hundred and forty-seven years ago, he wrote this: "I was led into these thoughts by the beauty of the morning operating on a sense of Idleness—I have not read any books—the Morning said I was right—I had no idea but of the morning, and the thrush said that I was right—seeming to say,

> O thou whose face hath felt the Winter's wind,
> Whose eye has seen the snow-clouds hung in mist,
> And the black elm-tops 'mong the freezing stars,
> To thee the Spring will be a harvest-time.
> O thou, whose only book has been the light
> Of supreme darkness, which thou feddest on
> Night after night when Phoebus was away,
> To thee the Spring shall be a triple morn.
> O fret not after knowledge—I have none,
> And yet my song comes native with the warmth.
> O fret not after knowledge—I have none,
> And yet the Evening listens. He who saddens
> At thought of idleness cannot be idle,
> And he's awake who thinks himself asleep."

If the time comes when you can't pray, don't try to. If the time comes when you can't believe, don't try to. If the time comes when you can't do what you think you ought to do, don't try to do it. If you can't breast the waves, ride them. If you haven't the energy to swim, float. The well will begin to fill, I promise you, from the bottom, the way a wound heals from the bottom.

Then, paradoxically, get up and do what you have to do. John Keats wrote another letter to his brother George, and I now read a passage from this letter because it shows you how he kept both of these things in balance, passivity and activity. "Whenever I find myself growing vaporish . . ." (that is a word we don't use now; it simply means depressed, in low spirits), "Whenever I find myself growing vaporish, I rouse myself, wash and put on a clean shirt, brush my hair and clothes, tie my shoestrings neatly, and in fact adonize [beautify myself] as though I were going out—then all clean and comfortable I sit down to write. This I find the greatest relief."

The interesting thing is that the way you feel does not necessarily determine what you do. On Friday we heard the Boston Symphony Concert, the Eighth Symphony of Beethoven, and in his incomparably good notes, John Nicholas Burk told us that the Seventh and the Eighth Symphony were written only four months apart in the year 1812. Each in its way is exuberant, the Eighth, to be sure, more quiet and more restrained, less passionate than the Seventh, but each overflowing with joy. Mr. Burk then looked at the events of Beethoven's life at that particular time, and writes that Beethoven "in the midst of his most productive years, with pregnant themes humming in his head, could be counted upon to work them out, despite physical distress and every preoccupation, sordid or otherwise." At that very time he had bad health, unhappy love affairs, and a terrible row with his brother, but it was his business to compose and, when he sat down to write, he wrote music the world still hears, and hears only the overtones of his joy and gladness.

You will find that you can do what you have to do; and, if you are anything like me, sometimes when you feel least like doing it, you will do it better than you know.

Now, after you have done these three things, after you have rid yourself of the delusion that you are a peculiar person, after you have begun to learn how to do nothing, and after you have done what you have to do, then go to someone whose well is not dry. Some of you, I fear, are too proud to do it, and some are too shy but, over and over again, during the years that I have been in the ministry—and I realize that it is because of my office, not because of my self—people have come to me and said essentially the same thing. In one way or another they have said, Normally, I can handle things like this myself, but I have come to the point where I need to talk to somebody. They may go away with only a cup of water, but it is all they need to prime the spring.

Sometimes you can find a person between the covers of a book. I remember so well one of the times when my well was dry, and late at night I got up and began to read Dietrich Bonhoeffer's *Letters from Prison*. I had never read them before, and I read on, and on, and on. I thought to myself, if this man could do this kind of thing under circumstances like these, I can do any of the things that I have to do under circumstances that are so much easier. It was as though my well began to fill because I had been in the company of someone whose well was not dry.

There are times when you need more than any ordinary person. I think so often of the line in the 61st Psalm, "Lead me to the rock that is higher than I." Go to the Gospels. Whether you understand every line or not, read one page, and let Jesus speak to you. Let something of his extraordinary vitality be transfused into you. Come to the Lord's table and be fed. Even though you do not understand how this can happen, how common elements like bread and wine can contain and convey to you the life and the vitality of the Lord Christ, come and be fed by Him.

Doing these things I can promise you that the time will come sooner or later, sometimes sooner and sometimes later, when you will know what the psalmist meant when he wrote, "Who going through the vale of misery use it for a well; and the pools are filled with water."

When our energies recede and our vitality is inadequate to meet the needs of the day, help us, O Lord, to learn to sit still, to care and not to care, to do nothing; and then give us the will to rise up to do the things we have to do, and go to those who can fill our empty wells, even unto Christ Jesus whose well is never empty. Amen.

The Sting of Death

᭡

Near the end of his first letter to the Christians in Corinth, after Paul had dealt with various problems and questions that had come up in the young church, he plunged into one of the most profound questions that any man has to face and hurled at his readers, as it were, the question, "O death, where is thy sting?" Before we give him a chance to answer the question, we think we know the answer.

We know where the sting of death is because we have been stung by it, or we know people who have been stung by it. Someone we deeply loved all our life long, someone knit together with us in a lifelong relationship, is taken from us. The sting of death is that person's absence. A man or a woman upon whom we depended in every sort of condition and circumstance is no longer "there"; we cannot depend on him. The sting of death is our loss of someone to turn to, someone to lean on.

Others we have known, and many we have never known, are mowed down by accident, or by deliberate action. A careful driver on the highway is killed by a careless drunken driver. A policeman with five children is shot in a riot. A cab driver is killed by a passenger. A young man is killed "in action," in an action we call a war. The sting of death is the injustice of it, the futility of it, the cruelty of it.

The thought of our own death seldom occurs to us, but when it does we begin to feel the sting of it, in different ways at different times. We know what life is like here; it is the only place we've ever known. It isn't always to our liking, but it's familiar to us. It's our home. We know where we are and where we are going. Not always, but generally, we know where we belong. We know nothing about any other life that may be beyond this one, or about any other world that may be over and above and beyond the one we now know. Whatever it may be, we know nothing about it whatsoever. The sting of death is the fear of the unknown.

Some have been taught that after death they will be called to account for everything they have ever done. They believe that they will be called before the judgment seat and every wrong thing they have done will be read from the ledger and balanced against the good they have done. The sting for them is the dread of facing the Judge.

Whether or not you have any of that particular dread (I confess that I don't) nevertheless no one can think about his own death without the knowledge of the things he has not done that he might have done, and the things that he has done that he should not have done; and the sting of death for him is in the knowledge of his shortcomings, the things he's missed, the people he's hurt.

Others there are who have no expectation of anything but extinction. One of the most distinguished people I have ever known once said to me as I tried to help her think through the imminence of her own death, "I am afraid of extinction!" At that particular time, rightly or wrongly, I turned it off lightly and said, "It is inconceivable to me that so distinguished a person should or could be extinguished." Nevertheless, the sting of death for many people is the fear of annihilation.

St. Paul repeats the question. "O grave, where is thy victory?" (It is interesting, parenthetically, if you are interested in texts, that the King James Version is mistaken because St. Paul used the same word *death* in both questions: "Death, where is thy sting? Death, where is thy victory?" Also, the English translation reverses the order of the questions!) Again, we know the answer, or we think we do.

The victory of death is its complete, utter finality. Once the curtain of a person's life is rung down, it has never yet been rung up again. There are no curtain calls at the end of life's performances. Once a person dies we never see him again as long as we live save in our memories, or our dreams, or our visions. We never again hear his voice, or take his hand. We may wonder why Paul asks this question, "O Death, where is thy sting? O Death, where is thy victory?" The answer seems so obvious to us that there is no use asking the question. It is like asking, O

Sun, where is thy light? We know where the light is, even if it be hidden for a few minutes as it was yesterday by the passing of the moon between it and the earth. We know that the sun is there when it shines, and we know where it is at night. So we know where the victory and the sting of death is.

We also know that our instinctive answer is not Paul's answer. If you do not know it, then I must tell you. The answers that I have been drawing together from our personal experience, and from the knowledge we have of human beings, these answers are not Paul's answer. His answer is quite different. St. Paul says, Death has lost its sting! That's where the sting is; it has gone! Like a bee that has not lost its life but has lost its power to sting, death has no more power to sting. Paul would be frank to admit that the struggle between life and death still continues and still tears people apart, but he would say, The victory is on the side of life. And before asking those two questions, hurling them out without intending any answer to be given because he already had the answer, not asking for the information he already had, he said, *Death is swallowed up in victory*.

St. Paul, you know, was an amazing person; he was a realist. He was a Jew and therefore it is hard for us to put ourselves in his place. His mind works differently from ours. And we who talk so much about *victory* are interested to see that St. Paul, in all the letters he wrote, uses the word *victory* only three times and all three are in this very passage from his letter to the Corinthians (I Cor. 15:54–56). When we hear him say, *Death is swallowed up in victory*, we reply, What victory? Whose? Certainly not ours.

We are not well acquainted with victory, even over ourselves, when we are honest with ourselves. We may be able to celebrate some minor victories over temptations and handicaps but we are not in a position to celebrate any major victories over the self as the dominating principle of our lives. And certainly, if we are not able to do that we are in no position to celebrate a victory over the powers of life and death. It is only fair that we remember that the human race has won enormous victories; the victory of knowledge over ignorance—think of the clouds of ignorance that have been pushed back as men and women have patiently tried to understand the nature of the world they lived in. As you watched the eclipse yesterday, on the screen or in the sky, the knowledge that men now have of the orderly movement of the heavenly bodies is staggering, and you realize that it wasn't so many years ago that men had not the slightest idea of either the cause or the nature of that celestial event. We have recently won another victory, the victory of earth over outer space; we are now able to break through the environment of the atmosphere which wraps this little planet and move out into the outer space of the other planets. But when it comes to death, death has the last word. We can see no sign of winning that victory.

Paul says that the victory over death is not a victory that we win; it is a victory that God gives us, through Jesus Christ. The way He gives it is not always understood in the same way by all people, at all times. We can do our best if we try to understand it in our way, imperfect though it be. This is the way the victory is given to me through Jesus Christ.

Jesus walked through life, loving life not death; giving life, freely, gladly. He once said that the purpose of his coming was that people might have life and that they might have it more abundantly. When death came toward him he walked straight toward death. There was no bypassing it. He walked right through it and came out on the other side. He came back, not as he was but as he is. He is the Victor. He is the one who took the sting out of death. He didn't take death away. He didn't even take the pain of it away. He left all that behind him. He did something greater; he took the fear of it away, and once death loses its power to frighten us it has no dominion over us. He drew the sting of guilt; he took away the sting of self-pity.

In him—I wish I could make you feel it the way I feel it, but I can only say that I feel it, for we cannot speak of it in rational, logical terms —in him Death was swallowed up in the vast dimensions of Life. He took away the sting of death because he lost himself in something far greater than either life or death; he lost himself in the Father's love. Picture it. Standing beside the Father, whose love reaches the uttermost parts of the earth, death shrinks into relative insignificance. This was the victory that Paul thanked God for. It is the victory of one man in which all others can participate, if they choose to. They don't have to, and many don't. No one shares it automatically, but if they want to, and are willing to pay the price, they can. One Man's victory can be theirs.

To drop to a very much lower level, to make plain if I can how one person can share in the victory of another, let me tell you about myself, something that I remember as vividly as though it were yesterday. I was born and brought up in a small town on the border of Connecticut and New York. There were 17,000 residents at the time. It was a town of middle-class people, and it didn't have much to be proud of, and not much to be ashamed of, I'm bold to say. It was often referred to as "the backyard of Rye and Greenwich." It had a good public high school and the high school had a basketball team. While I was still in the junior high school, the Port Chester High School basketball team won the state pennant. It doesn't sound like a very great thing, but when those boys came back the town went wild with delight and pride. And, what is more, I, who cared nothing about basketball, knew nothing about it, was enhanced by it, enlarged by it. Along with all the others, I was part of their victory. The mother of one of the players was a friend of my mother, so I knew him. He was older than I was, but not much, though I thought of him then as much older; when I could catch up with him on the street and walk along with him, I felt ten feet taller! We shared in the victory of one team. So you—many, many people—can share in the victory of one Person who took the sting out of death.

Two brief, final observations. Paul's conclusions are always greater than his arguments. His massive convictions are always more impressive than his reasons for them. He is not alone in that. Abraham Lincoln's conclusion that slavery was wrong is far greater than any of the arguments that he used to prove it. So, true to form, when Paul raised those two questions he went on to say, "The sting of death is sin, and the strength of sin is the Law." "The strength of sin is the Law"—that doesn't speak to me. Perhaps it does to you. I think that when I listened to a learned professor of New Testament expound it in the seminary I began to grasp it, but I am not sure I do now. After all, I haven't the brilliant mind of a first century, rabbinically trained Jew! Sometimes he speaks to me. When he says, "As in Adam all die, even so in Christ shall all be made alive"—that speaks to me, for Adam is my mortality and in

Adam I die. Christ is something more than my mortality, and in him I live. The extraordinary thing about us is that we are mortal; and being mortal we will die; but of all the creatures on the face of the earth we are the only ones who know that we are mortal! Hence, we may well be more than mortal. That is the first observation. When you read St. Paul keep your eye on his conclusions.

And the second is this. Whether or not death has lost its sting depends upon one of two things. Either you have lost your power to feel pain, drugged yourself to face the facts without feeling, in which case death loses its sting; either that, or you have found something greater, a spirit, the Christ-spirit which embraces death and in which you find a life too great, too far-reaching to be washed away by the tides of time and circumstance.

One of the most extraordinary figures in English literature is John Donne. For ten years—1621–1631—he was the Dean of St. Paul's Cathedral. Coming to the ministry late in life, he speaks to us now in a way that many other English poets do not because in spite of the fact that both his poetry and his prose are elegant, they are gnarled because he was always in a state of tension between his doubts and his faith, between his shortcomings and his achievements. His Holy Sonnets are some of the greatest poetry that has ever been written in English. I was tempted to read the familiar one, *Death Be Not Proud*, but instead of that I am going to read his *Hymn to God the Father*, which he wrote not long after his wife had died. I think you will see why I read it, having said what I have said about mortality and what it implies. Even though we may have no fear of Judgment, we have some fear of extinction; and we have some sense of failure that might have been avoided. This is the hymn addressed to God:

> Wilt thou forgive that sin where I begunne,
>   Which is my sin, though it were done before?
> Wilt thou forgive those sinnes, through which I run,
>   And do run still: though *still* I do deplore?
>   When thou hast done, thou hast not done,
>   For I have more.

66

THE STING OF DEATH

Wilt thou forgive that sin by which I've won
    Others to sin? and, made my sin their door?
Wilt thou forgive that sin which I did shun
    A year or two: but wallowed in a score?
        When thou hast done, thou hast not done,
        For I have more.

I have a sin of fear, that when I have spun
    My last thred, I shall perish on the shore;
Swear by thyself, that at my death thy son
    Shall shine as he shines now, and heretofore;
        And, having done that, Thou hast done,
        I fear no more.

The sting of death is gone!

Deepen our roots, O God, in the things that are true and beautiful and good. Grant that we may never turn away from the harsh facts of life, but with thy help and grace rise above them and trust the soul's invincible surmise, through Jesus Christ our Lord. Amen.

The Kingdom

T HE LORD'S PRAYER begins with something like a paradox. You call God, *father*. Contrary to all your instinctive and habitual manners, you drop all the formalities of royalty and high position, all the cosmic implications of deity, and approach him the way a small child approaches his parent. You call him Abba, *father*. Immediately, you draw back, as it were, and say, *Hallowed be Thy Name*. In other words, after you have spoken to him in that natural, familiar way, there is a hush that falls. Why? Because he with whom you dare to be so intimate is also ultimate.

It's always like that, even in the relationships we have with other people in everyday life. The more intimate you become with another person, the more you realize that there is something ultimate about him, something that you stand in awe of, something that you dare not touch, something that you will never completely understand, and something that you certainly do not take liberties with. And the greater the person, the more you are aware of the distance between you and him, in spite of the intimacy of your relationship with him.

Do you see what I mean? In the most intimate of all relationships in human life, the relationship between a man and wife, the more intimate, the closer it is, the more surely each one realizes that there is something ultimate in the other, an area that he dare not invade, a mystery that he will not probe. Therefore, after they address each other in the most endearing, intimate terms, they then say something comparable to *hallowed be thy name*. There is a hush that falls between the two; the silence not of estrangement but of adoration, the recognition of sanctity.

So it is with God; intimate, yet ultimate; close, yet distant. "Our Father, who art in heaven, Hallowed be thy name." It is not surprising therefore that the prayer continues in this same paradoxical vein: *Thy kingdom come.*

The word *kingdom* as we use it suggests a country or a state that is ruled either nominally or actually by a king or a queen; it has boundaries, a capital city, a citizenry, a court, an army, and a navy. It is a political unit of organized social life. God's kingdom isn't anything like that. It has no boundaries, it has no capital city, no court, no diplomatic corps; it has no foreign office, no cabinet, no army or navy. It is a community. It can't be a kingdom with a single citizen. It is a community of those who recognize the supremacy of God, and live as well as they can under his rule; or, better still, as members of his family. It doesn't mean that they deny all the political organizations under which they must live; they cannot. But they put him first, and as a consequence, in that community there is a climate, an atmosphere that you can feel the minute you step into it. Fear and suspicion have been left behind, and there is a quiet joy even in the presence of sorrow.

It is not an organization, certainly not a "power structure," even though there have been times in the history of the Christian religion when the Kingdom of God has been identified with the church. It must not be. The church is an institution, and has all the fallibilities and weaknesses of every other institution. Neither is the Kingdom a political form of government. It is a state of life, a state of being in which the will of God prevails. So in that sense, the Lord's Prayer is a paradoxical prayer: we ask for something that is a Kingdom, yet not a Kingdom.

There is another way in which it is paradoxical. You ask in the prayer that the Kingdom come, which implies that it is not here now. If you talk about Christmas coming, it is quite plain that Christmas isn't here. It is in the future. Yet you ask for the Kingdom to come in the future because in a sense it has already come! In still another sense, it has been here always. Nations rise and fall, they break against the wall of God's will. "The Lord is king, be the people never so impatient."

When Jesus came, the Kingdom came as it had never come before, like flashes of lightning. A lame man stood up and walked, a deaf man heard for the first time, a blind man saw. Things happened that set people free, free from whatever it was that confined them, and these were signs of the Kingdom. The Father made himself both perceived and felt in the action and person of Jesus: chains dropped; men were free both literally and figuratively (more especially figuratively, I think), free to walk and talk, free to see and hear, live and love as they had not been before.

The people who followed Jesus saw this happening. When they prayed *Thy kingdom come*, they were not reaching out for some impossible dream, instinctive as that is in human beings. They were not simply hoping for the better days that never seemed to come. They were asking for the completion and the fulfillment of something that had already begun, something that they had seen, something that they had been a part of.

It never occurred to them that they themselves could bring it to pass. They could only be in a position to receive it when God brought it about. Other Christians at other times have talked about building the Kingdom. This would never have occurred to the early Christians; they never thought of the Kingdom as something that they could bring about. They couldn't bring it about any more than they could have brought Jesus about. Jesus came out of the blue. They didn't bring him to the earth, he came; suddenly he was there, like a light, life, right in their midst; at a time when they least expected him, when everything else was crumbling, there he was. So the Kingdom would come.

When he came, some were ready and others were not; some were drawn to his company and were blessed, and some rejected him and brought upon themselves the only hell I think that there is, the hell of missing life when life comes to you.

Something in my personal experience may help you understand what the prayer for the Kingdom means. When I was in the seminary, the whole subject of the Kingdom quite frankly bewildered me, and the more I tried to find out what the New Testament said about it, and particularly what our Lord said about it, the more bewildered I was. In some places he talked about it as something present in him and in his ministry. On the next page he talked about it as something yet to come.

One minute he talked about as it something that you could enter, something that you could be in. On the next page he talked about it as something that could be in you. All this was very puzzling to me, and the more I pored over the multitude of references to the Kingdom in the Gospels, the more puzzled I was. How could something be coming if it was already here? How could Jesus speak of it as something past, present, and future?

Then something happened that in a small but vivid way—and it is usually the small things that happen to you that illuminate the great things—illuminated the whole question of the Kingdom.

When I was in college I was exposed to the theater in general. The theater in Boston at that time was very active, and there were many live theaters; we had a chance to see every great actor and actress in every great play there was on the boards, and I took full advantage of it. I was exposed to the theater in general, and I was exposed to Shakespeare in particular. I took the famous course English II under George Lyman Kittredge, perhaps the greatest of all the Shakespearian scholars at that time. In one year we read four plays, two each term, and we studied them under a microscope. We learned the meaning of every single word and the interpretation of the action. We memorized long passages; I remembered them long enough to reproduce some of them on the examination, after which I promptly forgot them. The course did a great deal for me. I knew something about Shakespeare, and something about four of his plays; I knew the plays philologically.

After I was ordained and was teaching in the seminary, a person crossed my path. The theater was his life, Shakespeare was his love. As I got to know him, he touched the plays as if with a wand of light, and for the first time they came alive. He would come up to my room, sometimes late at night, and say, "Let's do the second scene from the first act of Hamlet." He knew all the parts, and without the book, would begin quietly, in a conversational tone of voice, to say the lines. For the first time I realized that Shakespeare was beautiful! I had known the meaning of the words, but I missed the beauty; I lost the music in the mechanics.

So you see what I am trying to lead you into: Shakespeare was there to begin with, but Shakespeare came alive in that friend. Then what about the future? Shakespeare, as far as I am concerned, is still to come; he is still beyond me. I have just lately been working on the sonnets. I found a new edition of them last summer in Florence by John Dover Wilson, that veteran of Shakespearian critics who has finally brought to a conclusion the Cambridge Edition of Shakespeare with his volume on the sonnets. I am going through once again the insoluble mysteries connected with those poems, the poems that C. S. Lewis called 'the supreme love poetry of the world.'

I look on my shelves and see dozens of editions, paperbacks mostly, of the plays. Why? Because I am always finding a new one and I buy it to read the introduction to see what that person, that editor, thinks the play meant, see what new light he throws upon its meaning. So it is always ahead of me, and I reach out for it because once it was with me.

The Kingdom came with Jesus, and it is still to come, but you wouldn't pray for it to come if it hadn't come once, not to you in Galilee because you weren't in Galilee, but to you where you are, when his spirit takes hold of some one person, or a group of persons and draws you into it, so that you say, I know what the Kingdom is because I've been in it; I've had a taste of it.

This prayer, then, about the Kingdom makes plain a few things about a Christian's world and the way he looks at it. God's Kingdom is greater than any empire that man will ever build, and it is just as well that we now recognize the vastness of its dimensions. It includes all living creatures, all nations, all cultures, all classes, all races. We can't say, Thy kingdom come for me and my kind, for me and the nice people that I like and associate with, because his Kingdom is not selective. Not all people will respond to it, but when it comes, it comes to everyone. A tidal wave doesn't pick and choose its victims; you are either prepared for it, or you are not prepared for it. A renaissance does not discriminate; it sweeps through the whole land; some miss it, others are made by it. So it is when the Kingdom comes.

It includes also the mysterious universe around us, the floods and the earthquakes. We think of them now because both have been ravaging other countries; the earthquake in Peru, followed by floods. God's

Kingdom is made not for man's comfort or even, I would say, for his happiness; that is, not happiness in a trivial, superficial sense. It is made for his growth.

Another thing that it makes plain about our world and our view of it is that it will never be a perfect world in which man will be safe and comfortable; in which there will be no chance of failure, no possibility of suffering; no friction by fire, no challenge to do the right thing, and no temptation to do the wrong thing. There will always be a tension between things as they are and things as they ought to be; and in one sense a Christian can rest in that tension, but if he ever becomes unaware of it, he's lost.

The world will never be perfect; Christianity promises no Utopia of a classless society or an order in which there is no such thing as violence or injustice. Nor will it ever be completely lost. It is never out of God's control, never has been, never will be. It is not now. From time to time man's freedom leads him out of bounds. He forgets where he is. He oversteps, and God lets him overstep. He respects him enough to give him the freedom to go wrong. Then something happens. From time to time some stranger crosses his path and sweeps the dust away, clears the air so that he can see things as they are. The Kingdom comes, and when it comes to you, you want to do what God wants you to do.

"Thy kingdom come. Thy will be done, On earth as it is in heaven." The second phrase is often spoken of as a "gloss." A gloss is an explanation. "Thy kingdom come" is explained as God's will being done on earth. I have been wondering recently if it is an interpretation of the Kingdom, or a consequence. For me, I think it is more likely to be the latter. When the Kingdom comes, I want to do God's will. When Shakespeare came alive, nobody had to tell me to find out more about the plays. I wanted to. So for me, the prayer, *Thy kingdom come*, means something like this:

> Lord Jesus, come my way and give me the sense and the courage to go your way; to do what you want, not what I want. I want to be secure; you want me to be a free spirit, free because I'm bound to something. I want to be happy; you want me to be

joyful. I want the things that money can buy; you want the things that no money can ever buy. I want to keep; you want me to give. Help me to go your way and to do what you want, for if I don't, I'm lost. If I do, I'm found; and when I'm found by you, I can somehow find myself, and take to others the breath of that life that comes to me from you. Come now, out of the dark; in some small, unexpected way come out of the blue. Make me ready for you when you come; and let me not be slow to reach for the stars, for the stars once fell upon me.

Thy kingdom come, O God, and when it comes let us not be blind or dumb or stubborn, too set in our own way to take it in. We have no choice. We can be taken in by it, or washed away by it. Help us to see always those who are already in it, who shine like lights in our dark world. Gather us together, and keep us close to each other, that we may give to those who are looking and longing for the life they want. Amen.

The Story of Stephen

T HERE IS A NEW SERIES of biographies published by Alfred Knopf called *Great Lives in Brief.* So far ten of them have been published, and they are about people as different in time and place as Elizabeth I and Mahatma Gandhi, with Gilbert Stuart, the portrait painter, in between. None is more than two hundred pages in length. I read six of them this summer, and they did two things for me over and above the obvious pleasure and information that they gave me. First, they reminded me more vividly than I had been reminded in a long time that the most inspiring thing on earth is an inspired human life. There is nothing that will put wind in your sails more quickly than to spend a few hours with one of the great souls of the earth. And another thing they did for me was to give me an idea for a series of sermons. We biblical Christians live in a gallery of great lives. Most of them we think of very seldom; we hear their names occasionally on Sundays, we know one or two things about them, and that is all.

What I propose to do from time to time, not on successive Sundays but from time to time, is to take one of the great lives from the gallery of the Bible, and try to hold it up to you, in brief, so that you can see it, know it, and enjoy it, and let it breathe, perchance, into you some of its surplus energy and life. And we begin today with Stephen. Stephen's life was brief not only in the number of pages it takes to tell it, but in the number of years it took to live it. I have divided it into three chapters, and the first is *How he got his start.*

I

This is rather interesting. It all started with a complaint—not a promis-

75

ing place to start from. And this was the complaint. The widows of the Greek-speaking Jews in Jerusalem, who belonged to a group of Jews who had been brought up abroad and had only recently come back to Jerusalem to live, more highly cultivated perhaps, and more cosmopolitan than their less-travelled neighbors, complained that they were not getting as much attention as the widows of the native, Jerusalem-born Jews. They sent the complaint to the leaders of the church. It probably had to do with the distribution of the relief funds that the early Christians always made available for the people who needed it. It was as if the people on Commonwealth Avenue should complain to the clergy of Trinity Church that they were not getting as much attention as the people in the South End. I regret to say that it is usually the other way around, but to make it fit the story I have imagined it that way. The disciples, of course, did exactly what the clergy of this church would do. They surveyed the situation, and realized that they could not assume any more responsibilities than they already had. They said to themselves something like this: our task is growing every day and we need more people to help us, and particularly some people to help us with the important but secondary part of the work; the preaching and teaching must not be neglected in the interest of these other relatively unimportant matters. So they picked out seven young men and assigned them the particular work of seeing that whatever was to be administered to the widows of the Greek-speaking Jews was administered to them safe and sound and that they were not slighted in favor of the home-born Jews. Stephen was one of them.

We are not particularly proud of a situation like that; I think we ought to say that in the very beginning. For one thing, it grows out of the fact that two groups pursuing the same end are not getting along together. We dread to see dissension creeping into the little group of Christians who were so closely knit together and so thoroughly united at the beginning. We are sad to see any intrusion of friction, but here it shows its ugly head at the very beginning of the stream of its life, and it never completely disappears thereafter. Two groups, with different backgrounds and different interests, one complaining about the other, that the other gets more attention than it should, working not in harmony but in tension. This is something we recognize easily as an all too familiar sight and we are not proud of it.

Also, when the disciples did the only practical thing they could, namely, divided the responsibility and increased the staff, so to speak, they did a dangerous thing. What they did, you see, was to give the less important part of the work to the young men, assuming that they were keeping in their own hands the most important part. But which is more important, to preach or to wait on tables? Which is more important, to speak to hundreds about Christianity, or to get one old-age pension worked out satisfactorily? Who would dare say, remembering Jesus? We are conscious, therefore, of the dilemma into which the disciples were moving when they began to divide the responsibility on the basis of the nature of the work, and they made it possible right at the beginning for people to assume that one part of Christ's ministry to his people was more important than another part.

However, it was just such a rather unpropitious human situation that gave Stephen his start. What great things in human life often have miserable beginnings! He appeared almost out of the blue, so far as we know, to meet an emergency created by this situation. Apparently, he had the qualifications that were required. He was young to begin with; he was full of enthusiasm and, above all, he had the one thing that was needed. He was a Greek-speaking Jew and, therefore, he could speak to and please the people who had been neglected. In the very brief account of him in the Acts of the Apostles, it describes him as "a man full of grace and spiritual power." In other words, this man who appeared to meet the emergency was a man of some stature. He was a man of considerable dimensions. And the amazing thing is that if the situation had never arisen, Stephen might never have been heard of. If this particular circumstance had not called out of obscurity a young man named Stephen "full of grace and spiritual power," that young man might never have been heard of in the history of mankind.

If the conflict between the states had not come to a head in 1860, Abraham Lincoln might never have been heard of outside the city limits of Springfield, Illinois. If a door had not opened, a parent died, an accident occurred, a depression set in, a war begun, a teacher made the right move, you might not be where you are today. For a man, you see, is not only the result of what he does himself, but of what God does *to* him, and all of us, whether we are prominent in the galleries of the world like Stephen or not, are the result of these two component factors —the action of God calling us out from the wings to meet the emergency of a situation and our own capacity and will to respond to God's call. The lesson, therefore, of this first chapter of Stephen's life is simply this: a man is the product of the times he helps to produce. And, the moral of it is: when the times call, don't hang back in the wings.

II

The second chapter—*Why he got into trouble.* Why in the world did this young man with every talent anyone could have for a particular task, with the road open straight ahead of him, why did a man like that get into almost immediate trouble, and finally into the very serious trouble in which he lost his life? Why should this be? Why does it ever happen that way? Not that the answer to the question about Stephen will answer the question about every one of your lives that have been crippled when they should have been strengthened, and thwarted when they should have been free, and ended when they should have continued, not that that will be true, but we may get a glimpse of the answer from the life of Stephen.

There are two good reasons why Stephen got into trouble. This, I suppose, as I often say is an oversimplification, but remember this is a great life "in brief." First, he wanted above everything else to see Christianity grow. He had seen it begin; whether he ever saw Jesus himself we have no way of knowing, but he had been very close to the beginning of it and felt the throbbing life of it. This, he was convinced, was the spirit of God moving through the world of human affairs. The future belonged to this new way of life, and he did not hesitate to say what he thought about it. He was on fire with the new life. He saw it stirring men into a new and more vivid existence than they had ever had before, and he wanted it to grow and, in order to grow, everything that might obstruct it must be removed.

There were others who wanted to see it die. It is appalling as we sit

78

here now and look back quite objectively at the situation to realize that that was true, and yet it should not surprise us, should it? When you stop to think of it, there has never been a movement forward that has not been resisted by multitudes. I say it again. There has never been a forward movement that has not been resisted by great numbers of people. Did you ever stop to think about that and wonder why, whether you might be one of the resisting forces in the way of life's forward movement now? The movement to free the slaves, a movement which I suppose every person in this country would acclaim now and take for granted, that movement was resisted generation after generation by enlightened men and women like you and me. The movement to pay labor a fair wage, which most of us now would say is taken as a matter of course, was resisted decade after decade by some of the finest people in the English-speaking world. The movement to give the vote to the people, and to take the power out of a few chosen rulers, was resisted for centuries by people who thought that they knew what life was all about. And I think we ought to say this, that the church is not exempt from this weakness, for the church resisted the movement to know the truth about the stars and the moon and the rocks and the earth; it resisted that movement for decades. Indeed, in some quarters it is still rigorously resisting it!

Christianity, then, was no different. When it began, and often throughout its history, but particularly when it began, it was resisted bitterly by two sorts of people. I think we ought to make allowance for both sorts. One was the sincere conservatives, people who were afraid that the new movement was going to destroy something precious in the old society. I personally have great respect for people like that. Even when I disagree with them, I realize the dignity of the position they take. The church was also bitterly resisted, of course, by the selfish vested interest of people who knew that if the Christian movement went forward, they would go down to destruction.

Here, you see, were two strong-minded, irresistible bodies—a young, passionate man convinced that in this little seed of life was the life of the world for future ages and, on the other hand, a group of stubborn, redoubtable, sturdy men and women who refused to let that new movement grow. They were bound to clash, sooner or later, and they did. First, quite informally in debates between Stephen and the rabbis in the synagogues. It made matters worse because of the fact that Stephen always won the debates; he was more clever than they were. It did not enhance his popularity in their minds because the jealousy that had already been felt toward him was fanned and intensified by his success in argumentation. Finally, they brought him to the Council Chamber, which we might call the Court Room, to put him on trial, to give him a hearing, so to speak.

It is a dramatic scene, and almost impossible for us to reproduce, but there sitting, or probably standing, alone was Stephen. You will remember the things we have already said about him, the kind of person he was, the quality of life that was in him. The whole court room, the story says, fastened its eyes on Stephen. There wasn't a person distracted or looking at anything else, and the account goes on to say this, that as they looked at his face it was like the face of an angel. Even his enemies had to admit that there was a kind of radiance about him that the people in their ranks did not have. He shone like crystal; and they were dull, like lead.

Finally, when they asked him to speak, he did speak, and the account in the Book of the Acts gives a long speech, which some scholars think was probably not the original speech Stephen made. Very likely it wasn't but certainly the essence of what he said is made plain there, and I think we have no reason to question it. The point that he made, finally, toward the end and which was really the thrust which did something to the enemy that they never recovered from, was this. He said to them: You always resist the spirit of God! You resisted Moses, or your forefathers did. When God sent Moses to get you out of the slavery of Egypt, to take you across the Red Sea and lead you through all the perils of the wilderness to the Promised Land, no sooner had you crossed the Red Sea than you began to complain about Moses and to say that because you had difficulties and dangers to face he should have left you in Egypt. You resisted him; your forefathers have resisted all the others along the line. The prophets they have resisted consistently. Now, he said, you are resisting Jesus. Him in whom we see a new life for the world, a new order for society, a new hope for men and women, in whom we find an expression of the love of God such as we have never known before, you are resisting him.

When he finished you can imagine that they were furious. People don't like to be told, you certainly wouldn't like it if I told you, that they are deliberately resisting the spirit of God, but he didn't even look at them. He was looking up and, without giving them a chance to say anything, he said to them, "Look, the heavens are opened, and I can see the Son of Man standing on the right hand of God." What does it mean? He saw nothing in one sense, and yet he saw everything in another sense. Jesus not dimmed by the mist of confusion into which he had been plunged, but made brighter than ever before, over and above the smallness of humanity, their resistances and obstructions to the life of God, over and above and through that the heavens opened, and there was the greatness of God standing, still calling men on. There isn't anything, I think, more uplifting than to be in the presence of a person who in spite of all obstacles and all opposition, and all the pain that he has to encounter, still goes on his way, and still at the end, looks up and sees the heavens open, more assured than ever before, more confirmed in the thing that he believed in; his ideal, brighter and more alluring than it had been before.

III

They quickly led him out of the Sanhedrin and, of course, this action leads to the last chapter, which is very brief because it happened so quickly: *How he died.* They stoned him to death on the spot. No attempt was made to hide the fact of mob violence. No attempt or pretense was made at justice; it was a demonstration of organized passion and rage. It is a warning to us, and a solemn warning that we thought once we did not need to hear before the Second World War, that when the passions of people are left undisciplined so that they run down into the lower levels of life, when they are in that condition they can be aroused and they can perform acts of brutality and cruelty almost beyond our imagining. And that holds for people like us, you know; the most refined ones might be capable of the worst brutality.

While they were stoning him, he prayed. This was the real thing with Stephen. There are people we see all along through life who have what we think is the real thing, but when the actual test comes, they do not. But this was the real thing; he followed through. It was not any pose, he was not talking to people for the thrill he got from public speaking and from swaying the feelings and emotions of multitudes. He was saying what was in his heart and what was on his mind and what he believed with all his soul. This rang true and this is what he said, "Lord Jesus, receive my spirit. Lord, lay not this sin to their charge." It makes you feel mean, first; small, when you remember all your little resentments and grudges and desire for revenge. And then, somehow, it makes you feel great, proud to belong to a race that can so emerge from the lower instincts of the animal which are in every one of us as to reach from time to time, more often than we sometimes think, heights like this and, as you stand in the presence of that life, you begin to feel the currents of air from other worlds blow through the cramped and crowded ways of your life.

It isn't any wonder, is it, that a young intellectual Jew named Saul, from Tarsus, who was standing there watching Stephen, could never get that face out of his mind? First it haunted him, and then it changed him into the man who turned the world upside down for Christ.

We thank thee, O God, for the lives of thy chosen ones in whom there has been grace and power; draw us more closely into their fellowship that by association with them our lives may be quickened, and that we may be encouraged to strike out into the deeps of our own lives and live them with as much honesty and courage as they lived theirs. Amen.

The Unexpected Christh

❧

THE SUBJECT of the sermon today was suggested by a new book by
Loren Eiseley. Dr. Eiseley is the Benjamin Franklin Professor of Anthropology and History of Science at the University of Pennsylvania.
He is a distinguished anthropologist, but perhaps even more widely
known to the general public as a man of letters. He writes as a scientist
with the hand and the eye of a poet.

As an anthropologist he studies the origin and development of man
through the ages, the ages before history was written down. That means
that he is also an archaeologist. His business is to dig up the past, the
past that has long been buried, not in the subconscious mind where the
psychiatrists look for it, but in the earth where it has been buried by the
ice, the sea, and the rocks. Buried though it be, it has left traces for those
who have the eyes to see them. It may be just a scratch on Mt. Monad-
nock left by a glacier two million years ago; or it may be a stone that
once was a bone in the body of an animal. These are the things he looks
for.

This particular anthropologist not only digs up the past, but he also
digs into its meaning. I have already said that he is a poet by nature; he
is also a philosopher by temperament, and an artist as well as a scientist.
His first book that caught the public's imagination was *The Immense
Journey* (1957). It may surprise some of you, but I can quite honestly say
that if a person came to me who had no preconceptions about either
Christianity or religion, but wanted to know something by way of
background before he approached the subject of religion to which he
was more and more strongly attracted, I would not give him a book
about theology; I would give him Loren Eiseley's *The Immense Journey.*

83

That would spread the screen high and wide. Eiseley never talks about God directly, and only seldom mentions Him by name. I know nothing whatever about his personal religion, or whether he is attached to any particular religious institution. But I know that he says to me more about God than many of the theologians say who talk about Him all the time.

The new book is called *The Unexpected Universe*. I think what he is saying (and I say *I think* because quite obviously I am out of my field, and I am not quite sure that I have correctly understood him), but I venture to summarize the sum and substance of what he is saying. It is something like this. What happens is not always what we expect. We thought we had wrapped up the universe in a neat package of law and order; the scientists of the Victorian period were almost all convinced of this. They thought they had gotten down to the rock bottom of fact; and there it was, forever. It was all quite rational and dependable. The universe operated by law, not by chance or fancy, and the law was immutable. Now we are beginning to discover the surprises in the universe, the things we had not expected, things we had no way of predicting or foreseeing. Who would have thought, for instance, that man would first appear when ice covered most of the planet? You wouldn't choose that as the most auspicious time for the beginning of a new race!

There is something about our universe, about life, he is saying on almost every page, that slips through the fingers of the mind. There is something beyond the rational that points toward an unexpected, unforeseeable future; and to a present in which life is strangely mingled with death.

As I read his book, I who am not a scientist, I get the impression that the book is a gentle hint to all scientists, all would-be scientists, and to us who are prone to make dogmatic statements that are not open to question, that might be put in these words: Don't be too sure; keep looking, but don't be too sure; remember that time is always open-ended, and we don't know exactly what is going to happen.

On the first page of the book he quotes a line from Heraclitus, not the line that every schoolboy knows, but another line. "If you do not expect it, you will not find the unexpected, for it is hard to find and difficult." It's the unexpected universe that he continues to explore, and because he expects so much he is continually finding the unexpected.

You may wonder why that book suggests a sermon, particularly at this time of the year in the middle of Advent, the season of expectation. The answer is not hard to find. I couldn't read a book called *The Unexpected Universe* without thinking about the Unexpected Christ. Dr. Eiseley's book started me off on my own train of thought along which he might have no desire to follow.

You say immediately, Was anyone ever more expected than Christ? Anybody ever more looked forward to than he was? You know that on February 15, 1564, Michelangelo died and Galileo was born; and that on the 23rd of April in the same year Shakespeare was born. There are three men who shaped our thinking. No one had any reason to expect any one of them. But surely it was not so with Christ; a whole nation was expecting him! They had been waiting for at least two or three hundred years for his arrival. They were looking everywhere for him, and every time that they saw someone like John the Baptist they wondered whether he might be the one. The hope of his coming kept them going through the humiliation and the indignity of their exile, and through the coming of the Greeks with their temples, and then of the Romans, with their efficient management of government. So, certainly, you can't say that they didn't expect him.

And yet, the fact is that when he did come, they didn't know it; and they didn't know it because he wasn't the Christ that they had expected. They expected him to come with a fanfare, to cause a stir. But he didn't; he came quietly. The story tells us that a few shepherds knew it, but no one else; and in Malcolm Muggeridge's extraordinary book in which he describes his own rediscovery of Jesus, he writes, "Probably no child born into the world that day seemed to have poorer prospects than Christ did." They didn't expect that kind of Christ.

They expected (at least, most of them did; and I must warn you that when we say "they" we are not including everyone, because there were always exceptions, then as now), but in general, they expected a Christ who would liberate them from Rome. He didn't. He liberated them from Satan; from sin and from guilt. They expected a Christ who would dazzle them by miraculous feats. He didn't. He healed the sick and he fed the hungry; but he didn't jump off the temple just to dazzle them into belief. He refused to do that.

What is more, they expected a Christ who would instill in the young a love of the *Law*—the Law with a capital L because it was the Law of God that Moses had given them, and it covered every aspect of life with rules and regulations, both ceremonial and moral. People were neglecting it, and they were expecting a Christ who would rekindle a love of the Law with a capital L. He didn't. He talked about the Law of Love, which was quite different. He said that love is the fulfilling of all the laws.

They expected a Christ who would make life easier, reduce the taxes, increase the employment, bring down the prices. He didn't. If anything he made it harder. He talked about crosses, not crowns. It is harder, infinitely harder, to change yourself than to change your surroundings. I am not saying that it isn't important to change the surroundings of other people from time to time, for it is; but the essential thing is to change the person, and it is much easier to change the surroundings in which a person lives than to change the person who lives in those surroundings.

Above everything else, they expected a Christ who would be a smashing success. He wasn't; he was a dismal failure. They expected a Christ that they could keep to themselves as a nation. They couldn't. He was like a river, the current of which is so strong that no bank can contain it. They expected a Christ who would promise a happy ending. Everybody likes happy endings. He didn't promise the kind of a happy ending that all people really long for. He never let them forget about the girls who might have gone to the wedding, but didn't because they were too late, and the man who missed the dinner because he was too busy to accept the invitation. He never let people forget the fact that the door can be closed, and that it can be closed forever; that there is the possibility of missing the bus.

They didn't expect anything like that; only a few of the most perceptive ones could see the possibility of a Christ born in a manger and crucified on a cross. So it is no wonder that they hardly recognized him, because he was not the Christ they expected. They weren't ready for the Unexpected Christ.

Now we come to another Christmas, the middle of another season of Advent. We know that Christmas will come in the normal course of events. It always has come, the calendar always gets around to the 25th of December, and if we all live for another ten days, we will all have another Christmas. We know that. And we also know that Christ will come, in one way or another, but instinctively we look for him to come in the way we expect him; and there is a sense in which he will come in that way. He will break through, here and there, the crust of our fierce, competitive world; he will soften a hard heart, here and there. He will heal an open wound; he will manage to find a small place on the thousands of cards and messages, even the ones that have not a single reference to himself, because the one who sends it expresses his own love and affection on that card. So he will come that way.

But there is also a sense in which he is always the Unexpected Christ. We expect him to come in the usual place, which for us is either the church, or the home, or both. For many people he may come in neither of those places. He may come in the streets; he may come on the college campus where there doesn't seem to be much sign of him at the moment; he may come on a ski slope where a family spends the holidays. Or, he may come like a shining light in a scientist's laboratory, the flickering of a new idea that will open one of the secrets of the world. We expect him to come in the familiar music of the carols we love and have heard all our lives and will hear again next Sunday, and all through the Christmas Season. For many of us he will come in that music. But for thousands he may come in the more primitive rhythm of music that is called Rock. I don't understand it, but I am prepared for the fact that that is the way he will come for many people.

We expect him to come in the familiar language of the Bible, especially the King James translation, and the Book of Common Prayer. He may come in our time in some strange, new tongue that sounds to us so vernacular that it borders on the vulgar. Before you make any judgment about it, remember that the first translation of the Scriptures from Greek into Latin was called the *Vulgate* for that very reason, because people thought it was a vulgar language.

We expect him to come in the structure of our long-established manners and morals. He may not. He may come to some little shed completely outside our sheltered lives, in some new way of loving each other in a world in which love has been almost forced out of the picture by the sheer size of the human family.

This is disturbing to people over thirty. It would be so much easier for all of us if he came in the same old place, in the same old way. The old decorations would do; and save us such a lot of trouble, and an enormous amount of money. But he won't. He will not leave us alone; that is, he will not let us alone. He wants to keep us alive. Instead of solutions, he gives us problems for Christmas, if you can believe it. A man can settle down and die in a solution, but in a problem he is more sure to stay alive.

Christ comes as the angel that troubles the water. He says something like this to me, and he may say it to you; but he says it to me this particular year. You can't wrap God up in a proof-sheet of logical, rational reasoning. You can't have me gift-wrapped for a Christmas present. You can't preserve me in your theological formulas or even in your ecclesiastical institutions, because I will always be slipping out for a breath of fresh air. He says, If you want the serenity that I can give you, you must take the restlessness that goes with it, without which the serenity would be nothing but smugness. He says, When I come, I come as I am—like the wind, like a breath of life. If you don't expect me, you will not find me. If you do find me, don't be surprised if I am not the one you expected.

George MacDonald, the Scot who left the ministry because it was too tight for his mind, wrote a great many novels and stories for children. In 1883 he published a book of poems, one of which has been included in two of our hymnals. There are only three stanzas. The language is Victorian, but you can see why I end this sermon with these three verses.

THE UNEXPECTED CHRIST

They all were looking for a king
  To slay their foes, and lift them high:
Thou cam'st a little baby thing
  That made a woman cry.

O Son of Man, to right my lot
  Naught but thy presence can avail;
Yet on the road thy wheels are not
  Nor on the sea thy sail!

My fancied ways, why shouldst thou heed?
  Thou com'st down thine own secret stair;
Com'st down to answer all my need
  Yea, ev'ry bygone prayer.

The Unexpected Christ coming down his own secret stair!

Sharpen our minds, O Lord, humble our spirits, and open our hearts to take in the love that once became flesh, that comes amongst us again and again, that we may not only take him in, but show him to others and let others see him in us. And we ask it in his name, and by his power, and for his sake. Amen.

The Woman at the Well

THE SERMON TODAY is a commentary on a dialogue between Jesus and a woman. There are five such dialogues in St. John's Gospel and they are quite different from anything in the Synoptic Gospels; nothing like the short, brief encounters reported in the first three Gospels. These are long, we might call them "conversations in depth." There are some who believe that every word of the dialogues is a verbatim report of what was said. Others, more congenial to myself, believe that the dialogues are related in their nature and purpose to the Platonic dialogues. At the heart of each one of them is a real situation, and the writer of the Gospel uses that situation to develop ideas which he has come to believe are essential to the Christian faith.

In this particular dialogue Jesus began the conversation. He met a woman at the village well and asked her to give him a drink. The woman was there because she needed water for her household. The well was the center of the village life. Even today, the well is the center of life in the Italian village of San Gimignano, and the Piazza della Cisterna is still a place of attraction even though no one now comes there to draw water as they once did.

So the woman came to get water. He was a stranger, just passing through, on his way from Jerusalem to his home in Galilee. It was high noon; it was hot, and he was tired and thirsty. He had been walking all morning and it was only natural that he would be weary, and the walking plus the heat made him thirsty. When we think of Jesus we usually think of someone who is drawing the weary to himself. "Come unto me all ye that travail and are heavy laden, and I will give you rest."

Isn't that the way you think of him? Sometimes it is good to think of him as being weary himself. Anyone who gives out as he gave out, gave to people of all kinds and at all times, has to take in, needs the things that other people can give him. He was weary, and he sat down at the well.

Also, we are most likely to think of the things he did for other people. He healed them, he forgave them, he lifted that terrible burden of guilt that paralyzed some of them, he taught them, he aroused their conscience, their curiosity, their will; he often cheered them, gave them confidence, and finally died for them. We don't often think of the things that he asked other people to do for him. Give me a drink. Watch here for an hour or two while I go and say my prayers. Give up your business and follow me. Feed my sheep. Visit me. Feed me. Clothe me. We don't often think of those things.

In our time the church has often made its appeal to people on the basis of what the church can do for them. It is quite right that it should. Many times it can steady people who are not steady by themselves. It can often help them in practical ways. It sometimes can feed them. It can befriend them, and make friends for them. It can find a place for them to live, and on occasions, give them enough to live on. That is good; the church is in the world to serve as well as to save.

Sometimes I wonder if it might not be well to start the other way around with the things that you can give the church, not necessarily this church but the church as a whole, the Christian community; whether it might not be well for us to start out this way: Give us your hand, give us your interest, your attention, your concern, your time, your money perhaps, if you have any, your presence. We need you. And isn't it true, at least it seems more and more true to me, that we don't really help anyone only by serving him, although you do serve him; but you don't really help him by serving him until he reaches the point where he is ready to serve someone else. It is when you ask him to do something for you that you know whether he is really alive, whether he has changed for the better or worse.

The woman replied to this simple request for a drink, How can you ask *me* for a drink? It was quite natural for her to say that, and on two scores. First, he was a man. In the Oriental world such as the world he lived in, men and women did not mix together in public. A Jew was forbidden by the law in Leviticus to salute his own wife in public. The Women's Liberation Movement had never been thought of, and I can see how they might have had something to work on if they lived in those days. So the fact that he was a man and began the conversation with her was startling.

Also, he was a Jew and she was a Samaritan. Without going into the history of that long, deep-seated feud, and it has a long history—you can do it for yourself; I am not going to do it now because this would turn into a lecture and not a sermon—all I need to say is that the Jews and the Samaritans were not on speaking terms. It wasn't only that they were not on polite speaking terms; most Jews, if they had to travel northward from Jerusalem, would cross the Jordan and go up the other side of the river to avoid going through the Samaritan country.

Jesus, on this occasion, went directly through Samaria. Why he did it we don't know, though scholars have guessed and speculated about it ever since. In the Authorized Version is this wonderful phrase, "And he must needs go through Samaria." He didn't have to; he could have gone the way he came, up the longer but much easier route of the Jordan Valley; but he did go through Samaria. Although it was shorter, it was much more difficult because it was a mountainous country. Whether he did it because he wanted to do it is not said. But at any rate he did do it, and this gave the woman another reason for wondering why he spoke to her.

It makes us realize that there is nothing new about Iron Curtains, those walls that separate us from other groups of human beings. The Wall of China that was built in 225 B.C.; the Maginot Line that the French thought would protect them from the Germans; the English Channel which the English always thought of as sure protection against invasion from the Continent; the Berlin Wall that now separates East Berlin from West Berlin. Then you think of the invisible walls that for centuries separated Catholics from Protestants, and still do in many cases, but thank heaven they are now coming down; the wall that separates the Jew from the Gentile, the white from the colored, and even in

our own company, the liberal from the conservative. Where these walls
exist there is no passage, no transit, no crossing. Jesus refused to be separated from anyone by any of the artificial conventions of life. He ignored the walls of isolation. If a person chose to reject him that was his
business, but he did not exclude anyone.

Jesus characteristically didn't answer the woman's question. He must
have been a disturbing person to meet in conversation because he seldom answered a question directly, not as a rule. He had a good reason
for doing it; he wanted to draw the other person out.

Remember, he asked her for a drink and she said, How can you ask
me; you are a man and I am a woman; you are a Jew, and I am a Samaritan, how can you ask me for a drink? Instead of explaining the fact
that he didn't care a rap for the difference between the Samaritans and
the Jews, and that he despised the convention that men and women
should not speak in public, he said to her, "If you knew who I am, you
would ask me for a drink and I would give you water that would satisfy
your thirst forever." The woman was completely confused. Why
wouldn't she be? As we look at it now whether this be a verbatim
conversation or not, this is one of the ways a good teacher leads a person
out, by asking questions that confuse him and make him think further
than he would ordinarily think.

In the first place, the woman, like most people, had a literal mind. I
hope that I am not being unfair, but that is what I have come to believe
as I have grown older; most people have minds that are strictly literal.
She said, How can you give me a drink? You haven't any bucket to
draw with. And then she went on to say, What kind of water are you
talking about? He was comparing the water that he would give her
with the water in the well. He said, I would give you living water, that
is, running water. She said, This is the best well in the whole countryside, and it is here as a memorial to Jacob. Are you greater than he?

This is the kind of confusion that is bound to occur when two people
use the same word but in a different sense. Take the word *way*. Someone asks you the way to New York and you say, The way to New
York is the Massachusetts Turnpike; follow the signs. Another person
asks you the way to New York, and knowing the person you say, The

best way to get to New York is to do the best you can where you are. In the first instance, you are talking about a way of travel, and in the other, you are talking about a way of life. So, with water. Water to the woman meant something that came out of a well. To Jesus it meant something that came from God.

Here we shall pause briefly to make the comment that Jesus always directed a person's attention from the immediate necessities of life to the ultimate satisfactions. All of us need food and drink and money, and let no one ever underestimate those needs; but we need so much more than those. We need spirit, motivation, desire, aims, goals, without which all the money, all the food and the drink in the world makes nothing much better than a jet set. A person asks for prayers for someone who is dangerously ill. He needs the prayers, and we say the prayers. But he needs more than that. He needs the willingness to accept whatever comes his way and the confidence that God's will is such that he will have the strength to meet and deal with anything that happens to him. It is tragic, isn't it, the way so many of us settle for the basic needs like Social Security, color television, cars, all the gadgets that make life easier and pleasanter, and neglect the ultimate things, the "inner" things —whatever you want to call them—peace, unity, direction, happiness, usefulness, spirit, zest.

Puzzled as she was, the woman asked him to give her this water. It would, of course, save her a great deal of drudgery. She wouldn't have to come to the well day after day if the water that Jesus gave her was going to last forever. Then Jesus said, Go and get your husband. Again, the speculation that has been poured out upon this one line would take volumes to record. I don't know what the answer is. From my own experience in dealing with people, it has become clear that you can't have anything really precious by yourself alone. Go get the person nearest you; you cannot have it in private. Nothing great, not even the Christian Faith, is ever really possessed until it is shared.

The woman said she didn't have a husband, and she didn't; she told the absolute truth. She had a lover, and she had had a succession of lovers. Jesus knew it; he sensed it. You don't have to have ESP to know things like that. Even I can see things like that; and so can you if you have had any experience with human beings. But the woman was astonished. She thought he must be a prophet who could see the invisible. So she sidestepped the whole moral issue by raising a theological question. Never before in the dialogue was she more human than at that moment, and never afterwards.

She raised the question, Where is the right place to worship? The Jews said that Jerusalem was the place, and the Samaritans said that it was Mount Gerazim. Sometimes in a confirmation class I have tried as hard as I knew how to tell people the meaning of the cross, what it meant to them, what it asks of them. I ask at the end of an hour, Are there any questions? And someone says, Why are there six candles on the altar? Without realizing it, perhaps, he is sidestepping the great issue by way of a minor liturgical detail that makes really no difference at all. Or, you hear a plea from me or from someone else for regular attendance at Sunday worship and you say, I can't do it on Sunday because I do thus and so. Why don't you have it on Wednesday? One of the most common tricks of the mind is to use a valid question as a loophole out of a tight situation.

Jesus answered this question. I shall read it as it stands because no other words could replace them. "The hour cometh, when ye shall neither in this mountain, nor yet at Jerusalem, worship the Father . . . The hour cometh, and now is, when the true worshippers shall worship the Father in spirit and in truth: for the Father seeketh such to worship him. God is spirit: and they that worship him must worship him in spirit and in truth" (St. John 4:21–24). In other words, the question is not *where* you worship, but *how* you worship, and *whom* you worship.

I have been thinking a lot about Phillips Brooks this month because I wrote a paper for a club that he started a hundred years ago, and he died seventy-eight years ago yesterday. On his first trip to Europe in 1865 he went to the Holy Land and in one of his letters he wrote, "Of all the associations with Christ, I found the most pleasure in Nazareth, Jacob's well, and the Mount of Olives." Why Jacob's well? He told us why. Because it was "the scene of his highest announcement of truth." God is spirit, not to be contained in any building, in any theological system, in any doctrinal formula, or in any liturgical pattern, in any

95

sacramental act—God is spirit, energy, dynamic power that makes all things live, move, and be. You can worship him wherever you are, in any place, at any time. You cannot fence him in. All your theories, all your rites and ceremonies cannot hold him.

That was too much for the woman! She said, When the Messiah comes he will give us all the answers. She was doing just what we do. She was putting off into the future answers that are demanded today. And then Jesus said to her, according to St. John, "I that speak unto thee am he." It is just about the most dramatic moment in the New Testament, whether it is historically accurate or whether it isn't. The Messiah? This ordinary man, this stranger met by chance, by accident, sitting by a well, this man who asked me, a woman and a Samaritan, for a drink, this man with needs like mine, this man is the Messiah? Nonsense!

We, like that woman, are looking for something extraordinary to happen to set the world to rights. It may be sitting right on our doorstep now, something for us to do, something for us to cope with, staring us in the face, so familiar that we don't see it.

There is no attempt to describe what the woman felt. One famous line that the commentators never miss and, as Scott Holland says, thanks be to God, it can never be allegorized. "The woman left her waterpot." In other words, she went back home, but she intended to return. She went home and said to her friends, "Come, see a man who told me all that I ever did. Can this be the Christ?" That is what we are saying today, every day. That is virtually the message of every sermon even though not said in so many words. It is an invitation: Come, see a Man. And the answer to the question, Can this be the Christ? is up to you. It is for you to answer.

> Dear Lord, help us to live this week quietly, easily;
> To lean upon thy strength restfully, trustfully;
> To wait for the unfolding of thy will patiently, serenely;
> To meet others peacefully, joyously;
> To face tomorrow courageously, confidently. Amen.

The Key to a Split-Level Life

Not so very long ago—perhaps twenty-five years, more or less—the split-level house was an architectural novelty. The rooms were not on different "floors" stacked on top of each other, but were strung-out horizontally, you might say; but not all on the same level. One level led to the next with a few steps up or down. That was a novelty.

But there is nothing new about split-level lives! People have been living split-level lives for centuries. In fact, it's doubtful if many ever lived any other kind of life. If you think of it simply from a temperamental point of view, you can see the different levels. Sometimes a person is up in what we call "high G," sometimes he is down below "sea level," and the rest of the time somewhere near the octave of middle C. In other words, temperamentally he lives on different levels, and moves from one to the other quite easily, often without any perceptible cause.

Different people at different times in the history of the world picture these levels in different ways; they give them different names, not always with exactly the same meaning. The Greeks thought that man lived essentially on two levels, one was his body and the other was his soul. His body was his physical equipment and his soul was the part of him with which he soared into the upper region of eternal things. The body was a temporary container for the continuing life of the soul.

To skip across the centuries to Freud, he pictured man as living on three levels. One was the *id*, that is the libido, the unconscious level; the second was the *ego*, the conscious level, and the third was the *super-ego*, that is the level from which the commands, the directives came which produced in him guilt, some healthy, and some unhealthy.

St. Paul is the one we are really interested in right now, and he had his own picture of the levels on which people live, patterns which he inherited from his mixed inheritance from Greece and Palestine. The first level was the *flesh*, 'all this earthly part of me.' The second was the *psyche*, the mind. The third was the *spirit*; and the whole organism was the *body*. If this were a lecture I would stress that point and develop it further; don't mistake in Pauline theology body for flesh, because they are not the same. The body was that which identified a person as a person, the whole of him, including his flesh, his psyche, and his spirit. Flesh decays and dies; the body changes, but does not die and cannot be left behind.

People often miss the point of what St. Paul was writing about because they get lost in his terminology, his anthropology; I confess quite frankly that this sermon comes as a result of the portion of his Epistle to the Romans (8:1–10) that was read to you a few minutes ago, because as I read it over I thought to myself, What on earth will the people get when they hear St. Paul going on about the flesh and the spirit and the law? Knowing that a few of you are well trained theologically in Pauline thought, I also knew that most of you would get next to nothing, and the reason that you would get so little is that you would be lost in the terminology. Hence, this attempt to shed a ray of light on what you heard.

Sometimes we come closer to his meaning by looking first at ourselves and the levels of our own live. On the first level, usually partly below ground—if we keep the picture of the split-level house built on sloping land—there are the instincts, the impulses, the compulsions, the desires and passions, the anxieties and the fears, the hopes and the dreams—those invisible drives. Over these we sometimes seem to have no control whatsoever; as a matter of fact, they often control us. We say they "drive us"; they sometimes "drive us to drink"; sometimes to anger. We sometimes say things that we wouldn't dream of saying ordinarily and doing things that we can't conceive of doing at any other time. They drive some people to murder, or at the other extreme to say something mean, something that cuts without shedding a drop of blood. Sometimes they "drive" us to bitterness and despair.

On the other hand, they often drive us to do great things. Where would we be without any ambition, which one biographer of Vincent Van Gogh called the "lust for life." Where would we be without it? Where would we be without any desire or passion for anything, lukewarm, neutral about everything? Probably back in the caves where we started. But we also know that this very same energy can get us into the most serious trouble. We can drink too much, then drive a car, hit another car, and kill a whole family. It has been done. We can desire too much, take what doesn't really belong to us, cut too many corners, and land in jail, or whatever may be the equivalent of it for the guilty who is never caught. We can be free, up and about the streets, but still imprisoned, behind the bars of a guilty conscience that can do more damage to us than the bars of a prison. We can spend our passion on people we neither love nor even know just to use them for our pleasure, and sometimes ruin them, and slide down the slippery slope a little further ourselves. This, you see, is the level that St. Paul would call "the flesh," not bad in itself, but often the cause of suffering and evil, as well as beauty and greatness. So that is the first level.

Then there is the level of consciousness, intelligence, and knowledge. We may sometimes act in a blind rage but sooner or later we know that we did it and we wish we hadn't. We may, under certain circumstances, go mad with jealousy but, sooner or later, we know what we are doing even though we can't stop doing it. Sometimes the lower level can smoke out entirely this higher level. A man can be so consumed with ambition that he no longer knows that he is destroying another person's life. Sometimes I wonder, and I imagine that you wonder, about a person like Hitler, how much he knew what he was doing, or whether he knew and didn't care.

What we also know and ought to think about at this particular time is that none of us is beyond this possibility. None of us is beyond the possibility of those lower energies smoking out the upper level of the psyche, the mind. We can become so habitually possessive that we are not even aware of it, so continually self-centered that we haven't the slightest idea of it, and if anybody said we were we would think he was absolutely crazy. We can become so used to having our own way that we never give a thought to anyone else's way and haven't the slightest idea that we are doing it.

I doubt if there is anyone here who hasn't had that experience, to some degree. If any of you live alone as I do, you must have it because most of the time, at least in your private life, you have no one to think about but yourself and you find that you are likely to forget that there is anyone else to think about. But most of us, at least some of the time, know what we are doing. We know that when we drink too much we are "sailing close to the wind"; so we measure our drinks. We know that we are temperamentally moody; so we steer clear of the things that are most likely to bring on the darker moods, and if we can't do that we try not to let the shadow of darkness fall on other people.

The trouble is that no matter how much we know about ourselves we cannot always stop doing some of the very things we despise most. We know the rules and regulations of society and, by and large, respect them. But we break them. We know that alcohol and drugs can be harmful, and at the same time we can't stay away from them. We know that money isn't everything in life, but there is something in us that can't resist taking one more chance on the stock market, or offering a bribe, or taking one for a good deal. This leads us into a serious predicament. We know what to do but we have neither the will nor the power to do it. This is where the psyche failed St. Paul. He knew the Law of God. He had been brought up on it all his life; he was taught to obey it. He wanted to keep it, but he broke it (Romans 7:18–24).

So that's the second level. The psyche, the mind, the intelligence, the conscious level and the part it plays in our life.

Mercifully, there is another level sometimes rarely used, sometimes like the guest room only partly furnished. It is the level that I call *Motivating Spirit*. Some of it is part of our natural endowment; some people seem to have more than their share of it and some people have almost none; why this is I don't know and I know no one else who knows. For instance, an older woman in her eighties was run over by a bus. One leg was broken, one arm. She has been in a hospital since a year ago last September. Everything under the sun that could happen to anybody has happened to her. Yet when you see her you would never know it. She is cheerful, she never complains, and you come away saying, What a spirit she has! If you know her well, as I do, you have the feeling that this is part of her natural endowment. She has always been that way.

But sometimes that spirit is a visitor from outside, someone comes in from the outside and changes the color of a person's life. The classic example of this in recent times is Elizabeth Barrett stretched out on an invalid's couch in Wimpole Street, living under the thumb of a puritanical father who ruled every move she made. Suddenly, from the outside, from a different world, in walked Robert Browning! That was the end of the invalidism; they went off and were married, had a son, and lived in Italy for the rest of her life.

It isn't always as exciting as that. One of the major poets in this country (I have often said the "greatest" but perhaps I shouldn't say that) is Edwin Arlington Robinson. To say the very least, he was one of the few major American poets. He was a man without a home, once he left the family home in Maine, and he wandered about from friend to friend until finally quite early in life he found in the summer a haven where he could be at home. It was the MacDowell Colony in Peterborough, New Hampshire. He went there summer after summer and shared the life of other artists, musicians, and creative people all the rest of his life. Unfortunately, for a long time he nursed his loneliness in alcohol. He often drank too much, and this was difficult for him, and for his friends; and it didn't help his creative work. In one of his biographies this line comes: "In gratitude for what the MacDowell Colony had given him Robinson resolved to give up drink." And he did. That was the spirit that moved in from outside.

Francis Thompson, the man who wrote the poem I read at the end of the Price Lecture but didn't mention by name, wandered the streets of London for six or seven years, a drug addict, living in the gutters, selling matches to buy food. He broke the drug habit when Wilfred Meynell published one of his poems, and the Meynells took him in and started him on a whole new life so that he became, if not one of the major poets of the English language, what you might call a minor major poet, writing at least one major poem, *The Hound of Heaven*.

Malcolm Muggeridge, a different man from either of these, a journalist, first moved by his trip to Palestine and the walk to Emmaus, and then moved once again by a trip to Calcutta when he met Mother Teresa. Something happened to him, he is a different man now than he was before he met her. Again, something moved in from outside and settled in that upper level. He still has his original prejudices and peculiarities, but his whole temper has changed.

This is something like what happened to St. Paul. He had what you might call a permanent visitor on the top level of his life, whose presence went all through his life, right down to the lowest sub-basement of his flesh. That visitor was Christ. Christ lived in him and he lived in Christ. The climate of his life was completely changed. He was no longer straining, striving to obey rules and regulations that he knew he could not always obey, and frustrated because he couldn't.

He learned to accept himself as God had accepted him. He who was never married and may never have known what it means to be in love, had a love-life. Suddenly he had that. God loved him, and he was sure of it because Christ died for him just as he was, and he began to glow in the warmth of that love. His response to it was a life that changed the course of history. The lower level was still there, occasionally it got out of hand, sometimes very much out of hand when people tried to oppose him, but most of the time it was at the service of the Spirit. He had found the key to a split-level life.

Now the question is, and I can only raise it, Is anything like that possible for you, if you haven't already found it? I do not dare to say, but I can say that I know that it still happens to varying degrees and at different levels of intensity; but it does still happen. I read an article about the young man who plays the comic character in "Godspell." You know that that particular presentation of St. Matthew doesn't speak to me the way it does to some people, but I think that I appreciate the intention of it, the purpose of it, and I was moved by that article. He is a Jewish boy, but he said he found something in playing in that particular musical that he has never known before in his life. I am not saying that this is the Christ; I don't know what it is, but it certainly has something to do with being associated with the personality of Jesus. And if that happened to him it might happen to other people.

102

Why don't you try and see? Get into the story. Play the part in real life and see what being a member of the Christian cast might do for you. It might give you the key to a split-level life.

Christ, be with us as we try from day to day to work out the thorny questions and problems that perplex us, and try to use the talents and gifts that have been given to us so that other people may be helped and benefitted by them, and we ourselves may enjoy them and delight in them. Help us to find in him the motivating spirit which will guide, direct, and keep in control all the rest of us so that we may move on in joy and gladness, in the freedom to live without fear. Amen.

The Humanity of God

%

"Like as a father pitieth his own children; even so the Lord."
Psalm 103:13

THE SERMONS on the Sunday mornings during Advent are on the general theme Barriers in the Bible. Last Sunday we considered barrier number one, the miracles. The second barrier is an even more imposing one than the first. It is the humanity of God. Many a person turning to the Bible with intelligence and a fresh and alert mind is somewhat shocked and surprised to find that the God of the Bible looks like a magnified man. He does everything that a man does; He speaks and sees, and walks in the garden in the cool of the day. He pities and punishes; He gets angry and is jealous; He laughs and even changes His mind. He builds and blesses, and begets a son. He does everything that a man does, except make mistakes. And many a person, coming up against that kind of a God, says something like this to himself, "The universe that we live in is too big for a God like that, and I am too grown-up to believe in Him. To be sure, when I was a child, I believed in Santa Claus and I believed that on Christmas Eve Santa Claus visited every house in the whole world and left his gifts. But when I became a man I put away childish things. Indeed, when I was a child I might have believed in a man-like God, but now that I am become a man, I put away such a childish idea of God."

Before we cavalierly dismiss the God of the Bible as being far too human to be God, we had better understand more clearly than perhaps some of us do what the Bible means by faith in a personal God. Some of the most important things, some of the deepest things in life, are things that we cannot see, and if we are to describe them to anyone, we must describe them by comparing them with things that we do see. For example, when Anne Sullivan Macy was first attempting to lead Helen Keller out of the prison of her deafness and blindness, little Helen asked her one day, Teacher, what is love? Anne Sullivan Macy made one attempt along these lines. "She drew me closer to her and said. 'It is here,' pointing to my heart. Her words puzzled me very much because I did not then understand anything unless I touched it." Miss Macy had a bunch of violets in her hand and Helen smelt them and asked her, " 'Is love the sweetness of flowers?' 'No,' said my teacher. The warm sun was shining on us. It seemed to me that there could be nothing more beautiful than the sun, whose warmth makes all things grow, and I said to my teacher, 'Is not this love?' But Miss Sullivan shook her head." Finally, she tried once again; she spelled out into Helen's hand these words, "Love is something like the clouds that were in the sky before the sun came. You cannot touch the clouds, you know, but you can feel the rain and know how glad the flowers and thirsty earth are to have it after a hot day. You cannot touch love either but you feel the sweetness that it pours into everything. Without love you would not be happy or want to play." Love is something like the clouds from which sweetness pours into life. Then, writes Helen Keller, "the beautiful truth burst upon my mind, and I felt that there were invisible lines stretched between my spirit and the spirit of others."

So men from the very beginning have asked, What is God? We cannot see Him; we cannot touch Him; we can only describe Him in terms of something that He is like. The Bible is one answer to that question. And the Bible began by saying that God is like the most powerful thing that we know. For certainly, our first and primary impression of God is the dynamic, vitalizing energy which makes things go. Now for people who lived in a desert, the most powerful, the most awe-inspiring thing that they knew was a volcano in eruption, and so the Bible began by saying that God is like a volcano. He is like a cloud of smoke by day and a pillar of fire by night. And there in that tremendous dynamic power they found the first clue to the likeness of God. But as they lived more deeply and experienced life more completely, they began to see that the power they were surrounded by was directed toward a purpose. It was not just power running rampant, but it was power directed toward roses, and suns, and stars, and the building of a nation, toward the formation of a character. Furthermore, they discovered that it was not only power directed toward a purpose but it was felt as a presence. When they were going through deep waters they felt as though someone were with them, undergirding them, supporting them. When they went through great experiences of ecstasy and exhilaration, they felt as though someone were there and said, "Surely the Lord is in this place and I knew it not."

Now, power plus purpose plus presence equals person. There is nothing that you and I know in the whole universe except a person that combines those three things, power and purpose and presence, and so the writers of the Bible said this: You ask what God is. We cannot see Him; we cannot touch Him; we can only tell you what God is like. God is not a person, but God is more like human personality with all its self-consciousness and its direction toward purpose, with all of its gathering together into a presence that we can know and feel. God is more like that than anything else we know, and when they looked around them they saw that human personality was at its best when it was stripped of all its pettiness and when they were asked what God was like; "Like as a father pitieth his children; even so the Lord." That is something of what the Bible means by faith in a personal God.

Look now for a moment at our own situation. The times, to be sure, have changed. We live now not in a small compact earth, but we spin around on one planet that belongs to a solar system, and that solar system is one in a galaxy of systems. We are staggered as we face the prospect of interstellar space and light years, and it seems to us many times that the universe has become too big to be personal. It is like a hospital that gets to be so big that we wonder if there is any heart in it, any personal touch there. And as we stand in the presence of all these frightening demonstrations of sheer power, we say to ourselves, at least secretly: personality—once we thought it was such a powerful thing, so decisive, so ultimate and basic, that we could describe God in terms of it, but now it looks as though personality were at the mercy of power, atomic energy, and all the demons we have unleashed, as we have explored the mysteries of this expanding universe. Why, personality has no more chance in a universe like that than a butterfly with a hurricane! We feel something the way Darwin felt after he had made his discoveries of the long prehistoric past of mankind. He wrote this: "Sometimes I feel a warm sense of a personal God, and then—it goes away."

Before we settle down in that mood, we would do well to remember two things. First, granting all the changes that have taken place in the universe and in our understanding of it, we as human beings have not changed very much. We are very much like the people who found the God who was like a father. When we need a God, we need the God of the Bible. We may talk about a God in terms of a dynamo, but when we really need God, we need the same God that the Bible found. In one of Thomas Wolfe's novels, *Look Homeward Angel*, one of the characters, a young sophomore in college, could discuss academically and theoretically all the latest knowledge about God, and that knowledge had led him into such mysterious depths of understanding that he dismissed as puerile all the traditional knowledge of God that his fathers had held. He had outgrown God. Yet, when his brother died, one of his closest companions as well as his blood-relative, he sat by the deathbed through the long night watches, and this is what he said, "Whoever you are, wherever you are, be good to Ben tonight. Show him the way." An impersonal God, a dynamo, a cosmic force? Not at all! When he really needed God, he needed a personal God. "Whoever you are, wherever you are, be good to Ben tonight."

So you and I, when we are going through some of the more difficult ways of life, which we certainly do from time to time, and when we are right down in the depths of experience that we describe as rock bottom, we certainly never cry out, The life force is my shepherd, I shall not want. *It* maketh me to lie down in green pastures. *It* leadeth me beside the still waters. We never have that kind of an experience of God when we are going through the deep waters. So, when our hearts are overflowing with gratitude and all life seems to be rising toward one great peak of happiness, we are never satisfied to cry out, Bless the Cosmic

Ether, O my soul and everything that is within me bless its holy name. That does not ring true at all. Our gratitude overflows to a personal source of all the benefits and blessings of our lives. And so, when we have missed the way in life and broken life's basic rules and are conscious of our blunders and failures, whoever among us as we knelt down in the shadow of our guilt ever prayed, O Unmoved Mover, have mercy on me. We say, in justice to everything we feel and know, Lord, have mercy on me. Indeed, we may discuss God in impersonal terms and we do over and over again, but when we get right down to God, we need and find the same God that the Bible found.

One of the most eminent scientists in this country does us the honor to read the sermons that come from this church. He has been going through difficult ways in his personal life recently, and yesterday I got a letter from him. He had just read one of the sermons about God. This is what he said, "Just keep that surge of faith pressing on for many of us need it when we least expect it." Faith in some kind of an impersonal, unknowable, infinite power, an intellectual hypothesis, a chemical formula? Not at all. The thing he is talking about is faith in the kind of a God we all need when we are right down at the bottom of things, faith in a God who knows, and plans, and understands, and cares. In all our sophistication and advanced knowledge, we have not outgrown a God like that.

The other thing that we would do well to remember is this: in spite of all the changes that have taken place in our understanding of the universe there is one thing that has not changed, although sometimes it may appear to have done so. The most powerful thing we know in life is the power of personality. It may seem to us sometimes that the astronomical universe has swallowed up the minds of men. I remember once being very much excited by this conversation that took place across the Atlantic Ocean. One scholar over there made this comment and sent it back to us. "Astronomically speaking, man is negligible." When Professor George Coe in New York heard that, he made this retort. "Astronomically speaking, man is the astronomer." Man's mind reaches out to contain and grasp, imagine and appreciate, and stands there dumbfounded before the majesty of space. Man swallowed up by the astronomical universe? Not at all! The personality of man is the master of it!

Some people have been very much impressed by the fact that life seems to be driven along its way by impersonal economic forces. Karl Marx was the one who described those forces and graphed them, plotted them out. He said that you can interpret all of life not by what a man thinks or what he hopes, or what he has faith in, but what he is driven to do by the wages that he gets and the social life that he is forced to live in. And yet, when you set those impersonal economic drives side by side with the personality of Karl Marx whose mind first understood them, through whose personality they were interpreted to the world, and by whose genius men were lured to rally round them, is it the impersonal drive that is the powerful thing or the mind and the personality of the man who had the wits to discover them?

I suppose that the most powerful thing that we know anything about now is atomic energy, and when we take time to think of it seriously and realize what it may mean in our world, we shrink even more deeply into the shadows of doubt and despair. But can we not say this without withdrawing into a false optimism? Granted the power of atomic energy, when you compare it with the moral purpose that at least exists potentially in man, the capacity to discover that energy, to release it, and, if he wills, to control it and direct it toward creative ends, which in the long run is greater, the energy or the man that directs it? Again, if we were to look back two thousand years, we would see the whole world ruled by Roman legions. It looked as if brute power were in the saddle and over against it one stark personality, nailed tight to a tree, helpless, unmovable. And yet, as we travel down those centuries and on into the future, which is the power that really influences the lives of men and women for better, the power of the Roman legion or the power of the crucified personality that was in Christ Jesus?

So, we come right back to where the Bible began, when we try to interpret our experience of God and try to describe Him in some kind of language which is least inadequate. We say that the best, the greatest, the most powerful thing we know in life is the power of personality, and God certainly, whatever else He may be, must be something like that. We find in the Bible a kind of ladder pitched between the things that we can see and the things we cannot see. On it men have climbed from power through personality to God. They began in a very primitive sense with the eruption of a volcano—God was like that; they ended on the highest rung of the ladder, when they said that God is more like personality than anything we know. So Paul wrote to the Colossians, "To us there is but one God, the Father." That, I am convinced, for those of you who are sophisticated and for those of you who are simple-minded alike, that is the God that you need. When you come up against God, that is the God you find, and when you search all the avenues of your reason that is the God you see out there in the mysterious spaces of the universe, and you kneel down in the presence of that God and thank Him for those who first said, "Like as a father pitieth his own children; even so the Lord." That is about as near to God as we can ever get. Outgrow Him? Grow more and more up to Him!

Does God Hear Us When We Pray?

᭟

Every once in a while you meet a person who has prayed all his life, he was brought up to pray, he has prayed regularly and naturally, and then he gradually stops praying. If he tried to explain to you why he stopped (under most circumstances, of course, he wouldn't try to explain or would you ask him), but if he did try to explain why he had stopped praying when he had been in the habit of doing it all his life, he might say something like this, "I felt as though I were talking into space; it was as though I were on the telephone and no one was on the other end of the line. I felt something like a child who had written letters to Santa Claus all his early days and then stopped and, when someone asked him why he stopped, he said, Well, why bother? They just go up in smoke!" What this person is trying to say is that he stopped praying because he thought God did not hear him when he prayed.

Our question this morning is, Does God really hear us when we pray? The answer, let it be said at once, is Yes, he does. "When I was in trouble, I called unto the Lord and he heard me." But it is not so simple as that, and it is not enough simply to say that and nothing more. It may be well worth our time to think about this great matter as we have thought about some of the other questions about God, knowing in the beginning that we are not coming to any final answers, that these questions are too vast for us to pretend to plumb the depths of them in twenty minutes. People have spent a lifetime pondering them and have not reached the bottom of questions like these. But we can skirt about

111

them, make little inroads into them, and perhaps some light will be shed for some one person here and there on what to them has been a baffling mystery.

One of the reasons why you wonder from time to time whether or not God hears you when you pray is that it is almost impossible for you to visualize it. Isn't that true? You can't picture it. You may have a picture of God as a great man, a magnified man. I don't mean a man with a gray beard; you have outgrown that long ago. But, nevertheless, you picture God in human terms, the great Cosmic Executive with the management of the universe in His hands. And then you go on to picture Him getting calls from all over the inhabited world. One person wants a child made well, another man in prison wants to be set free, somebody else asks for $25.00 to be sent right away to pay the rent so that he will not be evicted. Someone asks for rain so the crops won't perish, and someone else from another part of the earth pleads that the rains may stop so the people won't be flooded out. A heartbroken man appeals to Him to heal the unhappiness of his home. A troubled parent sends in a call to break up an affair between his son and a Roman Catholic girl. And from this side of the world come prayers that the Russians may be destroyed, and from the other side come prayers that the Western powers be set at naught.

When you stop to think of the number of people and the vast variety of requests that they make upon the God of the universe, and the calls that cancel out each other, the whole thing seems fantastic. This is something that you cannot picture; no matter how hard you try to stretch your mind to take it in, you cannot do it. And you come to the general conclusion that the whole thing is too much for any one person to handle even if that person be the super-person God. You can't picture it so you put it out of your mind.

You may have a less personal picture of God. Your image of God, as you think of Him either consciously or unconsciously, is the God of the suns and the planets, the great cosmic God who keeps the universe going and, if you have that sort of picture of God, you can hardly imagine His being interested in the likes of you and your rather unimportant needs and desires. They seem of great urgency to you, but when you stop to think of it you cannot presume that they would be of any great concern to the God of the whole earth and the solar system. The God of the Milky Way cannot be greatly concerned as to whether or not your child gets home safely from a dance.

You know that the sun shines graciously and gloriously on everybody and you can praise the sun; you can expose yourself to the light and warmth of it, but it never occurs to you to think that the sun singles you out for special attention. And so, in this picture of God, it isn't that it is too much for God; it is beneath Him. He is too great to bother with all these little concerns that come up like mist rising from the surface of the earth. You can worship Him, but you can't expect Him to single you out for special attention.

Whichever your picture of God may be, it becomes increasingly difficult for you to visualize the fact that God hears you individually, and so you may come to the conclusion that He doesn't hear you at all, and if He doesn't hear you, there isn't much use in praying.

Just two or three suggestions. First, because you are a human being you are bound to visualize; you will never get away entirely from pictures and the deeper the thing is that you are thinking about the more you will depend on pictures. For instance, when you think of the equator, what do you think of? A band around the middle of the earth. When you think of the North Pole, you think of something sticking up out of the top of the globe. Those are pictures. When you think of God, nine times out of ten you think of some picture of God, and my suggestion is that on the whole, the bigger picture of God you have the better it is. In other words, I think you are on safer ground with the picture of the big cosmic God than you are with the picture of the Senior Executive. Both pictures have drawbacks and dangers, but the larger picture is more likely to be the better one.

As you grow, your picture of God ought to grow and as you increase in imagination, understanding, and depth of perception, you ought to reach out to greater depths in the nature of God until God becomes vaster, more wonderful and majestic than he was when you were a child. After all, it is so in the Bible. God appears in the opening chapters of Genesis in very human terms as a God walking in the garden in the cool of the day, and in the last chapters of Revelation as the great cosmic energy of love who is making all things new. This growth in man's picture of God is right; it is natural.

This suggestion may help. Think of God not as someone at the other end of a long-distance telephone call, but as a Living Spirit within you. In other words, try to think of your prayer not as a long-distance call by which you are trying to reach someone way out there hundreds of miles away, but as an intensely local call, communing with Someone who is already with you. When a man prays, it is as though the particle of life which he is were becoming part of, and aware of the whole of life. If you think of it for a moment in these impersonal terms, imperfect though they be, it might be something like this. You are alive. There is no doubt about that; there is life in you. That life has conceived you, dreamed you when you did not exist, created you unlike any other creature ever made before or any other who ever shall be made here-after; and when you pray, that life that is within you is reaching out and appealing to the life that makes all men, the stars and the moons, and all other things. It isn't altogether impossible to believe that the life that took the trouble to become you is aware of your troubles and your needs.

This thought has helped me but, when I was thinking about it, I be-gan to wonder whether this was good New Testament religion, and I rather had my doubts about it until I stopped to think more carefully about it. I remembered that St. Paul talked about the body being the temple of the Spirit of God, and then I came across a line in his Epistle to the Romans. It was a line that was made clear to me for the first time when I read J. B. Phillips' translation of the Epistle. This is the line, "We do not know how to pray worthily as sons of God, but his spirit within us is actually praying for us in those agonizing longings which never find words." In other words, St. Paul is saying that the longings that you have in you, the reaching upward of desires that you may never know how to express, these longings are the Spirit of God in you praying for you. This may help you to overcome the feeling that God is far away.

And remember, finally, that there are things that you cannot visualize and yet you know they are true. I was told in New York last week that a jet plane had recently flown from the West Coast to the East Coast in three and a half hours and that this was possible because it stayed in the "jet stream," which is a current of air moving at such a tremendous rate of speed that the plane is pushed on in excess of its own speed. This whole thing—the plane, the stream, the speed—is beyond my visualization, but I am sure it is true. Nor can I visualize the splitting of the atom, but I know it is true. I cannot really visualize the love of parents for ten children, and I cannot really picture to myself how it can be that when one of the children dies the parents suffer no less anguish because nine others survive. Yet I know this to be the mystery of love. And I believe this to be the mystery of God.

There is another more practical reason why you sometimes wonder whether God hears you and that is that you don't get an answer. If you write a letter to a person and you get no answer in return, and then you write again and you still don't get an answer, you normally draw the conclusion that either he didn't get the letter or he threw it away. He didn't pay any attention to it, at any rate. So it is with prayer, you think. No answer, no one home.

But not *quite* so. The situations are not altogether comparable. In the first place, you don't expect a verbal answer to prayer as you expect it from a letter or a telephone call, or a conversation. The answers to prayer come in the course of events, the things that happen to you. If things don't happen the way you want them to, you assume that you get no answer. If you ask God to make you well when you are sick and you get well, you say your prayer was answered. But if you don't get well, but get worse, you say your prayer was not answered. There is another possibility, of course, and that is that the answer was No; that God heard you, but that His answer was No, or Not yet.

Why we always jump to the conclusion that if we do not get exactly what we prayed for God does not hear us is beyond me when I stop to think about it. Even though it is hard to take No for an answer from anybody, let alone from God, we know, and we know beyond the shadow of a doubt if we have lived very long, that we are not always going to get everything we ask for in prayer. Can we put that down now and remember it later on? We are not going to get everything we ask for in prayer, we know that ahead of time. An earnest and devout soul who knows the Gospels and has been taught by people who believe that prayer can accomplish anything will say right away, What about the words of Jesus when he said, "Whatever you pray about and ask for, believe that you have received it, and it will be yours." What about that?

That statement of Jesus comes in the eleventh chapter of Mark and in the immediately preceding chapter, when Jesus is going up to Jerusalem with his close friends, two of them, James and John, ask him to give them places of priority, sitting on either side of him in his kingdom. Do you remember what his answer is? "You don't know what you are asking. You may be able to drink of my cup and be baptized with the baptism that I am baptized with, but to give you places on either side of me, this is not for me to give; they will be given to those for whom they have been prepared." Jesus was saying point-blank that there were some things he couldn't give them no matter how often they asked for them, or how much they wanted them. Nor could God. Jesus was saying in the first instance that when you pray, you pray with the simple trust and confidence of a child. He was saying in the second instance that you also pray with the humility of a child, knowing that everything you want and ask for your Father will not give you.

You know also that Jesus did not get everything he asked for. Jesus on the very last night of his life asked to be spared from the agony of death. He went alone into the garden, he left his friends behind him because at times like that even your closest friends must stay behind. He went into the garden alone and said, "Father, all things are possible unto thee; take this cup from me: nevertheless, not my will, but thine, be done." But it wasn't taken from him. He wasn't spared. He was given the strength to meet and face the ordeal and to go through it in such a way as to save the world. When we ask for things in absolute confidence and trust as he taught us to ask, we ask also with the same kind of humility always adding to our prayer, "Nevertheless, not my will, but thine, be done."

And we shall always have before our eyes the vision of his cross on which he died, after he had asked to be spared and his prayer was not granted, and dying upon which he continued to pray for his enemies first, for the lost ones around about him in the same plight, for his friends, and finally for himself. It was the great sublime illustration of what Shorthouse had the boldness to put into a single line in *John Inglesant*, "Only the infinite Pity is sufficient for the infinite pathos of human life."

Rather than trying to bring these threads together in a logical fashion, I am reminded of a poem written in his early years by William Butler Yeats. It is about an old Irish priest named Peter Gilligan. He was a faithful priest, visiting his people at all hours of the day and night. But he was getting older now and he was tired. He had had a long hard day when a call came from a man's wife that her husband was dying, would he please come right away. He complained to himself, he didn't want to go, but he knew that he must go and he knelt down by a chair to say a prayer to ask the Lord to bless him on his mission. Lo and behold, as he prayed he fell asleep and the hours of the evening went by and the dawn came and when he woke up he was terrified and cried out, "The man will have died." Nevertheless, he went as quickly as he could, and when he got to the house, the wife met him with a peaceful smile on her face and said, "O Father, thanks for coming again, he died peacefully and with a smile after you left." And Peter Gilligan realized that somehow, in the mystery of God, the man and his wife believed that he had been there and that God had made up for his shortcomings in some way that he could not understand, that God had heard his prayer. What he said as he left the house, many a man can say when, in spite of all appearances to the contrary, he knows that the great God heard him when he prayed.

> He Who hath made the night of stars
>   For souls who tire and bleed,
> Sent one of His great angels down
>   To help me in my need.
>
> He Who is wrapped in purple robes,

With planets in His care,
Had pity on the least of things,
Asleep upon a chair.

In our prayers, O God, draw us closer to thyself; help us always to be honest and real, to say no more than we really think and really want, and yet keep us always reaching outward and upward to a more perfect image of thyself, until at last we are joined with Jesus our Lord, so that with him on his cross we know that only the infinite Pity is sufficient for the infinite pathos of human life. Amen.

From One World to Another

I

W<small>E WILL BEGIN</small> today with a hypothetical situation in which you may be able to see yourself. Suppose, for the time being, that as a child you were taught that every word in the Bible is true. If the Bible says that God made the world in six days, he did. If the Bible says that Noah took a pair of every living creature into the ark, and thereby saved life when a flood covered the whole earth, he did. If the Bible says that Joshua made the sun stand still, it did stand still; and if it says that Elijah went up to heaven in a whirlwind, he did. You accepted it without question. As far as you knew, the people who taught you believed it, the people around you believed it, and you accepted it as a natural part of your environment.

Then, suppose the time came when you began to wonder about it. For one thing, you wondered whether all the miraculous things that are said to have happened in the Bible really did happen; and if they did, why they don't happen now. In the Bible, both in the Old Testament and also in the New Testament, people are raised from the dead. In both Testaments food is multiplied instantaneously; and men ascend into the sky. You wondered whether things like that ever really happened, and if they did happen, why they don't happen now. Today you don't see men raised from the dead, you don't see food multiplied instantaneously, and you don't see people ascend into the heavens when they come to the end of their mortal life.

Also, as you read the Bible, you began to see inconsistencies and contradictions which you had overlooked, or which had been explained away. For instance, when you read the first chapters of Genesis carefully, you recognize that there are two stories of creation, not one. The later one is in the first chapter; the earlier, more primitive one, is in the second chapter; and they are quite different. Are they both true? You also saw contradictions in the Gospels. In one of the Gospels the risen Jesus appears in Jerusalem only; but in the other three, he appears in Galilee. In three Gospels the Cleansing of the Temple comes at the end of his ministry; in one, it comes at the beginning. Are both historically accurate? These inconsistencies, contradictions, are innumerable; they began to bother you.

As you grew older, you also began to notice that there is a great difference in the quality of the thought that you find in the Bible. For instance, one of the psalmists sings about his enemy, "Let his children be fatherless, and his wife be a widow. Let his children be vagabonds, and beg their bread" (Psalm 109). Then you turn to the Gospels and Jesus says, "Love your enemies, bless them that curse you, do good to them that hate you, and pray for them which despitefully use you, and persecute you." The level of the thought is absolutely different, and this disturbed you.

Above all, and this can be as disturbing as any of the other things which you observed as you read the Bible, what you did in an attempt to do what the Bible says didn't always work out. Jesus said, "Ask, and it shall be given you." You did ask, and it was not given.

Finally, good and intelligent teachers told you that the Bible is not true, not literally true; not the people who say it carelessly, like the person who tells a child that there isn't any Santa Claus just for the fun of shocking him; but serious, intelligent teachers in your schools and colleges told you that the Bible is an inaccurate record of history, and you began to wonder what you were to think about it. You could feel the ground under your feet begin to move, like sand when the tide goes out.

What do you do at a time like that? It depends partly on the kind of person you are. If you are an impetuous, decisive person, you may wash your hands of the whole thing. You may be like the man who leaves a home no longer habitable; he walks out of it, slams the door behind him, and steps into another world free and full of promise; and he leaves the old world to take care of itself. You may do that.

Or, you may gradually be weaned away from it without knowing it; you may drift further and further from its center of gravity until you are out of its orbit altogether. In both cases you have moved from one world to another. You leave behind you the world of the Bible and strike out in another world of time, space, and reason.

II

That is exactly what Charles Darwin did. The more I know about Darwin, the more fascinated I am by that extraordinary human being. On the twenty-seventh of December 1831, he left Plymouth on the *Beagle* for a voyage around the world. He was gone five years. When he left Plymouth, he believed that the world was made exactly the way the Bible says it was made. Furthermore, the captain of his ship was an ardent believer in the literal truth of the Bible and one of the reasons he wanted a naturalist aboard was in the hope he had that he would prove the biblical account of the flood!

Here and there, during the years before the trip began, Darwin had met people who were beginning to wonder about the origin of life. One of them was his grandfather, Dr. Erasmus Darwin, who had skirted around the edges of the evolutionary theory. Another one was the great scientist Lamarck, but Darwin says in his autobiography that he was not influenced by either one of these two men. When he set sail from Plymouth, he had no doubt that the biblical account was the accurate one.

Then, of course, he began to see things that made him wonder. He saw so many things that no one could begin to list them all. He saw the fossil remains of animals that could not possibly have been crowded into the ark. They were too big. This made an embarrassing situation for him and Captain Fitzroy. He didn't say much about it, but he thought a lot about it. He saw the enormous variety of every species —plants, animals, birds, fish, every kind of growing thing the mind of man can imagine, things he had never seen before. They were different, though similar. How? Why? When?

In view of what he saw, he came to the conclusion that the world was not created the way the Bible said it was, not by fiat in six days, not by the God he met in the Bible, but that it evolved gradually and was still in the process of evolving. He read the Bible from that time on with entirely different eyes, the New Testament as well as the Old. Eventually he dropped the whole thing.

In his autobiography, when he was sixty-five, he wrote this: "Disbelief crept over me at a very slow rate, but was at last complete. . . . I can indeed hardly see how anyone ought to wish Christianity to be true; for if so, the plain language of the text seems to show that men who do not believe, and this would include my Father and Brother, and almost all my best friends, will be everlastingly punished. And this is a damnable doctrine."

So he left the world of the Bible, closed the door, slammed it behind him, and stepped out into a new world, the world of scientific experiment and knowledge. The interesting thing to notice is that he took with him the climate of the world he left behind. This invariably happens when a man moves from one world to another.

He had one of the most magnanimous spirits of any man who ever did anything of supreme importance in life. On June 18, 1858, when he was on the threshold of publishing *Origin of Species*, twenty years after he had made the round-the-world voyage on the *Beagle*, in the mail came a letter from his friend Alfred Russell Wallace, an English naturalist working in Malaya, with an essay for him to read and criticize. It was a brief essay in which was the gist of what he was preparing to publish in the *Origin of Species*. He was stunned. Another man got there ahead of him! To his friend Lyell he wrote: "I would rather burn my whole book than that he or any other man should think that I have behaved in a paltry spirit." He even offered to withdraw his publication, and it was only the persuasion of his friends that made it possible for him to go on.

Not only that magnanimous spirit did he take with him, but also a tenderness, a gentleness and loving care for everybody, his wife and ten children, and all his relations and friends, a gentleness and tenderness which seems slightly incongruous in his new world where "all nature is at war," and only the fittest survived.

That's what the great Darwin did; he took from the old world of the

Bible the atmosphere in which he grew up. He left the scenery behind, but he took the climate with him. That is what you may have done.

III

You may now ask the question, What else could I have done? If you are in any sense that hypothetical person—and you may not be; I never went through anything like that—but if you have been through anything like it, you might say, Well, what else could I have done?

You could have examined the Bible as carefully as you examine the world around you, and if you did, you would see that the Bible grew, it evolved. It wasn't written in six years. It took close to a thousand years to write the Bible. And if you looked at it carefully, you could see the layers that represent different periods, just as the geologist can see in an exposed surface of rock the different strata that represent the different ages in which the rocks were laid.

One layer in the Bible is the work of primitive man living a precarious nomadic existence in the desert, and his word is the word of imagination, fantasy, story, myth, which sometimes comes much closer to the truth of things than the bare facts of a scientist. Another layer is quite clearly the work of a city man, cultivated, sophisticated, with a conscience that scorches the country with fire, a man like Isaiah or Jeremiah. Another is the work of a singer; and still another, the work of a lawmaker. And in the layers you see high spots, low spots, regressions and advances, just as you would expect to see them in any growing thing.

You would also see that the words of the Bible are the words of men, but that the voice is the voice of God. You might not hear it; but if you listened, you might. Dr. Hunter, the Scottish scholar, has written a book called *Bible and Gospel*. He uses a simple illustration to show what he means when he talks about the voice of God in the Bible. You all know what the letters HMV mean, he says. They mean His Master's Voice, and when you buy a record marked HMV Caruso, you hear the voice of Caruso. But because it is an old record, you hear other disturbing noises, the needle scratches, and the sound is not always as good as it should be, but you don't pay much attention to them. In spite of those incidental sounds, you hear the master's voice. Likewise, when you read the Bible, because it is written by fallible men, you hear all sorts of sounds, but above them and through them all, you hear the Master's voice.

You might also see that the language of the Bible is often "picture language." The Lord God created man out of the dust of the earth, and woman out of one of man's ribs. That is picture language; what other language could be used? No one was there to observe it; no one photographed it.

Again, on one of the high spots of the Bible a singer begins, "The Lord is my shepherd; I shall not want." God is like the faithful shepherd who sees that his flock gets to a place where the pasture is green, not dry; where the water is still enough, not rushing in such mighty torrents that it will bruise him when he drinks. That's picture language. Again, in the New Testament, he reads that Jesus withdrew from his baptism into the wilderness, and had a conversation with Satan. That's picture language. You don't have a conversation with Satan, not in so many words. And at the end, he descended into hell when he died. That's picture language, too. No one was there to record it.

From this observation about language you may draw two conclusions. In some cases you conclude that the writers themselves knew what they were doing. These writers knew that they were using picture language. Do you suppose that the singer who began, "The Lord is my shepherd," really thought that God was a shepherd wandering over the hills of Judea, keeping a flock? Of course, he knew that he was using a picture to describe something beyond anything that ordinary plain, factual language could say.

In other cases, the writers may have meant what they said literally. For instance, when they said that Jesus was conceived by the Holy Spirit and born of a virgin, they probably meant it literally. Both Matthew and Luke, the only two who said it, undoubtedly believed it as a matter of historical fact. But what they said literally, we have a right to understand figuratively. Sometimes a child can make a simple statement of fact in which we see far more than the fact he states. Some of you have seen those two volumes of prayers called *Children's Letters to God*. The preface says that they are actual letters, prayers written by children. If they are, the children are precocious. One of them goes this way: "Dear God: My teacher read us the part where all the Jews went through where the water was and got away. Keep up the good work. I am Jewish. Love, Paula."

You know exactly what that child was talking about. Factually, it wouldn't stand up to much of a test, but you know exactly what was in her mind. And so, in the writing of men who were not always sophisticated, who told stories and sang songs to say what they meant, you know what they mean.

Reexamining the Bible, you see some of these things, and many more which you missed when you first read it. You may still reject it, but on other grounds, better grounds. If you accept it, you accept it as a *view* of life, as a *way* of life. It is a distinctive view of life which sees life as the work of Creative Mind, subordinated to love, and directed by purpose. That's questionable. Many people do not accept it, but it is the vast view that you get in the Bible, from beginning to end; Life is the work of Creative Mind, subordinated to love, directed by purpose.

The way of life is the way a Man once walked toward death and straight through to transfiguration; the way he once walked through weakness into power, through losing into finding. It isn't an easy way, and there is none like it. You may not be able to accept either the view or the way, but if you do, you will be standing on solid ground. You will weather that difficult period when you move out of one world into another. It is one of the most difficult periods in all of life, and it happens more than once. It happens whenever you move out of the world in which truth is imposed by word or law into a world in which truth speaks for itself and is embraced willingly, gladly. As you emerge into that world you may be bewildered. "Fresh light is always blinding." You may need time to get your bearings, and recover your balance, and to recognize in the new world how many invaluable things in the old world still cling to you.

Remember that after Paul was converted, the story says that he was blind for three days. Who wouldn't be? He had seen the glory of God in the face of Jesus Christ. He had moved out of one world into another one.

O God, as we read the ancient words, open our minds and our hearts to perceive the intent, the meaning, the glory, the beauty that is greater than anything that logic or fact can contain or convey, and lift us from the level of language, its accuracies and inaccuracies, to the higher level of truth in all its majesty and wonder, through Christ our Lord. Amen.

The Ministry of Sickness

༆

THERE IS A PASSAGE in a letter that St. Paul wrote to the Christians in Corinth that has always been read with great interest, especially in the twentieth century when scholars have examined it in microscopic detail for whatever light it might throw on the life of the great apostle. For the sake of freshness, I shall read the passage in Kenneth Taylor's paraphrase (II Corinthians 12:6-9).

> Because these experiences I had were so tremendous, God was afraid I might be puffed up by them; so there was given me a sickness which has been a thorn in my flesh, a messenger from Satan to hurt and bother me, and prick my pride.

> Three different times I begged God to make me well again. Each time He said, "No. But I am with you; that is all you need. My power shows up best in weak people." Now I am glad to boast about how weak I am; I am glad to be a living demonstration of Christ's power, instead of showing off my power and abilities.

Those who have read the Authorized Version all their lives will miss the beauty of two lines. In one God says, "My grace is sufficient for thee: for my strength is made perfect in weakness." And in the other, St. Paul says, "If I must needs glory, I will glory in the things which concern mine infirmities."

Volumes have been written about "the thorn in the flesh." What was it? What was the nature of the sickness to which Paul refers so vividly in this letter? Was it epilepsy? Some are sure that it was, and turn to the seizure that accompanied his conversion for supporting evidence. Others are convinced that it was a nervous disorder which would now be called a "neurosis." Still others believe that it was some sort of physical disability which may have manifested itself in a slight impediment in his speech. So the scholars continue their guessing game.

The fact is that the question has never been answered, and never will be. We do not know what the nature of his sickness was for the simple reason that St. Paul never saw fit to tell us. All we know is that St. Paul lived a rugged life of travel in spite of the thorn in his flesh that constantly nagged him; that he had the mind of a giant and often behaved like a boy; that he survived hardship of every conceivable kind; that he was one of the decisive men in human history, the man who "turned the world upside down"; *and*, that he thought the thorn in his flesh helped him do it!

The Bible is full of stories that tell of God's power to heal the sick; and when Jesus came, he came teaching and preaching, but it was his healing power that drew the crowds. So far as I know, this passage from St. Paul's letter is the only place in the Bible in which we find a man who uses his sickness to enlarge and intensify his work, and understands it to be not a curse but a blessing.

There have been thousands of sermons on *The Ministry to the Sick*, to which I have contributed my share. I could easily launch into a sermon on that subject right now, for I have felt more useful, more like a channel, in a sickroom than I have in any other single place. But this sermon is not on that tempting subject; this one is on *The Ministry of Sickness*.

Suppose, for the time being, that the sick person is you, yourself. You may be temporarily sick, or chronically ill, or virtually disabled. It may be a disability that everyone knows about and can plainly see; or it may be something that no one knows or dreams that you have. Whichever it is, you want to get well. There are so many things to be done; you can't afford to be sick, not only because you haven't the money; you haven't the time! And you don't like to put things on other people. If you are sick in bed, you resent the enforced idleness. And it hurts your pride! To be well and strong—not handicapped or knocked out—is what everyone wants to be; and at the time it seems, if you can look out of your window onto a city street, that every other human being in the world is well, up and about his business—everyone except you.

So, you grin and bear it; not exactly gracefully, and certainly not fruitfully. You may eventually get well; you may not. If you do, in time you will forget all about it, and the next time you are struck out by a virus or a fall you will go through the same thing. If you don't get well, you may die. If so, your worries are over. If you don't die, you may have to carry that annoying piece of baggage the rest of your life. You will learn to live with it and more than likely, you will do it with an inner grimness that even your best friends will not understand because they do not know what causes it.

This, I am glad to say, is not the only possiblity; something else can happen. It makes me think of the last line in the same chapter of St. Paul's letter even though it has no reference to his "thorn in the flesh." "And yet I show unto you a more excellent way." It is altogether possible that this sickness, whatever it may be, can do something for you; there may be a ministry in your sickness, there may be something in it reaching out to help you if you will let it.

For instance, you may realize for the first time the wonder of the human body; how complicated it is, how delicate it is in its incredible craftsmanship; how the muscles are so deftly put together, and how miraculously the nervous system transmits messages to the brain; how mysteriously the different parts are meshed—the mind and the body yoked together, both driven by the yet more mysterious spirit. You may turn to the 139th Psalm and say, "I will give thanks unto thee, for I am fearfully and wonderfully made."

Instead of complaining about the present discomfort that may interfere with the operation of your body, you will be grateful for the time it worked so well. If you can't see as well as you once did, you will be thankful that you once had two good eyes. If you can't walk as fast as you once did, you will be thankful that you ever walked at all. If you are depressed, you will try to pierce the heavy clouds and thank God for the brightness that has occasionally lighted your way.

We take for granted so many things so long as they work well. We don't stop to think of the unbelievable intricacy of the dial system when we call a person on the telephone until it doesn't work. When we dial a number three times and get either a wrong number, or a busy signal when we know that the line is not busy, or nothing at all, then we begin to think and talk about the dial system, and what we say is not always fit for print! It is something like that with our bodies, and one of the ways that certain kinds of sickness can minister to you is this: it may stop you from taking your body for granted. You will be grateful that so complicated a piece of machinery ever worked at all.

There are other ways. You may not be well enough, or "sharp" enough to read, but you can think (unless your mind is out of whack, or your body is racked by constant pain). As you think, it may dawn upon you that you are not quite so indispensable as you thought you were. You are the mother of three small children; you can't be sick; there is no one to look after them. You *are* sick; someone *does* look after them. You are the head of a business firm; there are decisions to be made and no one can make them without you. You *are* sick; the decisions *are* made; and the business goes on.

You suddenly realize that while you are not unimportant, you are not indispensable. The world was here before you came into it, and hopefully it will be here long after you have left it. You may have a decisive role to play in it, but if you are forced to drop out of the cast for awhile, the show will go on; and even if you should never return, someone else would take your part.

It may be an important part of the ministry of sickness to cut you down to size.

If you can think this far, you may go on and begin to think about other sick people: how many there are, in and out of hospitals; how many worse off than you (strange comfort this thought gives us!). You begin to participate in the largest of all human fellowships: *The Fellowship of Sufferers*. You think first of people you know: they are not in pain, not in any pain that you can observe; they are stricken with no disease; they are well and able-bodied. But you know that there is more than one kind of sickness, and you know that they are suffering behind a closed door. If this be true of people you know, think of the millions that you do not know.

You begin to wonder why. You turn instinctively to Jesus, and you see perhaps for the first time that he suffered all the way. His family didn't understand him; the people in his own hometown didn't want him there; the men he chose to work with him were often incredibly stupid; his critics called him a glutton and a drunkard; his friends deserted him when he needed them most; he was left alone to die between two criminals.

You say, Why is life like that? How can it be like that? You turn to him for an answer, but he never answers your question. In fact, he never asked it! That one loud cry from the cross, "My God, why?" is the only time he hinted at the question. But suppose he had not suffered; suppose he had gone along a way as smooth as silk, had an easy time of it all the way, do you think that you would ever hear of him now?

You think of other people who have made great contributions to life, well-known people, who have left their names in the history books. Are there any who have not suffered? There was an article in the *London Times* a few years back about William Hazlitt, the man whose lectures drew John Keats again and again. In the article was this paragraph: "He was the type of manic depressive who was able to use even the black moments to reach deep down into himself and find an extremity of meaning or experience which could be communicated to others." He was not alone in this ability to use his own darkness to light the way for other people.

This is all part of the ministry of sickness: to introduce you to the *Wider Fellowship of Creative Sufferers*; to make you more aware of yourself and other people; more sensitive, less self-centered, more tenderhearted, more open on more fronts, more tolerant of weakness, and less tense about the future.

There are times, especially in periods of enforced idleness, when your horizons begin to drop. Instead of standing around you like a prison wall of time and space, like a stockade in which you can barely move, they drop little by little so that fields you've never seen before begin to appear, one after the other like undiscovered countries you never ex-

131

pected to see. People from the distant past, and the not so distant past, people you thought had faded away into oblivion, are suddenly as plain as day. You can hear the sound of their voice, feel their presence, watch them as they move about the old familiar ways.

You may think that you are losing your mind, or that you are drifting into a state of coma. You are not; you are stepping into a larger world, more expansive than the one you have been concentrating upon when you were 'going strong.' You are beginning to see what Oscar Wilde meant when he wrote in *De Profundis*: "Clergymen and people who use phrases without wisdom sometimes talk of suffering as a mystery. It is really a revelation. One discerns things one never discerned before." It was for St. Paul; it may be for you. It may be a revelation if you will open your eyes.

The next time you are sick—whatever the nature of the sickness may be—ask yourself this question: Is it possible that this sickness can minister to me? If it can, Lord, don't let me miss it.

> *O Lord, make me well and strong;*
> *But if this be not thy will, help me*
>   *to use my weakness to strengthen others;*
> *And if this be not thy will, in my weakness let*
>   *me lean on Thee. Amen.*

The Lightship

⌘

ON THURSDAY, the twenty-fourth of August, just ten days ago, there was a picture of a ship on the front page of the *New York Times*. It wasn't the *Queen Mary*, one of the giants; nor was it the *Gipsy Moth* that sailed bravely around the world. Both of those ships have been very much in the public eye this summer. It was a picture of the Ambrose Lightship, anchored about eight miles off the Rockaways at the entrance to the harbor of New York.

There has been a ship at the entrance of the harbor since 1823. First it was stationed nearer Manhattan, just off Sandy Hook, and it was moved to its present position in 1908. The reason that there has been a ship at that particular place is that the channel is man-made. The article that went with the picture in the *Times* told me things about it that I never knew before. You may know it without my telling you, but I doubt if all of you do. The channel is 38,000 feet long, and exactly 2,000 feet wide. If you miss it, especially if you are navigating a large ship, you are lost; and in stormy weather, especially when the fog is dense, it is very easy to miss it. During the fog, therefore, every ship heads for the Ambrose Lightship's powerful fog horn, radio beacon, and five-and-a-half-million-candlepower light. It may also interest you to know that even in these days when shipping is declining in favor of air travel, one ship passes the Ambrose Lightship every seven minutes.

In the picture, just behind the lightship, was a four-legged tower which will take the place of the little ship. Purely functional in design, there is nothing beautiful or graceful about it. The picture was apparently taken very soon after the ceremonies which inaugurated the new tower and bade farewell to the familiar little red ship that has been showing

133

the way to New York for the last fifty-nine years; this particular ship for fifteen years.

A picture like that is bound to start you thinking, at least if you are anything like me. The first thing that came to my mind was this: how deceptive appearances can be! On a fair day the water at that point looks so wide and so deep that you might think, if you knew nothing about navigation and had never come into New York Harbor before, that anyone could sail anywhere he wanted to in perfect safety. But it isn't safe. There is only one place where the water is deep enough and if you miss it, you are lost.

Life is like that. Appearances are often deceiving. The world looks so flat and so motionless. But it isn't. It is round, and it is moving, constantly, in spite of all appearances to the contrary. And to turn to much more serious things, at least for us as human beings, when you are young, especially when you are young, the way of life, the way through life, looks so broad, the possibilities so many and so varied, that it looks as though you can go almost anywhere you wish and do anything you like in any way you choose. But you can't. The reefs and the rocks are often hidden; the dangers are not always obvious to a newcomer, and the consequences known only to the experienced traveller. To a person who hasn't had much experience, it looks as if you could do anything that is natural. It sounds so right. It wouldn't come naturally if it weren't right; anything that is natural must be right; but it isn't. It's natural to lie when you are in a jam, but it isn't right. It's as natural to lust as it is to love, but it isn't right. Often the very things that come naturally are the things that lead most directly to destruction. It looks as though you could live for yourself, by yourself, and of yourself, but you can't. If you try to live for yourself alone you will find your life growing more and more inward, less and less satisfying. Instead of opening like a flower as it blooms, you will close. You will know that you have made a mistake and missed the channel.

This accounts, perhaps, for those words of Jesus which are not popular in these days. He said, "Straight is the gate, and narrow is the way, which leadeth unto life." A straight and narrow path suggests restrictions and constrictions, and we don't like it. Perhaps it would be more congenial to us if we said, Deep is the way that leads to the real life; this is where you will find it and, if you go too far one way or the other, you are bound to strike the rocks and the reefs upon which you will come to disaster.

Perhaps it is this fact about life that led him to say that man shall not live by bread alone. It looks as if he could. We are physical human beings and if we only have enough to eat and to drink we can live. And yet Jesus made it clear that though this is how it appears to be, the appearance is a deception because a man or a woman who tries to live by bread alone realizes sooner or later that he doesn't live at all. Food and drink can keep his body alive, but he has something beside his body that must be fed with different food else it will die.

Another thing the ship made me think of is this: what a difference fog can make! On a clear day you might find your way by yourself. At least you could see the buoys that mark the channel quite clearly. You would not have any reason to look for any outside help at all. Then the fog descends. Sometimes it comes so quickly that it is almost unbelievable. When it comes you can see absolutely nothing. You cannot feel your way under those circumstances because there is nothing to touch. You can only "hear" your way. You can listen for sounds that will tell you what is near you and what to watch out for. So you make for the lightship because you hear the sound of its foghorn, and you may finally see, when you get near enough, the light that comes from its beacon.

Life is like that too. There are times when the visibility is high. You know it as well as I do. There are times when you can see clearly everything that lies ahead of you. There are times when your way is plain. You know exactly what you want to be and where you want to live. You know exactly what you think and what you don't think, what you believe and what you don't believe. Those times of visibility are wonderful. Then the fog comes. It may come down upon you largely from the world around you as it is coming down upon many people today, the fog of prejudice and hate, of despair and disenchantment, of violence and doubt. This fog is so thick that it is often difficult to see anything clearly. Or, it may rise up from you, yourself. It may come out of your own condition or mood. You can brew your own fog out of the breath of something that has gone wrong in your own life. Whatever it is, it rises up and blinds you to everything around you. Then you need some fixed point to steer by.

A student came to see me last year. He happened to have been brought up in this parish but I hadn't seen him much in the last year or two. When he came in to talk about his future, with three years still to go in the college in which he was then a freshman, he said something to me that went over me like a chill. He said, I live with three other boys in an apartment, and I like them; they are my friends. But, he said, I wonder if you realize what it means to say No, almost every day, to cheating, alcohol, drugs, and sex. And if he didn't say it in so many words he implied it that in order to do that he needed this place, more especially the people he knew here who would support him, not by anything they said, but by being the kind of people they are.

The church, in other words, is his lightship. And as I thought about that I wondered for how many others it points the way when the fog is dense. I know, of course, how many times it fails, but I also know enough about people to know that there have been others, many others, not necessarily young like this student, but in middle life when the way becomes even more bewildering, who have found the church—not the building, the people in it who make the building alive—to be the fixed point, the lightship, they needed. They have listened for the sound of it, they have looked for the light of it, they have trusted it to keep them in the open channel.

Another thing that the picture made me think of was this: not everything that looks alike is alike. This is related to the first thought about the deceptiveness of appearances, but it is not exactly the same. What is in my mind at this point is this. The Ambrose Lightship was a ship that looked like every other ship. It was made to float in water and to travel. But as a matter of fact, it was not like any other ship that passed it, and the difference was not only the obvious difference in size, color, and shape. It was a difference in nature that grew out of a difference in function. Every other ship was going somewhere, either into New York or out of New York to sea; but the lightship wasn't going anywhere. It was staying somewhere; it was anchored; its job was to stay, not to go.

People are like that, and institutions are even more like that. Most of them, if they are normal, are going somewhere. Some, I regret to say, are just going along with the times; some are going on a straight course to a fixed destination; some are returning; some are going around in circles; but most people are in a state of motion most of the time; they're going somewhere. Once in a while you find someone who isn't going anywhere; he *is* somewhere. You go away and you come back; he is *there*. It is not that he is static. He is riding the waves of the world just as you are. He is moving about doing his work just as you are. It is not that he is static; he is stable. He has arrived at a place where he can be himself, and you know where he is. Sometimes we think that people like that are looking for safety, that they are afraid to launch out into the deep seas and to go hither and yon, and try all the experiments of modern life. It is not so. The lightship never crossed the Atlantic, but it was never safe. It was always in danger of collision, especially in times of fog. In May 1947 the *Olympic* hit the Nantucket Lightship and split it in two; seven of the eleven crew on the ship were killed.

Jesus, in a sense, isn't going anywhere. He is riding the seas of life just as we are, and our picture of him changes with the changing times, but he isn't going anywhere. He *is* somewhere. He has never been safe. Standing where he stood, he was exposed to every potshot that anybody could take at him, and he took them all, and one of them killed him. It isn't a safe place to be, and no one who stands with him will ever be safe, but he will be at a place where he will know what he is doing and also have some assurance that he is pointed in the right direction.

The church, in many ways, looks like any other institution. Its construction is the same as the construction of a club or a college, of a museum or a bank. But it isn't like any of these. It isn't going anywhere in the same sense that other institutions are. Its business is not to promote either itself or anyone else, not even a system or a code. Its business is to *point*—by sight and sound, by being and doing, to the Way that leads to Life.

One last thing. The only thing that is permanent in life is change. This is an old theme that I have spoken of so many times that I hesitate to mention it again, but it is so much a part of this picture that it cannot be omitted. For one hundred and forty-four years the harbor of New York has been guarded by a small ship. Now its place is taken by a tower. If you are at all romantically inclined you resist the change, especially if you are familiar with the little red ship. You not only resist it, you resent it. The familiar red ship, bobbing about in the choppy seas, you will miss the next time you come into the harbor of New York. Why must they always be changing things? you ask. Then you begin to think in another direction. The light of the tower shines brighter; it is seen four miles farther than the light from the ship. Its radio beacon is more powerful. Its eight foghorns each have a six-mile range. And when you begin to think of the people on the ship, you realize that in your resistance to the change you have been thinking only about yourself. Life for them is much less monotonous and dangerous on the tower than it was on the ship tossing constantly in those turbulent waters, for the four legs of the light tower are driven one hundred and seventy feet into the ocean floor and it stands steadily no matter what the sea is doing.

Changes are easier for some than for others. I think they are easier for the young than for the middle-aged and the older, although of course there are always exceptions to that. Some of the oldest people in this congregation are the most prepared and ready for change. And changes are sometimes for the better, sometimes for the worse. Radical changes are taking place today and nothing more need be said about them; you know all too well what they are.

Changes are nowhere more radical than in the church. Changes are taking place in every area of the church's life, in its belief, in its behavior, in its organization, in its approach to everything that it does. I confess that some of us who have been in it for a long time resist those changes; we don't like them; we miss the old familiar things. Yet it may be like the lightship. This may be the time for it to change, and the change may be so radical that it will be unrecognizable in the future, as different from the lightship as the light tower. We don't like that. I must admit that I don't, but in my better self I know that the question is not whether it looks the same, but whether it is doing the same thing better. Is it pointing the way to the deep channel that leads to life? Is its light more powerful than the old candlelight of the old institution? Is its voice carrying farther even though the accents may seem strange to our ears? Those are the questions to ask. The answer may be Yes, and if it is, let us not be with those still clinging to the lightship as it leaves its place and goes into retirement.

This picture was of special interest to me for this reason. I passed the Ambrose Lightship just a few minutes before the picture was taken. I saw it as I have many times before. I saw the unfamiliar, and to me I must confess, ungainly tower. I wondered what it was, why it was there. I was, I think, on the last ship to pass the Ambrose Lightship. But I didn't know it! I didn't know it until the next morning when I saw the article in the *New York Times*. Sometimes we don't know that we are in the midst of change until after it has happened.

I think of the lightship often. I think of the church helping people to find the right way, not always *in* the same way, but always *to* the same way, for the Way is a Person who once said, according to St. John, I am the Way, and the Truth, and the Life. And so long as the company of all Christian people points the way to Him, through the fog, in time of storm and change, they will be fulfilling their ministry whether the church looks anything like the church that we know, or whether it rises up in a form completely different from anything we have ever seen or dreamed of.

My prayer is that this church, all churches, but this is the one for which we are particularly responsible, may be more and more in times like these a lightship, pointing not to itself but to the only channel which leads safely to the great satisfactions and to the ultimate things which make life worth living.

O God, thou hast committed to us thy church. Its leadership is in our hands. The world is sailing through troubled waters. Help us to keep the sound of our voice clear and unmistakable for those who wish to hear, and the light in this place bright enough to penetrate the thickest fog for those who wish to see, through Jesus Christ to whom we point and for whom we live Amen.

On Being Cast Down

THIS SERMON is about depression. The word *depression* originally referred to a sunken *place*—in a road, for example. Today, nine times out of ten, it refers to a *person* who is sunk in spirit. A depressed person is a person who is living, temporarily at least, under a low ceiling. The visibility is poor, the going is hard, and there is almost no joy at all. The days drag, and one is about as dreary as another. Some people are depressed more easily than others, some more often than others, and some much more severely than others. I suppose that there are people here and there who are never depressed at all. How I envy them, if there are any such people! I doubt if their number is very large.

Psychiatry in the last seventy-five years has wonderfully learned how to help people with extreme depression, what we might call abnormal or pathological depression, with causes that lie so far below the level of the conscious mind that there is almost no way to deal with them by the ordinary processes of thought. The success of psychiatry, for which we are all so grateful, has sometimes led us to forget that religion has always helped people deal with their fluctuating spirits; that is, religion has always helped people handle what we might call their normal depressions, the normal rise and fall of their emotional tides.

We have a perfect example of how religion does just that, how it helped a person handle his depression, in the man who wrote the 42nd Psalm, and we shall turn to him now as a focus for our thought, as a guide and help to us as we try to bring to bear our religious techniques and experience in handling our periods of depression.

The first thing that interests us about this particular man is that he had a

140

real reason for being depressed. He lived in a place where he didn't belong. He really belonged in Jerusalem; that is where he was born and brought up, and that is where he loved to be. He belonged more especially in the Temple. He was, as it were, on the staff of the Temple, he was one of the Temple musicians. He took great pleasure in directing the elaborate ceremonial of the Temple, and gathering the pilgrims together in great ceremonial processions. The Temple was his whole life. He was something of a mystic, but for him the Temple and God were virtually synonymous; to be separated from the Temple was almost equivalent to being separated from God Himself.

When he wrote the psalm, for some reason which we are not told, he was living up north in a rural, unfamiliar country. There was no Temple in that wild country, only the roaring cataracts and the forbidding hills. It seemed to him that he had lost God. This depressed him, and we can understand why. He was something like a man whose whole life was wrapped up in the theater and who had spent most of his life in New York, where he could see all the good plays and know the people who were acting in them and producing them, and who suddenly was forced to move to a small town in northern Maine. He might well be depressed when he realized that the only theater in the town was a second-rate moving-picture house.

There are usually some good reasons for our depressions. Sometimes it is something that has happened in the world. When you read in the morning paper, for instance, that a young man in Lincoln, Nebraska, has killed eleven people within two or three days, that is enough to cast down anybody's spirit. Or, when you read that another two-million-dollar Atlas intercontinental ballistic missile has blown up, that also is enough to cast your spirits down into the depths.

Sometimes it is something that has happened to you personally, just one blow too many. One of the mysteries of life, and I am aware of it more and more as I see more and more people, is that the blows of life usually come in rapid succession, one after the other. They hardly give a man time enough to get on his feet before he is struck down again, and sometimes it is one too many blows, a little more than you can take. Your spirits sink, and you travel with a heaviness that is impossible to shake off.

Sometimes it is something that happens inside you. You get upset with yourself, that is, if you have any sensitiveness at all to the kind of person you are or would like to be. You have done something on the spur of the moment that you know is foolish, that you should not have done, and you wish you hadn't done. I have done that so many times. This worries you, this frets your spirit, making it limp and feverish, restless and discontented. Or you know, or at least feel, that you are not the person that you would like to be; you are not the person that other people think you are. This does the same thing to you; this takes the light out of the sky, and you feel as if the clouds were pressing upon your shoulders so that you dread the thought of another day. You are sometimes caught in something that you cannot get out of, a way of life, that you are trapped in; you want to get out, but you cannot.

All these things can make you depressed. You can say with the psalmist, "O my God, my soul is cast down within me" and when you say it, you know that you have a good reason for saying it.

But the depression in the case of the psalmist, and I think the same thing is almost always true in our own case, was out of all proportion to the reason. It is as though he had a cause for the depression—that is, something started it, but it lingered too long, it went too deep, it wasted away too much of his life. He began to realize that while the fact that he was separated from the Temple and everything that he loved, and was living in a place where he did not want to live, that while this might be a cause for his spiritual depression, it was not an adequate reason for it. After all, other people had been through the same thing hundreds of times before and had not been in any such state of mind as he was in, and he began to see that the real trouble was not with the place where he lived, the real trouble was with himself. This is where real progress begins. To be sure, he would rather have been in a different place, but many people in life have to make adjustments to that situation, and they do. The trouble with him was that there was something in himself that was wrong.

Now this, I think, is the first step that any of us can take out of our depression. When a young man, for instance, who is depressed because he has lost his job, sees clearly that the loss of the job may be the initial cause of his depression, but is not the reason for it, then he is on his way out. Or, when a man who has lost his wife, or a woman her husband, realizes that his grief may be the cause of his low spirits, yet not the adequate reason for it, then he is on his way up and out.

It is interesting to see what this particular man did and, as you read the two psalms when you get home, quietly, you will see what I mean. You can almost watch him climb out of the slough of despond. The first thing he does is this: he pours it all out to himself. Perhaps it would be more accurate to say that he poured it out to God, but he began by talking to himself. It was a kind of self-analysis.

He had a gift for words, so he put it all down on paper, he wrote it out, and he didn't spare anything. He described exactly how bad he felt. He said, "My tears have been my meat day and night." It is not easy for a man to admit to himself that he weeps at the slightest provocation, and sometimes for no reason at all; but he did, he put that down. Then he went on to say, "All thy waves and billows have gone over me." I feel, he said, like someone in the depths of the sea. I feel as if all the storms of life had caught me up in their sweep and swell and tossed me back and forth for no reason at all. A man doesn't like to admit that he is the victim of circumstances to any such degree as that; but he put it down.

He went further. He said, "I will say unto God, 'Why hast thou forgotten me?'" He was a religious man. God meant everything in the world to him, and it wasn't easy for him to admit that he had come to the point where he really thought that God had forgotten him and that he had lost God. It was as bad as that, but he put it down. He wrote down one more thing. He admitted that sometimes he could not help remembering the old days when he was in the Temple, leading the great processions of pilgrims, how his heart rejoiced and how his spirit walked on the high places; and of course, the more he remembered the old days, the worse he felt. He put that down.

Here is a clue for you. When you are in a state like this, don't be afraid to pour it out, to put it all down. Don't pour it out to everybody, but to someone you can trust; it might be a doctor, it might be a minister; it

143

might be a friend or someone close to the family; or it might be to yourself. It might help you to write it down, to pour it all out on paper. Don't be ashamed of it. This is nothing peculiar to you; it happens to the young, old, and middle-aged. Put it down as something that you face and acknowledge, just as it is, frightening as it is, but nevertheless true.

That is the first thing he did, and then he asked a question: "*Why* art thou cast down, O my soul, and *why* art thou so disquieted within me?" I can imagine that he began to rehearse all over again the reasons and the causes. "My soul is athirst for God," he may have said, and I cannot find Him. He went so far as to compare himself to a wild animal that was dying of thirst and, when he got to the brook, the brook was dry. The thing he wanted most desperately in the world, he did not have and could not find.

I imagine, and I am using my imagination legitimately, I hope, that in the midst of his rehearsal of the legitimate causes of his depression, the things that started it, it dawned on him that there wasn't any good reason for it. Can't you hear that implication in the question, "*Why* art thou cast down, O my soul; and *why* art thou so disquieted within me?" There isn't any really good reason why I should be so cast down. "Hope thou in God, for I will yet thank him, who is the health of my countenance, and my God." It was as if he were gradually seeing the fact, anticipating it even before he could grasp it, that if he could find God in the Temple, he could find Him in the resounding cataracts of those rivers up there in the northern hills where the Jordan had its source.

He was beginning to see that if God was in one place, He was in another, and that he had no good reason for being so cast down. If you want to put it in less technically religious language, it may be said this way. He began to see what many of us learn as we climb out of these periods of depression, that life wonderfully and marvelously provides its own remedies. Life carries along with it its own restoratives. They do their work quietly, if we give them half a chance. The natural thing for a wound to do is to heal. The natural thing for a disturbed nervous system to do it to right itself. The displaced person tends to adjust himself, the grief-stricken person eventually straightens himself. This doesn't always happen, to be sure, but the healthy thing is to expect it to happen and, if for some reason it doesn't, deal with that situation when it comes.

The circumstances of life do not change, but the life that the person has been given enables him to make the changes that are necessary to match the circumstances, until he can rise above them and triumph over them. This, I think, is what the psalmist was beginning to sense, and what many people begin to sense, in the midst of their deepest depressions. Why art thou cast down? Hope thou in God. The God that I am thirsting for, the God that I seem to be separated from, the place that I would like to live in, the person that I have lost, the job that I want—in these very things as they happen to me, in these very situations, can be found the restoring, the renewing strength to enable me to handle them well. That is a great thing to know; and if you have ever been through it, you really know it.

Finally, he prayed. The prayer comes in the 43rd Psalm, which obviously is part of the psalm which we have been talking about (they were divided at one time for reasons which nobody knows). This is the prayer, it is familiar: "O send out thy light and thy truth, that they may lead me, and bring me unto thy holy hill, and to thy dwelling." I wonder whether he was still thinking in terms of getting back to Jerusalem. Perhaps he was, I don't know; but I doubt it. At any rate, his mood was different, for he followed the prayer with this: "Then will I go unto the altar of God, unto God my exceeding joy; yea, upon the harp will I praise thee, O God my God." And even if he were still lingering in the shadows of his depression, the light was beginning to break through.

There is the clue, the last clue for us. After we have thought it all out, and after we have asked the question and found that there is really no good reason for our being so cast down, then comes our prayer, O send out thy light and thy truth that they may lead me, and bring me unto something that is good in the future, which I neither anticipate nor expect at the moment, but toward which I move in confidence and trust. And our prayer is more than a matter of words. You are simply not to get down on your knees and repeat that prayer. The prayer is the expression of this in you, namely, that you trust the restorative powers of God and that you give them a chance to work. What you may need is rest for your body. Your emotions may not stand the strain that some people's do, and you may need to let them lie idle for a while. You may need to take a different direction in your life. The recognition of this is the sign that you really mean what you pray, and that you expect to give the restorative energies of God a fair chance to operate in your life, to lead you out into a fair place.

Some of you remember, I am sure, because you knew her personally, a woman who influenced generations of young women in Wellesley College as a professor of English, Vida Scudder. Most of you probably did not know her because she was a very old lady when she died a few years ago and had not done anything in public for a long time. But those of us who did know her, even though we didn't know her intimately, counted on her greatly. When she was over seventy, in 1937, she wrote the story of her life. I read it when it came out, and I shall never forget it. I happened to take it down the other day. If you want to read the story of a great life that found its way through shadows, as well as through light, take down Vida Scudder's story, *On Journey*.

One thing impressed me at the end of it, and I end the sermon with it. She had had her ups and downs in life and, at the end of the story when she came to her conclusion and rehearsed all the rises and falls in her life, her disappointments as well as her satisfactions, she had two things to say: " 'I feel it more than most.' . . . Never say it! 'That he overwent; this also may I'. . . . Always remember it!"

O God, guide us through the dark places in life. Grant that we may not fear the loss of thee, knowing that thou art always by our side, and that life will renew itself in us if we give it time and are willing to wait. And as we rise out of the low places through which we sometimes must walk, help us to be thankful for them, because through them and by them we may be able to help someone else through the darkness into light. Amen.

The Palm Sunday Sermon

❦

W HEN JESUS RODE into Jerusalem on the Sunday before the Passover, the city went wild with excitement. According to the King James
Version, "all the city was moved." According to the Revised Standard
Version, "all the city was stirred." According to J. B. Phillips' translation, "a shock ran through the whole city." And now in the New English Bible, "the city went wild with excitement." I was curious to see
the original Greek word. It's a verb that means to "shake" or to "agi-
tate," and might be used in reference to an earthquake. So the New
English Bible, I think, is correct in its implication that when Jesus rode
into Jerusalem the whole city was thrown into a state of intense agitation.

We can see why. For one thing, the city was in a state of hypertension
at that particular time, both religiously and politically. The pious were
swelling with religious zeal as the pilgrims poured into the city to keep
the great national festival of the Passover. The nationals were preparing
for a revolution which, incidentally, began just about thirty years after
this event. The collaborators were playing the game with Rome as well
as they could, trying to keep one foot in each world. The hierarchy
were trying their best to protect the beloved establishment, to save it
from destruction. The Romans were steering a steady, relentless course
of law and order.

Into that tense situation, with the friction so great that you can feel it
if you have any imagination at all, went Jesus in a way not calculated to
calm things down. He was a young man in the prime of life, riding on
an ass (a donkey, we would say), a beast of burden, reminding every
good Jew what one of the prophets had said, Your king will come to

you, meek, humble, gentle, riding upon an ass. And the crowd along the way hailed him as their king.

That would be enough to excite any city, particularly at such a time. If it happened in an American city today, he would probably be either mobbed, or murdered, or ridiculed; or simply ignored. In Jerusalem, however, the people asked a question. Do you remember what the question was? They asked, Who is he? Who is this who has come into our city in such a way, implying so many things? Who is he?

It was easy enough to identify him. He was Jesus, a prophet from Nazareth in Galilee. They were given his name, address, and occupation. That is enough to identify a man, but it doesn't really answer the question. Does it? They still wanted to know who he was, who he thought he was, who he claimed to be, who he really was. Was he a fake, or a freak, or the real thing? If you really wanted to know what a person was up to and what he was all about, it wouldn't be enough simply to know his name and address and occupation. You would have to know more than that.

The fact is that no one really knew who he was, not even his closest friends, and you can't blame them too much. For one thing, he would never tell them. They were looking and waiting for the one they called Messiah, God's Man, who would get them out of the mess they were in, straighten them out, and put them on the up-and-up again.

A few wondered whether this carpenter might not be that Man. There was just enough about him to make him seem a possible candidate for the high office. John the Baptist was in prison, but he sent representatives to ask whether he was that Man, but he never gave them a direct answer. He said to them, Look at what I do, and then you tell me who I am. He knew, I suppose, that you can't tell anyone anything unless he already knows it. I realize that there are exceptions to that, but when it gets to one of the great things in life, you can't tell it to anyone unless he already knows it, or in some way has an inkling of it, even though he is unconscious of it at the time. What you say to him sometimes simply brings to the surface of his conscious mind what was there already in the subconscious levels of his mind. No matter how often you tell him, it never registers until he sees it himself.

Suppose, for instance, I told you that the Bach B Minor Mass is one of the great moments in musical history. If you had never heard it, had never known anything about it, I could tell you that a thousand times and it would mean absolutely nothing except that there were people who thought it. Not until you heard it could you take in what I said.

Or, if I said to you, Florence is one of the most fascinating cities in the world, you could hear it, you could take it as a fact that I believed it, but you could not really take it in until you felt it yourself, until you had been there and had seen it, or at least until you wanted to see it.

So that is one reason why he didn't tell them. Also, he knew that his idea of the Messiah and theirs were as far apart as day and night. They were looking for a Messiah who would put them back in power. His idea of the Messiah was a person who would put them into service, put them to use. See how different that is. He wasn't thinking at all of the Messiah who would restore the national grandeur of the nation. He was thinking of a Messiah who would take the seeds of redemptive suffering that had been sown among his people and scatter them to the four winds of the world.

Another reason why they never knew exactly who he was was that they were baffled by the contradictory things he said and did. Think of some of the things he said. You know them, but I shall remind you by recalling a few of them. He said, for instance, that the peacemakers are happy because they are the children of God; and in almost the next breath he said, I am come not to bring peace, but a sword! He said, I am come not to destroy the law, but to fulfill it; and the next day he encouraged his disciples to break the law, to work on the Sabbath Day, to eat without observing the ceremonial laws about washing their hands. He told one man that if he wanted to have life that amounted to anything, one of the things he had to do was to honor his father and mother. In almost the next breath he said, I have come to set a man against his father and a daughter against her mother.

What he did was even more contradictory, and what he did on this very day. He rode into the city in such a way that it suggested to every good Jew the idea of royalty. They couldn't miss it. They could accept him on that basis or not, but they couldn't miss the intention of it; and yet not a hand was lifted against him, there was no violence, no troops were called out, not even the police. There must have been something unusual about him, because he had the people in the palm of his hand, and if he had wanted to ride to victory on the backs of the people, he could have. But he didn't. He did not take the city by storm.

Yet on that day he went into the open porches of the Temple and drove out the people who were conducting business there; and it wasn't secular business, it was church business! They were changing money because the church required that anything given to the Temple be in Jewish coin, not Roman coin, and they were changing it for them. And they were selling doves to poor people who had no better animals to sacrifice. He loved the Temple. It wasn't the Temple that he was protesting, not even the sacrifices, not even the practice of sacrifice. He was protesting against the idea that in this open place, the one place open to Gentiles, by the way, men conducted a business partly for their own profit. It was a place for worship, and anything that distracted from the worship of God was out of place.

He was angry, and, in one way, this was so out of character. You can see how it affected the people. But thank God he had the capacity for righteous indignation, and on occasion he showed it. Yet it is no wonder that they weren't quite sure who he was. One day he would reach out with his infinite compassion and touch a leper, the most loathsome of all possible diseases. The next day he would be angry with a leper who presumed to reach out to touch him. One day he said that his mission was limited to his own people: "I am not sent but to the lost sheep of the House of Israel"; and the very next day, in a foreign country, he was completely captivated by the wit of a woman, and healed her daughter, who was a foreigner!

Truth is seldom simple. It may be simple in its essential being, but as we comprehend it, it is not simple. It is far too complex to be put in any single sentence. Truth, as we comprehend it, has at least two sides, and the one side often seems to contradict the other. That's another reason why they were never quite sure who he was.

And to top it all, they were not endowed with an overactive imagination. Even his closest friends, we might as well admit it, were not exceptionally smart or perceptive. They often came close to the point and then missed it completely. Peter came close when he answered the question, Who do you think I am? He said, I think you are the Messiah. Then when Jesus began to speak about the Messiah in terms of suffering, Peter rebuked him. He missed the point.

They were always drawn to him, but they didn't always know quite why. By and large, I would say, people are like that. H. L. Mencken was not one of my primary guides in life but he often said things that were very penetrating. He once said that no one ever went broke by underestimating the intelligence of the American public. And I would now add, after thirty-five years of experience, nor did anyone ever go broke by underestimating the imagination of the American public. Most people prefer black and white to varying degrees of gray, and it is hard for some to appreciate that every man, including himself and myself, is a mixture of each. Even our heroes may have a dash of badness in their blood, if only to save them from being bland.

Those who knew him best didn't really know who Jesus was. We can't blame them too much. He was too subtle for most of them to grasp, and fresh light, don't forget, is always blinding.

Now to turn away from Jerusalem to Boston, to those gathered here now, what can we say to this question, Who is he? We think we know who he is. We say so every Sunday. We say that he is Jesus Christ, His only Son, our Lord and Master. We say that he is our Saviour, that for our sins and our salvation he came down from heaven and became man. We know infinitely more about him than they did. We certainly ought to, for we have had a long time to think about him, and take him in, and we have inherited the thinking and the living of thousands of people who have devoted their lives to him, so we ought to know more about him than they did.

At our best, we mean what we say, but there are times when we say to ourselves, Who is this strange man, so out of his element in this technological, distraught twentieth century? Who is he, so far out of his natural environment of thought and behavior, and yet in some ways so much a part of it? We can see him even in the revolt against conventions, machines, and materialism.

Who is this strange man who keeps coming back? We can't keep him away. He is still asking questions, still refusing to answer them for us, showing us all sorts of things, and then saying to us, Now, you answer the question. He is still putting up with our stupidity, still making allowance for our colossal blunders. Who is he? He is a paradox that we can't quite take in, yet never quite ignore. One year they say he is God Incarnate; this year they say he is the Man for Others; next year they will be saying something else. Words never quite capture what men feel about him.

What do you say? Do you say anything like this? This is what I often say; at least, it is a part of what I say.

I know who you are, but what I feel I cannot always find words to express. The ancient words of the Bible and the Creed are a great help. You are the Word of God made flesh; you are the Son of God come down from heaven to save us. But sometimes I must reach after words of my own. Through you and in you I meet God. In you the Infinite becomes Finite for the sake of me and my kind. Once I see God in you I see him everywhere. You make God real to me; you personify him. Your own personality is never usurped by God, never taken over by him. In a strange way, he doesn't have to, for you are in him, and he is in you. To put it in other words, you are both the Ground and the Goal of my existence.

Most of the time I am sure that I know who you are; but not always. If I were too sure, I would be sure that I was wrong. But I will follow you wherever you go, as well as I can; and when I fall behind, as I often have, and often will in the future, I know that you will come and pick me up. In some strange way, you are the King, like no other king; my friend, my master, and my king.

O Christ, we are following. We often falter, we fall far behind, we fail to see, to understand, but we try. We want to know, we want to do, we want to be the kind of person in whom you can live and love and save some of the world's suffering. Amen.

The Bread and the Body

IN A LETTER written about 55 A.D. the Apostle Paul reminded the little group of Christians in the Greek city of Corinth of what happened on the night before Jesus died. He told them that he had supper with his friends; it was a simple meal of bread and wine. As he broke the bread, he gave it to them and told them to eat it, and said that it was his body, broken for them. And when he poured the wine out and gave it to them he said, "Drink it, this is my blood; it is shed for you."

Christians have been doing that, in one way or another ever since— for roughly two thousand years. And we are about to do it now, once again. The setting has changed, the language has changed, the world has changed. But the words are the same. The question is, What do we mean when we say that a small piece of bread is the body of Jesus Christ, and that the wine is his blood? And when we do it, when we eat and drink it, are we doing what we seem to be doing? Are we reverting to cannibalism? Are we withdrawing into some mystical act that has no relevance at all to a world that is filled with turmoil and confusion, torn apart with suffering and bloodshed?

"Take, eat, this is my body, which is given for you." It is time we stopped once again and thought about those words and what they mean to us here and now.

The first thing to do is to go back to the event itself: the Last Supper in the Upper Room, the meal Jesus planned and shared with the twelve men who were closest to him. One thing is as clear as day. As Jesus sat at the table with those twelve chosen friends of his—chosen to be his apprentices, his students—as he broke the bread and said as he gave it to them, "Take, eat, this is my body," and when the disciples ate it, it is as clear as day that they were not eating the body of Jesus, for the body of Jesus was sitting right there at the table in their midst. Why, then, did he say it?

First, because he was a Jew, and Jews by nature do not theorize; they dramatize. When the prophet Jeremiah was aware of the fact that the kingdom of Judah was about to be swallowed up and completely conquered and forced into exile by Babylon, he talked about it to a certain extent, but he did something much more dramatic than that. He had a huge yoke made, and whenever he went through the streets of Jerusalem he wore it! No one could miss what he meant; he was dramatic, he acted out what he thought and believed. He knew that actions speak louder than words.

Jesus did the same thing, not only at the end of his life, but all through his ministry. One time people went to him and asked what he thought about paying taxes to Rome. Instead of giving a learned discourse on the principle of taxation, he said, "Show me a coin." They gave him a coin, and he said, "Whose face is that?" They said, "Caesar's." He said, "All right, if it belongs to Caesar, give it back to Caesar, and give to God what belongs to him."

Another time, a man went to him and said, "Who is my neighbor?" and instead of giving a discourse in which he tried to define exactly who was and who was not a neighbor, he drew a picture. A certain Samaritan came by and helped a man who had been stripped and robbed. He was the "neighbor," the Good Samaritan, who lives to this day. This dramatization was one of his natural ways of teaching, of communicating the truth to the learned as well as to the simple.

At this particular point he wanted to say something about his death. He knew that it was coming and that it was coming soon. He hadn't sought it; he was not at all like the fine Japanese novelist who deliberately committed suicide a few weeks ago to prove and commend his commitment to the old order of things. He wasn't like that. He tried to avoid death, as a matter of fact, up to the very end. When he saw that it could not be avoided without compromising the things that he believed to be essential, he accepted it. And he was convinced, in ways that we may not, and perhaps cannot understand, that his death would give other people life. But it has happened before on an infinitely smaller scale; the things that people have given, the self-sacrifices they have made, have been the bread of life to other people.

Jesus told them what he felt and believed, not by talking to them but by doing something. He took the loaf of bread, and when he broke it, he said, "My body, broken for you: eat it, feed upon it; it will give you life." The implication is that he expected them to share not only in his life but also in his death. In other words, he expected them to share not only in his healing and preaching ministry, in all that he did and said to make life richer and fuller for people, but he also expected them to share in his suffering, and to join him as one of the burdenbearers of the race.

That is one thing that is clear. There is another that is equally clear when you look at the event. After Jesus died, a small group of his followers continued this simple meal. In other words, the event survived, and for a good and understandable reason. His followers believed, and there is no question about this, that his spirit was alive. That is what the Resurrection means, that he was alive, and that his spirit was everywhere. But they *felt* his lively presence particularly when they shared in this meal. That is when they felt it most vividly. And I think you can see why. For one thing, it was so like him. It was simple, so bare, so stripped of all the nonessentials of life which make up such a large part of the lives of other people. It was a continual reminder of the way he pared life down to its bare essentials. It was so like him to give and not to count the cost, not to hold back.

And it was so natural for them to feel something by doing something; not just thinking, or talking about it. Sometimes you can do that, sometimes you can feel the presence of another person who is either absent or departed by talking about him. I can do that, but there are other times when I can feel it more vividly by doing something, by feeling the things that were associated with him. I have a small private communion set that was given to Mr. Brooks in 1860 by one of his classmates after they were graduated from the Virginia Seminary. I don't take it out very often, but when I do to show it to people somehow just the touch of it makes me feel his presence in a way that I don't when I simply talk, and talk, and talk about him.

Two things, then, are clear when we look at the event, the Last Supper. When Jesus said, "This is my body, take it and eat it," he was not referring to his own body of flesh and blood. When the words were first said the bread and the body were not identical. And second, when his followers continued the meal after his death they believed that the spirit of Jesus was alive and present everywhere, but they felt it more especially in that meal, and that the Bread and the Presence went together hand in hand.

As time went on and Christianity broke loose from its Jewish moorings, it became more and more intellectual. This almost always happens in the normal development of any event. When you fall in love, for instance, you don't at the very beginning stop and try to explain it, or analyze it. You just do it. You enjoy it. You don't have time to think much about it, to analyze it. As time goes on, perhaps, you reflect upon it, and if you are wise, you try to see what it means in the larger context of life. If you ever write your memoirs you may try to put it, years later, in its proper frame of reference—either as a passing romance or as the pole star of your life. But at the time, no. You are busy doing it, enjoying it, living it out.

This certainly happened to the first followers of Jesus. I think that it is fair to say that in the colloquial language of our time, there were people who "fell" for him. They were convinced that he was alive even though some of them had seen him die on the cross. They were absolutely convinced that he was the image of his Father, and they were sure that he was with them in this meal of bread and wine. They didn't try to explain it. As time went on they began to think about it, especially about the bread and the wine, and the relationship between the bread and wine and the body and blood of Christ. If he said that the bread was his body and the wine his blood, they thought it must be so. But how could it be? How could those simple, material things be identical with the living, vibrant instrument which once spoke, walked, wept, and prayed. They must be changed. How?

157

Through the ninth, tenth, eleventh, twelfth centuries they gradually worked out an explanation. They said that the bread and the wine are not changed in appearance; they look exactly the same as they did in the beginning. They have all the "accidents" of bread and wine; they taste the same, they look the same. But they are changed in "substance," in their essence. The way you might say a dollar bill is changed. It is still paper; it looks like paper, tears like paper, but you don't tear it because it isn't paper: it's money. The nature of it is different; it has been changed. The bread and wine have been changed from food and drink to the presence of a living body.

When does this change happen? At that time they said that it happened when the right words of institution were said by the right man, the man ordained and commissioned with the power to say them. Those words are the same words that come originally from St. Paul: "In the night in which he was betrayed, he took Bread: and when he had given thanks, he broke it, and gave it to his disciples, saying, Take, eat, this is my Body, which is given for you."

Since the Council of Trent in 1545 this has been the explanation of the Roman Catholic Church, and it is called the Doctrine of Transubstantiation. It is easy for the plain man to take it to mean that the bread itself becomes the body of Jesus. The English Church never accepted this explanation. Nor did it ever attempt another one. So, in this church we have no official explanation of what actually happens. I, for one, am thankful that we haven't. The mystery remains, and one can still appreciate it without trying to explain it. The more you explain it, the more commonplace it becomes. And, as so often happens, what begins as a mystery deteriorates into a miracle.

This means that we are left with the action only. We continue the meal, we say the words, we repeat the action, we share in the food, and we feel the presence. Some feel it more than others.

Some of you may say, I'm one of those who don't feel the presence; not intensely at least, if at all; I think about Christ, and I care a great deal about the church; the church means everything to me, and I couldn't live without it. But I feel the presence of Christ more, sometimes when

I am alone in the church and nothing is being said or done; or when I'm listening to music, or even listening to a sermon; or even when I'm out on the street, or at home at my dining room table with the rest of the family. What about me?

I say to you (to the others perhaps I don't need to say anything), Don't be ashamed of being the person you are, and don't ever try to be someone else; you can never do it. No two people are exactly alike. Never forget those two great Christians. Those of you who are my age are old enough to remember them both, even if you never saw them. On the one hand, Rufus Jones, the Friend, the Quaker, who never went to any sacrament in his life. And on the other, Baron von Hugel, the faithful Roman Catholic, who went to Mass every day of his life. When those two met they were absolutely in unison, grounded in their faith in God made man in Christ.

Second, remember that it is easy, and often very tempting, to draw back from suffering; the thought of blood may turn you away. You cannot get away from it. Life is full of suffering and stained with blood wherever you look, and there is nothing that you can do to change that. On Friday in the *New York Times* I read a review by Clive Barnes of a revival of Samuel Beckett's *Waiting for Godot*. There was one line that I noted. Clive Barnes wrote this in trying to interpret Beckett's extreme rejection of everything that means much to many of the rest of us: "Life is not the Charge of the Light Brigade, life is a succession of little deaths." I say the same, if I can add to that, Life is not the Charge of the Light Brigade; it is a succession of little deaths, often followed by little risings. And it's the risings that make the deaths not only bearable but often beautiful.

Jesus knew that. He went through many a "little death" before he shed his blood, and he has helped others go through those "little deaths"; not actual deaths, but the giving up of this, the losing of that, the disappointment here, and the curtain that falls at the end of a chapter, the sting of grief, the darkness of despair. We have all gone through those "little deaths" over and over again. And he has enabled some of us to go through those little deaths in such a way as to make them little victories. Little Deaths transfigured into Little Risings—that is what we see wherever and whenever the Spirit of Christ dwells in a man. What else is worth seeing?

And finally, be sure that you take into account the drama and poetry in the biblical tradition of the Christian faith, for they play an enormous part in it, and until you understand them you will be misled at every turn, and miss half of the meaning and most of the glory.

"The Lord is my shepherd." Does that mean that the God of the mysterious universe is a Keeper of sheep? "God so loved the world that he gave his son." Does that mean that the God of interstellar space impregnated a woman and produced a child? "Before Abraham was, I am." Does that mean that Jesus of Nazareth was already in existence before Abraham was thought of? "Take, eat, this is my body." Does that mean that Jesus intended his friends to feast upon his own physical body? The answers are self-evident in the questions.

When and if you come to the communion table, beware of the literal fallacy. It is a trap that has tripped up thousands of well-meaning Christians. They are like the conductor who sees the notes, but has not yet learned to see beneath them. Be open to the greater truth, the Presence —suggested by, communicated by, but never completely contained in, the material things like bread and wine. In them the Presence is felt and perceived in a unique way by those who are open to it. It is expressed, don't forget, only when you go out of this place to do likewise, in remembrance of him.

O God, who hast given us things that we can touch, handle, see, and feel, and in those things hast conveyed to us things that are beyond touch, beyond sight, beyond anything that we can see or hear, help us in these simple elements of bread and wine to feel the presence of him who gave everything he had, his love and his life, to the end that others might live. Amen.

The Mysterious Fact of Resurrection

❦

In him was life; and the life was the light of men. And the light shineth in darkness; and the darkness has never put it out." Those are two verses from the grand prologue of St. John's Gospel (1:4, 5). He began his Gospel by setting the background of the story he was about to tell, the story of Jesus of Nazareth. But the setting was not the events that were taking place in Rome and Jerusalem, not the names of emperors, kings, and governors who were in power at the time of the action. The setting was eternity. If it were ever set to music, the direction would be *maestoso*, with majesty.

"In him was life; and the life was the light of men." There are different kinds of light. There is the natural light of the sun by which the world around us comes back to life every morning, almost miraculously, each object resuming its shape, and the color that we thought the darkness had drained out of it is once again bright. By it we know where we are, we can see where we are going. Sometimes the way is beautiful and sometimes it is ugly.

Also, there is the natural light of the moon. Not so powerful as the light of the sun, and if clouds come across it we can't see it at all. But when we can see it, we sometimes see a beauty that is almost unearthly; particularly if the moon is full and the night is clear.

Then, there is what we might call "artificial light," beginning first with the light of a candle set in the middle of a room to make at least a center of light so that the family could see what they were eating. Then

161

came the gas lamp, and finally the incandescent bulb. Now, with electricity, we can light our cities so that they are sometimes brighter at midnight than they are at midday; alas, too bright for some of us! And by this artificial light signals start and stop the trains, the automobiles, and warn the pilots on their flights.

But there is another kind of light, the light of a life. Picture a room at night, already well lit. Into it steps another person. The minute he enters it the room is brilliant as it wasn't before. His presence makes it bright. It's the light of a person's life. Or, less dramatically, you are having trouble, if you are anything like me, with mathematics. You can't make the figures go the way they are supposed to go, or come out in the right way. They don't come out right, they never do; they don't make sense and you have almost given them up. You develop a definite dislike for figures. Then a teacher takes the class. It is as though a light were turned on. He knows exactly what to do, how to approach your anti-mathematical mind so that you even get to enjoy the figures and you can make sense of them; you can add and subtract, and even multiply them!

Still more significantly, you meet a man; perhaps not face to face, but only on the printed page. Even so, in his life there is light. I have met both men and women who did that for me, but I have chosen one because he did it to such an extraordinary degree. He was the French novelist and essayist Albert Camus. He made no pretense of being a Christian, not even a theist. He was an avowed atheist. It was in the fifties, and I found myself in some of the corners of the world that I had never really faced before. They were the dark areas of a troubled world; it was increasingly an unbelieving world, in which we were beginning to hear about the "absurd" and "the meaninglessness of meaning." I was lost in it, and he helped me find my way. His sensitivity, his kindness, his brilliant, intellectual power, everything about him, everything he did, shed light. In his life there was light—the way he accepted the poverty of his boyhood, the tuberculosis of his young manhood; his exuberant response to the sun and the sea; his moral response to the Nazi crimes and the part he played in the French underground; his novels, his essays, his notebooks; and particularly, his address to the Dominican monks in 1948. He was more Christian in spirit than many church people I have known, and he helped me find my way through some of the immemorial problems of the human race.

This is the kind of light that Jesus is. It was the life that was in his life that was the light of men. He lived simply, but he lived intensely. At times he burned with a white heat. His life overflowed, so to speak; he could not contain it. Everything he touched was more alive. He gave sight to the blind, not only the blind who couldn't see because their eyes were gone, but the others, many more in number, who couldn't see because they were "in the dark."

They were in the dark about so many things. About themselves; they didn't quite know who they were, especially in the presence of God. He said to them, you are not servants; you don't need to bow and scrape in the presence of God; you are His friends, His children. Stand up! They were in the dark about their mistakes, their violations of the law; or more often, I am sorry to say, about the violations that someone else had made. And he always implied, although I think it was never recorded that he said it, but I can hear him say it when people were criticizing others for violating the law, I can hear him say, which law? One of the relatively unimportant ceremonial laws or one of the basic laws like Thou shalt not kill? Most often it was one of the less important laws.

They were in the dark about their neighbors. Who were they? He tried to tell them. Your neighbor, he said, is not the one you like the most, not necessarily the one who lives next door to you, or the one who agrees with you. You have a natural affinity with those people, but your neighbor is the one who needs you the most. They were in the dark about failure. They thought that failure was a disgrace. It is now in the eyes of many of our people. If their son drops out of college or fails to pass, it is a disgrace brought on the family. It is sad, because it may be largely his fault. But he was saying to them, don't forget that failure, failure of a certain kind, may be the way to let the light through. And suffering—so many people were (and are) in the dark about suffering. They thought that it was something sent to them, directed to them personally by God, and usually as punishment for something they had done or not done. By his own suffering he showed them that suffering is the price you pay for being the person you are. If you are any kind of person at all, you will suffer, and the way you do it may be something like the light that was in him. *In him was life; and the life was the light of men.*

It is what follows that statement which captivates our attention today: "and the light shineth in the darkness and the darkness has never put it out." If you are familiar with the Authorized Version, you expect to hear, "and the darkness comprehendeth it not." Let me tell you that William Temple gave me the ground for saying that the verb can mean either "to comprehend" or "to overcome"; in this case he chose the latter. The darkness has never overcome the light that was in Christ. Darkness has never put it out.

Not the darkness of ignorance through the long night of barbarian darkness that came down like tidal waves from northern Europe in the fifth, sixth, seventh, eighth, and ninth centuries. That darkness, you would think, would have extinguished any light that Jesus might once have lit, but there were groups of monks here and there who kept it burning. It was dim, but it didn't go out.

Not the darkness of wealth and power in the thirteenth century. The church of Europe was so drenched with wealth and power that it almost forgot what it was there for. But even that darkness didn't put out the light entirely because there was a little Italian who went up and down singing about the Lord Jesus. He possessed nothing, yet had all things. Thousands of men and women were drawn to his light. He asked them to do only two things, to give away everything they had and to be cheerful. And in eighteenth century England the established church was almost in total darkness. John Wesley rode up and down the land and wherever he went, the light began to shine!

What is more surprising perhaps is that even now in this secular, materialistic, violent, cynical age in which we live, and in which every value that a Christian holds dear has been attacked, challenged, or just ignored. In this age of rapid, revolutionary changes there is *Jesus Christ Superstar* on records, and now on the stage; and *Godspell*. Some of you who know me know that I am not particularly drawn by either of them, but I am drawn by the spirit that animates them, by the incentive that leads the young people in the cast to do them, and that draws people to the theater to see it. I do not see in them my picture of Jesus, but no two eras have exactly the same picture of Jesus. They never do, for in Jesus every generation sees, to some degree, a reflection of itself; and this one sees violence, ugliness, and failure. There is also the Jesus Movement, and the Jesus Freaks. I am sure that a great deal of both movements would not draw me and will not last long. But this I know: there is a Life in Jesus that is light, and the young will not let it go.

This is something we can see and understand, but what we are celebrating today we can't always see and we may never understand it. This is it: not even the darkness of the tomb, or the darkness of death could put out that light. This is the key sentence of the sermon: *The resurrection of Jesus remains the most mysterious fact in human history.* How *could* it happen? How *did* it happen? *Did* it actually happen? Or was it an event that took place in the inspired imagination of devout followers? Or was it the fulfillment of an extravagant desire?

In some other years we have probed the resurrection narratives in the Gospels and the references to the resurrection in the letters and the rest of the New Testament. It is a fascinating subject for any student, or for anyone who has a shred of intellectual curiosity. To see where they coincide, where they contradict each other, and at what point they diverge —this is a fascinating exercise. But for the person who meets the risen Lord on his way to work, or as he sits by the deathbed of someone he loves, or waits for his first child to be born, that study doesn't help much, in fact, I would say it was almost completely irrelevant.

What is relevant in the New Testament is the men and women who walk through its pages—Peter, Paul, John, Barnabas, Mark, and Luke. A slave like Onesimus, do you know anything about him? A couple like Priscilla and Aquilla. A young girl like Rhoda, so excited that she didn't even let Peter in when he knocked at the door until she had gone to tell her family that he was there, just out of prison. And the prison guards in Rome. Do you remember what happened to them?

One thing they all had in common, different as they were, one thing they all had in common, they were all once "in the dark"; they were now in the light. And the light was not a brighter sun, or better weather, or even a better government, or better schools, or a more adequately administered welfare. The light was the light that was in Christ that not even the darkness of death could put out and now shone across their way.

But you may say, I have never met the risen Lord on my way to work or in any other place, for that matter. Neither have I. If you mean a person walking up the street with pierced hands and feet, I've never met him. Some have, but I never have. But if you mean the life that takes hold of a person and changes him from a self-centered brat into a companionable, loving human being, I've seen him. Or, if you mean the life that gradually developed an overgrown, spoiled teenager into one of the most sensitive, competent professionals in his field, I've seen him. Or, if you mean a middle-aged person whose life had gone down the drain either in alcohol or something worse, and suddenly he begins to live and stand up, throw back his head, have a job, be glad to be alive, if you mean that, I've seen him.

I have met that life. In fact, I think if it weren't for him I'd give up. For the darkness of life is deep and powerful. I cannot face it alone. I can face it because I know that in him is life; and that the life was the light of men. And the light shines in the darkness and the darkness has never yet been able to put it out. In fact, it is shining here now!

Thanks be to thee, O God, for the life that is in Jesus, and for the light that comes to us from him and guides us on our way and makes sense of life, that gives us a better direction. Steady us, Lord, for the way we have to go. Save us from unnecessary mistakes; and when we make them, help us to remember that thou art not only our Judge, but also our Father. Amen.

Filled with the Holy Spirit

ℰ

ONE OF THE THINGS that bother some of us is the fact that there are two people inside us instead of one. There is the person we know we are. He is basically selfish. He often makes extravagant gestures of unselfishness but, especially in times of crisis, he knows that his life revolves around his own interests. He is impatient when he ought to be patient. He is complaining when he ought to be filled with gratitude. He is prejudiced in his judgments when he ought to be objective. He is slow to respond to the needs of others when he ought to be quick. And there is likely to be a duplicity about him. With one hand he quite genuinely reaches for the stars, and with the other he clings to clods of earth. He believes in God honestly and sincerely and yet, when he looks at the future, he is filled with anxiety and when he approaches the darkness of the night, he is frightened.

Then there is the person we would like to be, single as the shining of the sun without the slightest trace of duplicity, willing one will, to do one thing in the world; steady like the stars, unshaken by any of the confusion or tumult of the world; and selfless as Jesus was selfless in the sense of handling a situation without reference to his own interests.

And the difficulty for many of us is that these two persons seem to be poles apart, and as the years pass they seem to grow not much closer together. At fifty we are just about the same kind of shabby, selfish people inwardly that we were at thirty. And our question is, Is there any chance of our ever becoming the person we would like to be, or shall we give up and settle down to keep house with the person that we know we are?

This sermon may not reach some of you at all because some of you are quite satisfied with yourselves as you are. But if there ever creeps into your consciousness that dissatisfaction, that desire to be more single, more steady, more selfless, the question may be a very persistent one. Is there any chance of my ever becoming anything like the person I want to be?

I

We can say at the outset that it has been done. It has happened. Let me give you a classic example. According to the story in the Acts of the Apostles, Peter and his friend John had spent a night in jail. We would say that they had been "thrown" into jail without any hearing or trial. In other words, the whole proceeding was completely unfair. They had been put in jail because on the day before they had healed a lame man who was sitting by the temple gate, and in explaining to the crowds about their healing, they had told them about Jesus and the power that there was in his risen life. The powers that represented the status quo wanted to squelch that resurrection movement so they put them in jail.

The next day the two men were brought before an investigating committee of what we might call the ecclesiastical "brass" of the day, the top ranking officials of the church, the high priest, his father-in-law, and all his family, all the church lawyers and officials. Like most investigating committees, the procedure was fair enough but it must have been a humiliating experience for the men who were to be examined. The cards were against them from the very start and the question was swiftly put before them, "By what power, or by what name, have you done this?" Then Peter, "filled with the Holy Spirit," began to speak, and this is what he said: "Rulers of the people and elders of Israel, if we are being cross-examined today upon a benefit rendered to a cripple, upon how this man got better, you and the people of Israel must all know this, that he stands before you strong and well, thanks to the name of Jesus Christ the Nazarene whom you crucified and whom God raised from the dead."

Notice the transformation that had taken place in Peter. Peter was by nature a hot-tempered person, impulsive, impatient, blustering, impetuous. Normally a situation like this which was filled with unfairness and injustice would have irritated him to the point where he would have lost complete control of himself and his passions. Yet when he spoke, he spoke quietly, all his passions completely mastered and in perfect control. Again, he was an uneducated and untrained man who had spent his early life as a fisherman and had no formal education at all, and yet when he spoke, he spoke with the eloquence of simplicity that is the sure sign of reality. In his earlier days he had been a very self-protecting sort of person. He had even gone to the extent of denying his Lord in order to save his own skin. Yet here before all the authorities he freely and completely exposed himself and stood there in their presence without any self-defense whatsoever. At an earlier time when Jesus took him along with two other friends to the mount which was to become the Mount of Transfiguration Peter was heavy with sleep, inert and unresponsive, and here was a man who was alive with a spiritual power that could handle the situation with apparent ease. It was a genuine transformation.

So it can be done. It has been done. The Peter that was, the vacillating, hot-tempered, restless, irritable, self-centered Peter, became the Peter that was to be. That is the first clue to the answer of our question.

II

We want, however, to explore the matter a little further. Granted that it can be done, that it has been done, not only of course in this case but in thousands of others in its train, we want to know how it can be done, if it is possible to know that. The clue to it in this particular case is in the phrase, "then Peter, filled with the Holy Spirit."

You notice that the story does not say Peter, mustering every ounce of energy that he could muster; it does not say Peter, taking a deep breath and gritting his teeth, set about to defend himself; it does not say that Peter drew deeply on his own reserves and resources and brought up from unknown depths strength he did not know he had in himself. It says, "Peter, filled with the Holy Spirit," which means, of course, that Peter himself did nothing. It means that something was done to him. It means that Peter had the human capacity to receive powers outside himself, and that into him were poured energies from beyond himself, and he was filled with a power not his own that enabled him to rise to heights that neither he nor any of his friends ever dreamed he could reach.

In Peter's case, that spirit was the spirit of Jesus, I am quite convinced of that. And the power that filled him was the influence of Jesus. Peter had been exposed to Jesus day after day for at least a year or two, probably longer. It was an intimate daily association. He knew what he thought, he knew exactly what he had done and what he stood for. And without any doubt Jesus was the greatest single influence in the life of Peter. He changed his career. He found him a fisherman, he made him a fisher of men. He changed his name. He found him Simon and named him Peter, the rock. Sometimes, to be sure, Peter followed only at a great distance. There were days when it seemed as though the influence of Jesus upon this man was negligible; that he had left no impression upon him whatsoever.

But now, in a case of extreme emergency, when Peter found himself in a situation which taxed his own strength beyond his resources, is it possible for us in our imagination to think that at that time Peter remembered Jesus, how he too stood before a humiliating investigating committee, how he too had questions that were unfair and unjust flung at him, and how he had stood there, quiet, self-possessed, protesting nothing, not defending himself at all and answered the questions in a single word, sometimes by complete silence. It was as though that greater life of which there was such an excessive abundance in Jesus somehow flowed into the life of Peter as one man can influence another man, and his vitality, his thought, his emotion can be transfused into another life to make up for the deficiency to revive him in his weakness. It was as though the promise of Jesus, "I will not leave you helpless. I will come to you," was being fulfilled then and there in Peter. And as he stood before that mocking group of investigators, nothing that he did made him a different man, but he was filled with the influence of Jesus and the spirit of his Lord took possession of him and he became for a moment at least the Peter that he longed to be.

III

Now we may begin to see the answer to our question, and the rest of

170

this sermon is an attempt very briefly to point out that answer and make one or two comments upon it.

If we do find ourselves in a state of dissatisfaction about ourselves, we must recognize at the outset that we cannot make ourselves any better. The only thing that we do by trying to make ourselves better is to make ourselves self-righteous and unbearable to those who live with us. The harder we try to approach this character that we would like to be, the stiffer we become, the more unyielding and unbending in our relationships with other people. We may end in the valley of despair and depression.

But, and this is the good news in this sermon, and is something which I wish I could make more real than words can make, on one side we lie open to eternity. We are like an electric light bulb that cannot create light but that can be filled with light; like a lake that cannot create water, but that can be fed by the springs from the hills; like a sail that cannot make power, but that can catch the winds and sail a ship. We too lie open to forces and energies from beyond ourselves and what we cannot create in and by ourselves we can catch. We have the capacity to take in powers, energies, vitalities and by them be enabled to do the things that otherwise we could not do.

And the greatest spiritual power to which you and I can expose ourselves is the influence of Jesus. It is in the air we breathe. Take it in today. It is in the nooks and crannies of our memories, no matter how they may be clogged with all other bits and scraps of information. The influence of Jesus is pushing itself through the blocks of our memory to make itself felt upon our immediate perception. Let it make its way.

It is in the best of the civilization which we inherit and which we live in in spite of all the criticisms we make about it, we preachers and civilians. This civilization is all shot through with the influence of Jesus, his compassion in the hospitals, his truth in the schools, his humanity in the sons and daughters of men and women who are trying to make life better for other people. Take it in! His influence is more powerful now than it was two thousand years ago. It is the excessive life that was in Jesus which, like the water of the sea trying to push its way up into the little rivers and streams of the land, is trying to make its way into your life and my life. And the wonder of it is that when it takes hold of us, then we become like him, not because of anything we do but because of something he does.

Of course, and I hesitate to say this because it is making a point of what is already so obvious, we must expose ourselves to that influence else like a room with the windows closed the mighty rushing wind of the spirit will pass by us and not through us.

If I may add just a personal paragraph here which is not at all in my notes, the thing that I want for myself more than anything else is that I may grow up more and more into him, that I may carry myself a share of his reconciling life in the world today. I know that I cannot do that by myself, only as I expose myself to his influence can he do it in me. Next to that I want you to be more and more like him, more charitable, more understanding, slower to speak, less ready to bear grudges, greater in your understanding, and more sure in your confidence of God. You cannot do that yourself but he like a mighty rushing wind can fill you with his spirit, if you will let him.

Fill us, O Christ, with thy Spirit. Give us the power to do the things we want to do but in our strength we are not able to do. Take the raw material of our lives and refine it. Cool our tempers, soften our speech, enlarge our understanding, deepen our love. When the test comes, we will trust in thee and not in ourselves, knowing that by thy Spirit we will be able to do all things. Amen.

The New Life

J ESUS HAD an almost uncanny way of putting his finger on the laws of existence, and the ability to state in unmistakable terms the unconditional requirements of life—not biological life, but life on its highest levels. Listen to some of the ways he said it.

Except your righteousness shall exceed the righteousness of the Scribes and the Pharisees, you will never enter the kingdom of heaven. In other words, unless your goodness is more extravagant than the law requires, you will never come anywhere near the higher life. That is one of the laws of existence when you begin to think of life in its highest terms.

Once again he said, *Except you become like little children you will never enter the kingdom of heaven.* Unless you add to the sophisticated wisdom of an adult the acquired innocence and naturalness of a little child, you will be lost. That is another prerequisite of life, the spontaneous, quick response of trust and joy.

Again he said, *Except you repent, you will all likewise perish.* A tower had fallen and killed eighteen people and there were some who thought that the victims of the accident were punished for something that they had done. He looked at the people who thought that and said, unless you change your course, you will *all* run on the rocks. There are times when nations as well as individuals must radically change their way of thinking and living, if they want to survive.

Another time he said, *Except a man be born again he cannot see the kingdom of heaven.* There are some people who need from time to time to be repaired. Sometimes the repairs are minor and sometimes major; but there are other people who need to be rebuilt from the ground up, and until they are, they will have no idea at all what he was talking about, or what life on its highest level looks like.

And once again, *Except a grain of wheat fall into the ground and die, it abideth alone: but if it die, it bringeth forth much fruit.* That brings us to the eighth variation on a single theme. The theme is, "Behold, I make all things new," and the sermons during Lent have been variations on that one theme. We began with The New Liturgy, then went on to The New Catechism, The New Restlessness, The New Christ, The New Man, The New Church, and today The New Life. This last one of Jesus' prerequisites of life brings us very close to the event we are celebrating today.

Jesus was speaking quite simply about a seed. He was a country man, you know, and while he was not a farmer by trade, he must have known something about what happened in the spring of the year, and what he said about the seed was so undeniable and so obvious that we wonder sometimes why he said it. You know, however, when you stop to think about it, that the most obvious things in life are the things that people are most often likely to miss.

What he was saying was something like this. If you want to keep a seed just as it is, you can. You can put it in a drawer and if it is out of the light, and if you don't give it any water, it will stay very much the way it is. It may sprout a little, but you can keep it there indefinitely until time finally wears it away. But if you are willing to give up the seed, put it in the dirt, knowing that you will never see it again, you will lose it; but in time you will have a plant. You may have a flower or a fruit, or both.

He then went on to say that this is one of the laws of life. If you want to keep your life, keep it safe and secure, never risk it, never spend it, never give it away if you can possibly avoid it, keep it locked up all to yourself, figuratively speaking in your safe-deposit box, you can. You can do that; but if you do, eventually it will dry up and disappear like a bit of dust. If you are willing to let it go, lose it, so to speak; if you are willing to put it into the soil of existence, bury it, invest it, involve it in the great issues of life, spend it, give it extravagantly, you may lose it altogether in one sense; but the miracle is that you will find another life, another kind of life, a life as different as the plant is different from the seed, fuller, richer, more beautiful, more creative; what the writer of the Fourth Gospel imaginatively called *eternal* life.

The law that he was enunciating was this—and it isn't altogether pleasant to listen to—you must die in order to live, and unless you do, you will never really live. Some people may be perplexed by that if they take it too literally.

Jesus can help us because he is one of those rare human beings who practiced what he preached, and did what he talked about. He started out in the very beginning by giving life to other people, his life. Now, after nineteen hundred years, you can almost see the sparks that leap from his life to the life of other people, as his vitality was infused into the weak, limp people around him. Sometimes by a word, sometimes by a look, sometimes by a touch of the hand, he would bring people back to life. He gave his confidence to people who had given up all hope for the future. He also gave his joy. He must have been a radiant creature. If he hadn't had joy, he wouldn't have attracted so many children to him. They are not drawn to people who are wrapped in gloom.

You might say that in his short life he died, at least figuratively speaking, a thousand deaths. He let go some of the things that must have called him: the companionship of a wife, the possibility of children, the satisfaction of popularity (he could have had it so easily, and he did in the beginning), the normal human desire to be liked by everyone, and to make no enemies because you stand for nothing that really matters; the desire to be accepted, to be successful, to see his dream come true.

I often wonder how many doors he closed in order to keep one door open, how many times he said *no* to little things, appealing things that were perfectly legitimate, in order to say *yes* to the great things. For him the great thing was to do the will of Him who sent him; and in order to do that, there were many other things he could not do. He went on and on with many a dark moment, many a misgiving. He went through Gethsemane, sweat it out, you might say, and finally stood before the Roman Governor on trial for his life. As he stood there, he spoke not a single word. He didn't answer one of the charges made against him, so that the Governor marvelled. There was nothing left to be said. He had said it, he had done it; there was nothing left to be said or done. So he was killed; he was put to death. Like a seed, he was put into the ground to die. And he did die.

Like a seed, he was raised to a new life. It was as though the mute had been taken off so that he could play on the open strings. He didn't look the same; even his closest friends didn't recognize him when they saw him after the resurrection, but he was the same person with a new and different instrument. He is alive now, not only as a part of our historic memory, not only as great people of all times live on in their influence, not in that sense only. He is alive now as an active energy. He gets into people and gives them the power to do things, to rise to new levels of being. He went through death and beyond it.

Every once in a while he finds another instrument, sometimes in a congregation of people very much like this, that he can use to do his work. This comes very close to us today. He is searching for instruments that he can use to heal and reconcile, to steady and reassure.

I can hear Jesus saying something like this:

> You are naturally curious about the future, your own future and the future of your world, but especially about your own future. You are made that way. The unknown fascinates you, and frightens you. What is on the other side of the moon you have always wanted to know, and you have just begun to find out. What is on the other side of death? You have always wanted to know that, not only for your own sake, but because you are thinking of those you love who are already on the other side.

> It is natural that you should want to know whether it is true that when the body goes, you go. It oftens looks that way. Many intelligent people think that and say it. When you are confused by what they say, look at me. I couldn't have done anything without my body, but when it was destroyed, put into the ground like a seed, I went on. So will you.

> Stop fretting about the future, I hear him say. Stop speculating about it. Make some experiments now. Throw overboard some of your possessions, and travel without them. Bury them

and see what happens; see what happens when you begin to let yourself go; see how the gates begin to swing wide; see how the future opens up.

I also remember what the anonymous writer of the Letter to the Hebrews said about Jesus. "Looking to Jesus, the pioneer of our faith, who for the joy that was set before him endured the cross, despising the shame and is now seated at the right hand of God." This year, for the first time, I asked myself what the joy might be that was set before him. He didn't have any of the joys of life that most of us count on; a few, perhaps, but not many. Surely his joy was not a plum held out in the future as a reward that would be given to him if he was willing to go through the valley of the shadow of death. It wasn't like a bicycle promised to a boy if he passed his examination. We can't conceive of that. It was the joy of moving in the great rhythms of life, the joy of being in step with the morning stars.

My hearing may not be as good as it should be, but I hear him saying to us now:

At a time like this, the world is battered, battered badly, but not beaten; sad and sorrowful, cynical and frustrated. But it is not bereft of joy, the joy of opening the door for another person; the joy of losing your own life, little bits of it here and there, and finding yourself in a larger room in which you can begin a new life; a life in which death, little deaths all along the way, and the great death at the end, is the very seed from which the new life springs. This is the joy of the resurrection, the joy of the new life for those who are willing to march behind me toward the Kingdom of God, in step with the morning stars.

Thanks be to thee, O God, for every glimpse of life that cheers us on our way, for everyone who rises out of the dust and ashes of despair and discouragement and goes forward to do the best he can in the world he lives in. We ask that we now be given the courage to enter that larger room where life looks out on distances greater than we have ever seen before. Amen.

177

The Gulf between the Ideal
and the Actual

ℰ

O<small>NE OF THE</small> most noticeable things about human beings is that they have ideals—standards of excellence—for themselves, their families, and their communities. They do not all have the same ideals. The ideals of an Oriental are not always the same as the ideals of a Westerner. And in our eyes, they are not all equally good ideals. The ideals of democracy we greatly prefer to the ideals of communism.

But it is worth noting that all human beings have their eyes set on some far-off goal. (The saying goes that there is honor even among thieves.) You look at a man once, and he looks like a worm crawling along the ground, miserable and mean. You look at him again, and he is like a creature with wings, soaring toward the stars.

It is equally noticeable that human beings seldom, if ever, realize their ideals. They seldom, if ever, grasp the things they reach for. Their ideal home life and their actual home life are often poles apart. Their ideal political society and their actual political society, the order in which they really live, are often as different as night from day. Their ideal characters, the men they would be, and the men they actually are too often seem to bear little resemblance to each other. In other words, there is always a gulf between the ideal and the actual. In life as we know it there is always a discrepancy, and sometimes an enormous one, between what ought to be and what is.

For a Christian this gulf is excruciatingly broad, and for the obvious reason that the ideal is so high that the performance is often embarrassingly poor. If your ideal is to live a comfortably adjusted life, there is some chance that you may come somewhere near reaching it. But if your ideal is to be perfect as your heavenly Father is perfect, the chance of anything but a poor performance is not very great. Christians are often compared unfavorably with followers of other religions on the basis of performance—that is, the degree to which they practice what they preach. To be perfectly fair in the comparison one must be sure that the ideals which the others preach are as high as Christian ideals. In some cases they are not.

What concerns me today is how you behave when you reach the gulf that exists between the ideal and the actual in your own life. What concerns me is how you behave when it dawns on you that your marriage is not the marriage that you dreamed of; or, when it becomes plain to you that the profession to which you looked forward with such high hopes is filled with corruption and ambition and tainted with the same poisons that you find in less lofty callings; or, when it dawns on you that the church itself is not the perfect place you expected it to be, that the people in it are not the models of the Christian life that you hoped they would be, and that the spirit in it is not always the spirit that you hoped to find in it. Especially am I concerned about how you behave when you see for the first time that you yourself are not the person you wanted to be, hoped to be, or as a matter of fact thought you were.

What do you do then? Do you say, if you are in the early years of your adult life, Well at last I've grown up? I have left my ideals behind me with my adolescence and I accept the advice that was given to the young senator, The only way to get along is to go along. Is that what you do? Do you become cynical and bitter and say to yourself, Well, I've learned a lot about life at last, and I know that people are not what I thought they were and I will never get caught again? Or, do you try to withdraw from the actual world and live in the clouds, separated as much as possible from the wear and tear of the market, the family, and the state? Or what do you do when you reach the gulf between the ideal and the actual?

In my experience with people, I am prepared to say that more people flounder in the waters of this gulf than almost anywhere else, and at no place do we need guidance more than we do right at this point, when

179

we become aware of the fact that we are creatures with ideals, but that we live in a world in which those ideals are virtually never realized.

Now forget yourself and your problems for a moment, and try to see Jesus. If anybody ever had an ideal, he did. And if one tried to put his ideal into words, perhaps these might be the words. His ideal was an order of society in which people trusted God completely and treated each other as the children of God. That is somewhere near it, isn't it? His ideal was an order of society in which people trusted God implicitly and treated each other as the children of God. Perhaps we should say parenthetically that this ideal was not a theory that he thought up in solitude, not something that he got out of a textbook. It was the result of his own personal experience of God. He had known God as a child, and increasingly as a young man, as his Father, intimately his Father, uniquely his Father, but the Father also of all men, and the ideal was the result of that experience. He would never have called it an "ideal"; he would have described it as doing the will of his Father.

He had an ideal. Between that ideal and the actual facts of life he saw a great gulf fixed, like the gulf between Dives and Lazarus. People did not trust God. Some of them did, to be sure, some of the time; but a great many of them, when they were put right to it, put their trust in their money, or their power, or their friends, or the influence behind the scenes. And they did not treat each other as the children of God. More often they treated people as means to their own ends.

Everywhere he looked he saw people selling their souls for money. He saw them striving for prestige in a pitiful way, because what they got was such a paltry thing, a seat next to the right person at the right time. He saw people bursting with ambition, ambition, often, for things that were not really worth having, and for things that would do them more harm than good. He saw people pathetically trying to be someone they were not. And he saw other people pinning all their hopes on either Rome or Zion, putting all their eggs either in the basket of the Roman Empire or of the Jewish cult and temple. He saw other people clinging to the past long after it was dead and gone because they felt that in this was their only security, and still others hoping for a future in which their vanity would be amply satisfied.

He believed, you see, that men were potential sons of God; he saw men constantly behaving like actual sons of the devil. Not only Pilate, mind you, but Peter also; not only Judas, but James and John. He was in the deep waters of the gulf between the ideal and the actual, and in that gulf he chose to remain.

He did not have to remain there. He could have sacked the world altogether and gone off to a hill-town by himself with a few chosen friends to live a "spiritual life," as free as possible from the distractions and disturbances of the natural world. He could have done that perfectly well. Or he could have scrapped his ideals and settled with the hierarchy, saying that these things that he hoped for were impossible and the best he could do was to come to some kind of settlement with things as they were. After all, the Kingdom of Heaven is a great deal to expect among the nations of the earth, too much, perhaps.

He could have done either one of these things and yet, knowing him, you know that he could not have done either one and remained himself. He could not have sacked the world. It was his Father's world, imperfect though it be, the world his Father made, and the people in it were the people whom his Father made and loved. He could not sack that world and go off and live in an ivory tower somewhere on a hill, aloof to, and independent of the needs and sorrows of the actual world of men. Nor could he have scrapped his ideal. His ideal was his life, and without it he was nothing.

He chose, rather, to remain in the world as it was, and I am quite sure, not grudgingly, but gladly, not saying to himself, This certainly isn't the place I thought it was but perhaps I had better stay here, stick it out, and do as well as I can; I certainly would rather be living under different circumstances but these are the ones I've been given so I will make the best of a bad bargain. Not that! He did it gladly as though he believed that in this very gulf his ministry had the greatest opportunity, as though he believed that with these ordinary, simple, little people he had the best chance of working out the purpose of God, that in this tragic world of men and women the Kingdom had the greatest chance. Notice that he did not choose as his closest associates the intellectuals, people like Nicodemus; he chose fishermen and tax-gatherers, men with little discernment and often no imagination, not by any means the cream of the crop, as if to say, if God cannot come into the world in these people, and for these people, He cannot come into it at all.

In other words, he worked willingly with the material he had, and most of it was not very good material. The people were rough diamonds at best, and some of them were not anything like diamonds, even rough ones. Nevertheless, he worked with the material he had, knowing that it was by no means perfect. Nobody ever fooled him. He knew the kind of people he had to deal with. He even knew—and this is one of the things that always staggers me when I stop to think about it—he even knew that his most intimate friends were capable of betrayal and denial. He knew that from the beginning. Yet he worked with the material he had, knowing that it was not perfect but believing that God could use imperfect materials as instruments of his purpose.

His accomplishment seemed almost negligible at the time. In Nazareth, you remember, his hometown, he could do nothing. So he left. According to one account he was expelled and would have been killed if he had not taken particular pains to protect himself and save his life. In Capernaum, a neighboring town where he was not so well known, he aroused a good deal of interest and curiosity and gave a great many people a new lease on life. In Jerusalem, he made a futile attempt to reform the Temple, but made no real impact on either the Jewish or the Roman authorities. Eventually, he was executed by the state as a dangerous character. In one sense his ideal was never realized. The Kingdom of God never came. In another sense, his ideal was supremely realized, for the Kingdom of God came in *him*!

I do not know whether you can see that or not. Perhaps it is not a thing that you can see, but only feel. I feel it more and more as I grow older and, if I could spread this mystery before you, I would feel that I had done my part. It represents a revelation about life that is different from anything that comes to us from any of the other great religions and cultures of the world. The revelation is this, that as he was torn between the ideal and the actual, he was obedient and, in that moment of obedience, the Kingdom came. As he did God's will in *this* world, under *these* difficult circumstances, given *this* poor material to work with, God's will was done in him! Do you see that?

What he says to us, as we stand in that same gulf, is something like this: You are living in an imperfect world in which there will always be a great gulf between the ideals you cherish and the actual facts you struggle with. You know this. You can expect no perfect state of affairs. You cannot look forward to a home that will be perfect, or a country that will be an ideal society, or to a profession that will be completely pure, or a life that will be perfect, or a situation in which all the circumstances are perfect. What is more, there are great forces of evil working against you all the time, and the longer you live, the more you will appreciate how great these forces really are. Don't ask where they come from. It is enough to try to meet them.

Nevertheless, he says to us, Whatever the circumstances may be, you are a son of God; act like one. You will not always act in exactly the same way. It will depend on the circumstances. For instance, you will not approach an unruly child in the same way that you will approach a grief-stricken adult. And you will not always act as much like a son of God at some times as at others. People around you will make it impossible sometimes; the resisting medium will be so great that you will not be able to act as you would like to act. On other occasions, unmanageable forces in yourself will prevent you from acting like a son of God. But always remember who you are, whose son you are, and when you fail, as you will fail, acknowledge your failures; but don't grieve over them. Get up and get going. God will understand the way your father and mother understood when you were a child.

And remember this, I think he would say to us, the Kingdom comes not once and for all, and to stay forever, a static state of affairs. The Kingdom of the Christian is not like that. It is not a utopia. It is not the classless society of the communist system. It is something much more like fire and wind. The Kingdom comes whenever a man responds to a need, or a challenge, or an opportunity by acting as much like a son of God as he can at that moment. Then the Kingdom comes. *This* is the time, and *this* is the place, and *this* is the situation, and *you* are the person.

Open our eyes, O God, to all the facts of life; give us the strength to face it with courage, not shrinking from the evil, but always striving for that which is right and true and good, knowing that we are sons of thine, and that in all things, thy love and thy power will be made known through us. Amen.

The Good Shepherd

❧

JESUS SAID, "I am the Good Shepherd," and as we listen to that simple declarative statement of fact we ask the same questions that we asked when we heard him say, "I am the bread of life." Those questions were: first, To whom did he say it? second, Did Jesus say it or did John say it? and third, What does it mean to us now? This time we will take the second question first and deal with it more briefly because a great deal of it will be by way of repetition.

Did Jesus say it or did John say it? Sincere Christians, as you might expect, give different answers to that question as they do to almost every question that they are asked. Within the Christian fellowship, there is room for a wide variety of opinion. Some believe passionately that Jesus himself said it, and for good reasons. What is more, they base their whole faith largely on the fact that he *did* say it. Not only on that patricular claim, but on all the other claims he made about himself. In other words, if you ask some people, Why do you believe that Jesus was the Son of God? thousands of them will say, I believe it because he said he was.

Others, including myself, believe that St. John said it about Jesus; and we believe that, too, for good reasons. The first three evangelists tell essentially the same story about Jesus from essentially the same point of view. That is why they are called the "Synoptic Gospels." They tell the same story from essentially the same point of view. They arrange the record of their memories—that is, their material, which includes the memories of many people kept alive by word of mouth—in slightly different ways, but essentially it is the same story.

The fourth Evangelist goes about his work in an entirely different way, and approaches his subject from a completely different angle. For one thing, he leaves a great deal out of the story which they included. He leaves out the baptism, the temptation, the transfiguration, the institution of the Last Supper, and the prayer in the Garden of Gethsemane. These omissions suggest at once that he has his camera set at a different angle. He does not include a single parable in his Gospel, and the Kingdom of God, which is the theme of Jesus' teaching in the first three Gospels, is never mentioned save once only in his conversation with Nicodemus.

St. John is not so much telling a story as he is telling the meaning of the story after brooding over it for many years. This leads us to believe that the spirit of the living Christ is using John, or perhaps we should say is speaking through John, as an interpreter, as a transcriber, even as a translator. The Kingdom of God, for example, is translated by St. John as "eternal life." No one who wasn't a Jew would have known what the Kingdom of God meant, but eternal life—every Gentile would know what that meant.

So, we believe that the spirit of the living Christ is speaking through John as an interpreter, transcriber, and translator and that he makes no attempt to recall or record the actual words that Jesus spoke, any more than Catherine Drinker Bowen does when she writes one of her biographical novels or fictional biographies. In the *Yankee from Olympus* there are long conversations between Oliver Wendall Holmes and his wife. She has no way of knowing what they actually said, but she knows enough about him to be able to say with a certain degree of fairness and accuracy that this is the kind of thing he would have said to his wife.

In much the same way, John speaks for Jesus. The claims that Jesus makes in this Gospel are claims that John is making about him. He is the Bread of Life; he is the Good Shepherd; he is the Light of the World. That is as much as we will say today about the second question.

The first question gets us into deeper waters. To whom did he say it? He said it to the last people that you would imagine he would say it to. He said it not to the people, not to the flock, not to the people who were lost like sheep without a shepherd, not to the people. He said it to the

186

religious leaders who had just put out of the synagogue the man born blind, the man whom Jesus had healed and who refused to say under their questioning that Jesus was a "sinner" because he healed him on the Sabbath Day, and therefore broke the law. They are the people he was talking to.

He said it, in other words, to the "shepherds" who were in a position to lead the people and who to his way of thinking were seriously misleading them. He was saying to them and in no uncertain terms, *You* are the blind men, and blind in so many ways; blind to the purpose and intention of the law. The Law was intended originally for man's good, to lead him to God, to help him know God and how to live in God's world; and you have made it like weights upon his feet and chains upon his hands; an end in itself, not a means to an end.

You are blind to the dangers of insurrection and violence, he said to them. At that time there was a great deal of political unrest and many movements to stir up and encourage insurrection against Rome. Jesus believed that insurrection against Rome spelled nothing but disaster for the Jews, as indeed it proved to be when they finally did rebel in the year 66. After four years of resistance Jerusalem was leveled to the ground in 70, though a group of less than a hundred zealots held out at the fortress of Masada until 73.

Violence, tempting as it often is, and apparently the only way as it often seems to be, was never the way of Jesus. We think of some of the people in the resistance movement in the Second World War in France and in Italy, and some of the people who now feel that violence is the only way. It is tempting, but Jesus believed that tempting as it often is, it is temporary at best; and that it violates the very essence, the heart of the order of life he came to inaugurate, namely God's order.

They were blind not only to these things, but they were blind to him! They didn't see what was happening right before their very eyes. They could see Moses quite clearly a thousand years before feeding the people with manna as they wandered about the wilderness. This, they said, was a miracle from heaven; but they couldn't see God feeding the people on the hillside when Jesus took a boy's lunch and satisfied their hunger then and there! They could see God working through the ancients, like Elijah who raised the widow's son from the dead, but when Jesus opened the eyes of the man who had been born blind they didn't see it, they couldn't see it. Why? Why couldn't they see it?

We don't know why. But what would you say? I would say—and this, naturally, is based entirely on what knowledge I have of myself and of other people— they weren't really "blind"; they had perfectly good eyes, but they were afraid to look. They were afraid of what they might see; it might mean that they would lose their position, their status, their whole way of life.

And how right they were, for if Jesus had his way they would lose their way, their way of looking at things. You might describe their way as looking through the wrong end of the telescope. Instead of looking at a *person*, they looked at a book and tried to see which rule applied. They made their ultimate judgments on the basis of outward actions. Behavior is important (don't misunderstand me) but they were making ultimate judgments solely on the basis of outward action; that is, on the observance of the letter of the law and not looking at the inward being of the person who might be keeping every letter of the code and still be rotten at the core.

Their way wasn't his way, and the two ways were incompatible. His way, mind you, wasn't the free and easy way. It was the way of giving yourself for the sake of the flock. It was the people's way, because the people were the Children of God. It was the way of the inward look. The difference between the two ways can be seen today by the way doctors look at a patient: one looks at the reports that come to him on sheets of paper, made on the basis of tests and analyses; the other looks at the patient, looks into him, at the whole of his life and work, and reads the printed analyses in the light of what he sees in the patient and applies them accordingly.

It is plain to see that Jesus was charging straight into the religious establishment of his day when he said these things to the "shepherds." At least, into that part of it that was trying to put an end to him and to the new order of life he came to begin. So it was to these men, these so-called "shepherds" of the sheep that Jesus said, You are like the thieves who climb up over the wall instead of going in by the door. You know why they climb over the wall, and what they want when they get there, and what they do. I am the one and only door, said Jesus through St. John, the shepherd's door. I am the good shepherd; and the good shepherd gives his life for his sheep.

Finally, but most important, what do these words mean to us? So far as I can see they don't mean anything to us unless we see that they are spoken directly to us, and therefore I shall begin with number one, namely myself. They are spoken to me for I, too, am a "shepherd." Not a real one, not in the literal sense; but figuratively, I am a shepherd, for I am the chief pastor of this flock, and *pastor* is the Latin word for *shepherd*. So I am one of the shepherds he is speaking to and, as he speaks, these questions I can hear him ask. Are you looking out for the flock or for yourself—your position, your security, your comfort, your future? What would you do in a showdown? You may be able to stand for what you believe now, but if it came to a showdown where would you stand? You see clearly what is written in the pages of the New Testament (and how I love to read it, and study it, and work on it, even though I've read it a thousand times) but do you see clearly, or miss completely what is being written today in Copley Square? Are you so wedded to things that have been that you refuse to see what they might become?

And of course, one of the most difficult questions that comes to me as I hear this address to the shepherds, one of the most difficult facts I have to face is that I am so attracted to the lovable sheep that I often neglect the difficult ones. Am I willing to go out to the ones who are lost, lost usually because no one really wants them?

So, he is certainly speaking to me; and he is speaking to you. I know that you aren't a shepherd, not even figuratively. Yet don't be too sure. If you are the head of a family, the teacher of a class, the leader of a group, the president of a firm, a big corporation, or a nation, you are a shepherd of those people. And Jesus is speaking to you, and he is saying something like this: Are you blocking my way, or opening it? Are you thinking of the flock or of your own future—the next election, so to speak, if you are in that field? Or your next promotion?

189

Once we have understood this and hear him speak to us and not only to others, it clears the way that leads us out into the open spaces where we meet the Good Shepherd himself. He, too, was not really a shepherd, you know. He never kept sheep. He lived in a sheep-raising country; he must have known many shepherds, and he saw them much more often than we do for we see them only occasionally, when we go to parts of our own country, or to England, or Scotland, or Switzerland where sheep are raised. So he was a shepherd only in a figurative sense.

Think what a modest claim it was. We keep talking about the claims that Jesus made. Even if he made it himself, think how modest a claim it was. Julius Caesar a century before him made a claim: "I came, I saw, I conquered." Louis the XIVth in the seventeenth century made a claim: "I am the State." Jesus made a claim, "I am the Good Shepherd." What a contrast! He claimed to be the keeper of sheep—sheep noted for their stupidity and their willingness to follow the leader who loved them, and for their value in the marketplace, their wool and their meat. There is only one thing implied in the claim. The good shepherd cares; he lays down his life for the sheep. He cares about his flock, and he cares about the sheep one by one.

I am told, though I have never been there, that the relationship between an eastern shepherd and his sheep is entirely different from anything we see. For one thing, he is always ahead of them, not behind them, driving them. He is ahead of them exploring, finding the way; and they follow him. He is always out in front, looking for the green pasture and the still water; going on ahead through the dangerous ravines, clearing the ground so that they can eat in safety.

We claim that he is "the King of Glory," that he is sitting at the right hand of the Father. His claims were more modest, yet more ultimate. They are claims that one of his closest friends could make for him without the slightest exaggeration. He is the Bread of Life, the food by which we live—because he cares. He is the Light of the World, the light by which we find our way and see the beauty that surrounds us—because he cares. He is the Way, the Truth, and the Life—because he cares. How much does he care? Enough to go out on a limb for the flock, to pitch into the roughest element of the opposition, and to lose his life in the end. To lose it only to find it, hoping that the sheep may find their life in his.

O Keeper of Sheep, I have the will but not always the power to follow. When I go astray, look for me and find me. Take me back where I belong and set me up on the right way again. Keep ahead of me, and point me to the stars lest I settle down in the nearest valley, or in some ditch. At the end, lead me to my Father's house and leave me in His care. Amen.

How Can We Be Sure?

"Surely goodness and mercy shall follow me all the days of my life: and I will dwell in the house of the Lord forever." Psalm 23:6

THIS SERMON is intended especially for those who are not sure about their religion. They participate in it, but they have no inner certainty about it. They may say something like this to themselves: There may be a God, and there may not be. I am not sure. There may be some great purpose in life, and there may not be. I cannot be certain. There may be a life after death, sometimes it looks as though there were, and there may not be. I am not sure. So, they travel in the twilight of uncertainty, staggering between their intellectual doubts and their emotional desires. They walk, so to speak, the tightrope of an open mind.

And yet, they are by no means happy about their lack of assurance. It troubles them. They would like to be sure and they ask of us who seem to have some portion of assurance, How can we be sure? It is to that question that I should like to speak today, warning them ahead of time that no one can give them the assurance which they ultimately must discover and develop inside themselves. We can, however, point the way.

I

One thing must be said at the outset and that is that you never can have the same kind of assurance in religion that you can have in some other realms of experience. There are some things that you are sure of because you can prove them. For instance, you can be sure that two parts

192

of hydrogen mixed with one part oxygen makes water because, when you put them together, you have water. You can be pretty sure that a straight line is the shortest distance between two points because when you measure all the other distances, the straight line is the shortest. And you can be sure that it is necessary to eat to live because if you stop eating you stop living. There are scores of things in life that you are sure of because they are demonstrable. You can prove them as you can prove a problem in arithmetic.

But there are other things that you are sure of in spite of the fact that you cannot prove them. For example, when a boy falls in love with a girl, one of his parents concerned for the boy and the girl is very likely to say to him, Are you sure you are in love with this girl? And the boy will say something like this: All I know is that I am more sure of that than anything else in the world. He cannot prove it, it is beyond demonstration, and yet he is absolutely certain of it. Likewise, when a man looks at a dogwood tree in full bloom he is likely to say something like this: I am sure that that is beautiful and I am sure that beauty is real. Ask him to prove it, and he cannot. It may simply be the strange reaction of the chemicals in his body to a particular arrangement of natural elements which he chooses to think are beautiful. Nevertheless, he is sure of it as he is sure of little else.

So, when one man says, "Surely goodness and mercy shall follow me all the days of my life; and I will dwell in the house of the Lord forever," he cannot prove it. He could not possibly bring together enough facts to demonstrate with any conclusive evidence that he was to have all his life long that security which we all crave, and that the goodness and the mercy of the Lord would follow him to the very end of his days; he could not prove it if his life depended upon it. And yet, when he begins the sentence with that single word *surely*, we know that he is as certain of that as he is of the fact that the sun will come up tomorrow morning, and his life rests upon it as surely as a building rests upon its foundation.

So, if you are looking in your religion for the kind of assurance that you have in the realm of demonstrable, provable things, I must tell you that you will never find it. For religion is in the realm of those things where assurance is more by way of the intuition than by way of the intellect. It is not that the intellect is left out (far be it from me to say that!), but the final, basic assurances of religion include far more than the intellect. They include not only the evidence that the mind can marshal, but also the testimony and experience of the whole of a man's personality that reaches out intuitively to grasp and appreciate the total meaning of life. Some people are not sure of their religion today because they have tried to approach it by the one-way street of the intellect.

II

Now, where does that kind of assurance come from, because that is the kind of assurance we want? In the first place, it is handed down to us from the generations who have gone before us. A child's first assurances are most likely to be the assurances of his father and mother. If, for instance, the father and mother are sure that the earth is round and not flat, the chances are that the child will be sure of that too, and he begins his scientific life by accepting that hypothesis on the authority of his parents. If his father and mother are sure that the family is worth every sacrifice that has to be made for it, the child is likely to be sure of that too. He has never had the occasion nor the necessity to prove it, but he accepts it. If the father is the kind of person who is sure that the only university worth the name is the university in Cambridge or New Haven, the child, unfortunately, is likely to be sure of that too,—for a while!

For it is true, is it not, that our most deep and basic assurances we inherit from those who have gone before us, and so it is not surprising for us to see that a man's first religious assurances are those of his ancestors, the ones that have been forged on the anvil, to use a trite expression, of experiences down through long generations of human history. We are members of a family that, by and large, has been sure, in spite of many facts which indicate the contrary, that there is within this whole complex situation which we call the life of man a purpose. Our family has been sure, by and large, that life has rime and reason, that it is not just a jumble of unrelated, chaotic facts tossed together by a witless power, for no purpose and to no end.

Likewise, we are the children of a family that has been sure that Jesus is the personification of the divine. They have expressed it in different ways. They have had different kinds of evidence to support that assurance, but by and large our family has been sure of that. They have been sure that life has a height and depth that is not comprehended completely by the calendar. They have been sure that individual men have a dignity which is worthy of our respect, for it is the dignity derived from the Creator, God. They have been sure of all these things. Of course, they have had their doubts and their questions, but we inherit those subconscious, deep, racial, social assurances that have been handed down from generation to generation.

And so, I say in the first place, that those of you who are looking for assurance in your religion must not turn too quickly and with impatience from your heritage, all that great body of faith that has come down to you; do not turn aside from it as you would from some things which are no longer worthy of your belief or loyalty until you have pondered it well and examined the weight of it and the meaning of it. For in that you will find your social and psychological link with the experience of the human race back through the ages. Our first assurance of things unseen is handed down to us from the generations that have gone before us and let us not thoughtlessly cast that heritage aside.

That assurance, however, must then be verified by the facts of a man's personal experience. No assurance, no matter how much we may want it, can long be sustained if it is contrary to fact. Several years ago there was a man in Memphis, Tennessee, who was so sure of the spiritual nature of man that he went on a fast and wanted to prove to the world that man, independent of the physical body, could live without eating. He finally came to the conclusion that his assurance was contrary to fact as his life quietly and quickly ebbed away and he had to revise his assurances to bring them into line with fact. And so, all of us who inherit assurances from our past and from our families must verify them by the facts of our own experience and sometimes the assurances of the past must be revised. Here is where the exercise of our critical faculties comes in.

For example, some of us inherited from our ancestors a Bible that they believed to be the verbal inspiration of God, a Bible in which every sentence was dictated by God, in which there could be no error, no inaccuracy, and no inconsistency. We soon found that that could not be verified by the facts, that there were errors in the Bible, that there were inaccuracies, that there were different levels of spiritual awareness and attainment, and that the Bible was the inspired word of God in the sense that through human channels, with all their fallibility and frailty, God made Himself known in different times and in different places and to different degrees to His people. We had to revise what we inherited from the past in the light of the facts of our own knowledge. That has happened more than once.

Other things that we inherit from the past are verified and confirmed and amplified by the facts of our own experience, and that to my mind is one of the greatest satisfactions in life. For example, to be told by your family, by the great Christian family that has gone before you, that there is a purpose in life and that all the extraneous and apparently irrelevant strands really can be woven together to make a pattern, to be told that is one thing, but then to go through the deep waters of life yourself, facing all the contradictions and acknowledging all the things which seem to point to the fact that life is chaos, and suddenly realizing, because you feel it in your own life, that there is some purpose toward which all the avenues of your own personal existence converge, that there is a pattern which slowly and painfully emerges, and that beyond your personal life there is a purpose which holds together, drawing them as a magnet draws steel, all the fragments of life, to feel that yourself and to verify that yourself in your own experience is one of the great moments in an adult's life. The heritage of the past has been confirmed by the experience of the present.

In much the same way, some people receive as their heritage the teaching of Jesus, and as obedient children they accept it and then they come to a period in their life when suddenly that teaching becomes alive because they see it working. I remember, for instance, how the line "He that loseth his life shall find it" always made a kind of appeal to me over and above the appeal of the authority of my minister and my teachers.

And yet, it was not until quite recently that the truth of that line, namely that you never have any kind of life worth calling life, until you successfully submerge yourself in something much greater than yourself, it was not until just recent years that the full truth and meaning of that dawned upon me. And so, these assurances of things unseen come to us by way of inheritance which, in turn, is verified by the experience of our own lives.

But, in the absence of complete proof, and there never is complete proof in these things, the evidence is never completely in, it is finally confirmed, this assurance we are speaking of, by the desire of the human heart. And here I recognize that I am on ground that is dangerous and difficult and will not be acceptable to all. All I can say is that the longer I live the more I am convinced of it. Perhaps we can take an illustration from another realm of life that will make it clear. Here, for instance, is a young scientist in the medical field who is sure that he can find a cure for cancer, he together with his colleagues. He has proved to himself that there is no fact that is conclusively against that. Otherwise he would have to give up the undertaking altogether. In addition, he has discovered some facts that support the possibility of it. They are like hints, suggestions, intimations. But he has not enough facts to prove it or to bring it yet to pass. What keeps him going, then? He goes on believing because he *wants* to find that cure, and the ultimate confirmation of his assurance when he has surveyed the whole realm of fact, providing there is no fact against it, is in the deep place of his heart's desire. Because he wants it so much, he believes in it so steadily.

Here, then, is a man who is sure of God and all that we mean by God —purpose, mind, meaning, love, goodness—he is sure of it. He can find in the universe no fact or group of facts which conclusively proves that there is not such a God. He has discovered some facts that very definitely favor it and support it, order, spirit, presence, purpose. There are not enough facts to prove it or to demonstrate it to the world. There are many facts that are in the neutral zone, that raise many an embarrassing question; facts like the suffering of the innocent. He goes on believing and trusting his assurance because he *wants* God, because there is something in his human being that is athirst for God, that craves for

197

the infinite, that looks up above the earth with all of its storm and travail for the serenity and the peace that abide in the heart of the Almighty. He wants something more than bread, and more enduring than the days of our years. He wants the assurance of purpose, he wants life to be good, he wants it to make sense and so, he goes out with no fact proving to the contrary and yet, without enough facts to prove his case, believing because in his heart of hearts he wants to believe.

That is where a man's assurance of things unseen finally is bound to rest. May I say to those of you who are in your younger years when your minds are alive and alert and are particularly curious about these things and are fearful of accepting anything that cannot be well substantiated, you are to be honored for that. Never distrust your minds or in any way violate them; but go out beyond them! You are more than a mind, as a ship is more than any one of its essential parts. Do not be afraid of the things that you sincerely desire, do not hold back from believing in the things you want to believe in: make the ground of your assurance that citadel of the human heart where your greatest desires dwell.

Strangely enough, what we have been trying to say one of the Victorian poets, who is not read much now as he was once read, and may well again be read, expressed when he wrote these lines:

> Strong Son of God, immortal Love,
>   Whom we, that have not seen thy face,
>   By faith, and faith alone, embrace,
> Believing where we cannot prove;
>
> We have but faith: we cannot know;
>   For knowledge is of things we see,
>   And yet we trust it comes from thee,
> A beam in darkness, let it grow.
>
> Forgive these wild and wandering cries,
>   Confusions of a wasted youth;
>   Forgive them where they fail in truth,
> And in thy wisdom make me wise.

"Surely, goodness and mercy shall follow me all the days of my life and I will dwell in the house of the Lord forever."

Give us, O God, the confidence that comes when we put our assurance and trust in the things that are real; grant that we may never be afraid of our sincere desires; give us the courage also to test them by the facts of existence; and then give us that strength of mind and body and spirit to make the leap out into the uncharted areas where the heart has reasons that the mind knows not of. Amen.

What Christianity Has to Say to Those Who Have Lost Someone They Love

❧

THERE ARE very few people in this congregation who have not lost someone they love. There may be some, still young, whose circle of family and friends has not yet been disturbed by death but, sooner or later, it will. When it happens, you will be shaken by it, and shocked, no matter how well prepared you think you are for the event, and no matter how inevitable it may be. Your whole world will seem to crumble. If it is a parent you lose, you will seem strangely alone in the world, out in front for the first time, even though you may not have been dependent upon that parent for years. If it is a friend, you will seem to be deprived of something that was an intimate part of your life from day to day. If it is a wife or a husband, how can I say it? But those of you who have been through it know it, you will feel that a very part of your life has been torn away from you, and you will go through periods of physical anguish and pain. The road ahead at that time will look so bare that you will hardly be able to bear the thought of travelling it alone.

And at those times, the same questions come up over and over again. You ask yourself, What has happened to them? Where are they? In what state are they? Do they exist at all? Have they simply disappeared? And then you ask yourself, What is going to happen to me now? How am I going to go on with the life I now live under these conditions of loneliness? And what is going to happen to me later when I come to the same inevitable event? Am I going to see the people that I have loved and lost?

What has Christianity to say to people in whose minds these questions are rumbling around during the long night watches? Before I attempt to say what Christianity has to say to them, I should like to say on my own behalf that Christianity at its best has no easy, quick, glib answers, and I am thankful for that. The subject is too thoroughly enshrouded in mystery to be glib about it or facile. And Christianity has no answers that overlook the agony out of which these question spring, or that seem to belittle the faith of the person who dares to ask such questions. Rather than giving quick answers to questions like these, Christianity makes two broad, bold affirmations, and I should like now to make those affirmations, and to expound them, and explore them as far as we can within the limitations of a sermon.

I

The first is that the person that dies is not lost. People in this world are pretty much divided into two big camps. The people in one camp say that this life is all there is, there isn't any more. Life is what there is by way of existence between the date of birth and the date of death. There are a great many people in that camp; that is where the Communists who were executed last week in Teheran stood. When one of them was offered the Koran and invited to pray that he might enter into Paradise, he said, "Paradise was the place we were going to make in this country. We know no other paradise." And there are a great many people in the world who stand in that camp; this life is all there is, there isn't any more. They are not necessarily cynical about it; they often enjoy life and contribute greatly to it, but that is where they stand.

Those in the other camp are those that say there is something more, that there is a life beyond this life, and that death is a transition from one life to the other. They don't like to be too explicit about it, they can't say too much by way of proof, they resort to images and pictures, and they think of the ranges of mountains that you see in our great Western country, where range after range stretch away until they reach far beyond anything that your eye can see, and yet you know that beyond the furthest one there lies still a further range. And the people in this camp feel that beyond this life, with all its interests, enthusiasms, possibilities, and disappointments, there lie further ranges of life beyond, and beyond, until you get to the furthest one; there you rest for a moment and then you go on to further ones still.

Christianity stands foursquare in this camp, along with most of the great religions of the world and many of the great philosophers, from Plato to William James. When we begin to think about it and what it involves, and when we try to imagine all the people who ever lived in all the generations that ever existed on the earth, try to imagine them living together in some other life beyond this, we stagger under that, and we say it is hardly possible. We cannot, by our very nature, imagine any other life but this one, this life circumscribed by time and space, in which we move from one day to another until we finally come to the end of the sequence. We cannot imagine any other kind of life and therefore, we are inclined to say, quietly to ourselves, There can't be any other life. As a matter of fact, we couldn't have imagined this one before we actually saw it and lived it, so that the fact that it is hard to imagine another one need not discourage us. If only what we can imagine is true, we live in a miserable world indeed.

When we look at it from the lower levels, it seems natural that we, like the falling leaves in the autumn, should be worked back into the earth to enrich it. It seems perfectly natural to us when we look at this whole matter from the physiological level, from beneath so to speak, that we, like the crops and the falling leaves, should be plowed back into the earth and lose our identity. Enough it is that we should make the little plot where we have lived richer by the fact of our existing. Why should we be any different from the rest of the created order? The answer is, of course, that we *are* different! We are *not* like a crop of wheat; we are *not* like falling leaves. We are, for better or worse, creators and lovers of beauty and truth and goodness, and we have a sense of something over and above our own transiency which leaps up and over and beyond these temporal things, thirsting after that which is eternal and unchangeable. The leaves fall but do not know that they fall. We fall, and we know it. There lies the difference.

When we look at it from the higher level, it seems hardly possible that it should not be so. In other words, when we change our point of view from our own limitations and try to look at this whole thing from

God's infinite possibilities, it seems hardly possible that it should be any other way. For example, when you think of a man like Albert Schweitzer, who has achieved the heights of spiritual and moral life and who has brought to flower the gifts that all of you have potentially, can you conceive that a God like our God could think of nothing better to do with Albert Schweitzer when he dies than to plow him back into the earth? That to my mind would be the inconceivable; a God who has the creative imagination and power to make this spectacular universe, who has the genius to create a Schweitzer, and who can think of nothing better than that to do with one of His creatures who has reached the heights of achievement. The possibility of another world, it seems to me, is no more fantastic than the fact of this world. So the first thing that Christianity has to say to you or to any person who has lost someone he loves is that the person you love is not lost; he is with God.

II

What is more, Christianity goes on to say this: he continues as a real person and he lives a real life. That is the second affirmation that it makes. There are two major insights into the mystery of the life beyond. One comes from the Greeks, and the other from the Hebrews. Let's look at them just for a minute. The Greeks watched a man release a homing pigeon from his cage and watched that pigeon spiral tentatively upwards until apparently he came to a height from which he could see some recognizable horizon, and then he made his way homeward with an incredible precision and an unerring sense of direction. Now that, said the Greeks, is what death is like. The spirit of man is captured in the cage of the body, in a strange and unfamiliar, uncongenial world and, when death comes, the cage is opened and the spirit is released, and it goes instinctively homeward to his Maker. In other words, the stress that the Greeks put upon this whole matter and the insight that they are famous for originating is that death is the release of the spirit from the body.

The Hebrews, a very different sort of people, not abstract in their thinking at all, practical, concrete, dramatic, historical, rather than philosophical, watched a man put a seed in the ground. They knew that within a few days or a week, the seed would completely disappear and die; and they knew also that as they watched the place where he put it, the life that was in the seed would reappear in a new form appropriate to the new life above ground. That, they said, is what death is like; it is not so much the release of the spirit from the body as it is the resurrection of the body for a completely new life.

Both of these aspects are insights into the truth, and I personally think it is unwise to try to claim that either one is the only and exclusive way to the truth. A truth as great as this must inevitably have many avenues of approach and while I feel at home in the Hebrew position because it has come to me by way of Christianity, nevertheless, I am perfectly glad and free to say that both of these insights together make one of the great comprehensions of this mystery.

But the Hebrew insight has this to commend it. In the first place, it is completely realistic about this world and it gives due credit to this world. One of the things that has impressed me recently, and I would like to know what some of the scholars would say about it, is this: it seems to me strange that the Greeks who seemed to enjoy the world more than the Hebrews did, were more suspicious of it than the Hebrews, and were afraid to give it much credit, and talked about death in terms of getting out of it. The Hebrews were always willing to acknowledge the fact that while we are not completely fulfilled in the life we live now, while we thirst for the things that we never get in this life, while in one sense we are pilgrims and sojourners here, nevertheless, this world is our home; God made it for us and in many ways we are extremely well adapted to it; we love it, we enjoy it, and it is not something that we think of as a cage to get out of. The Hebrews were also extremely realistic in that they admitted that finally the world as we understand it and enjoy it comes to an end for us when we die. They did not see any inherent capacity in man that would make him immortal. When he died, he died.

Also, the Hebrew insight has this to commend it. It promises a completely real life in the next world; that is, a life of personal identity that is recognizable. That is why, I suppose, they put so much emphasis upon the resurrection of the body, because if it were not for our bodies, we wouldn't recognize one another; there would be no way to distinguish our identity, and the Jews, and the Christians following them, wanted to say, If there is any life beyond this, and we realize that it is a gamble, we know that it isn't proven, but if there is any, if it is worth looking forward to at all, it is a life of personal identity in which a personality is known for the person he is and for what he is. Otherwise, it is nothing but a shadowy existence that no one would look forward to at all.

We certainly do not expect the next world to be an exact reproduction of this one, heaven forbid, but we do expect to get some hints about it here. That is, if the principles that are locally valid, and this is one of the platforms on which the scientists stand, if the principles that are locally valid here are also universally valid, then we can expect to get some clues about the next world from life here. We move always from the known to the unknown, not with complete certainty, but with a good deal of encouragement that if we take seriously the known facts, they will give us little inklings, here and there, into the unknown. If in this life personal relationships count for so much, there is every reason to suppose that they will in the next.

I think that most everyone of you would agree that if it were not for the relationships you have with people, this life wouldn't be worth the effort, and the older we grow the more we appreciate that. As we look back over the years the stars that make them bright are simply the wonderful people we have known and loved, and if that is so much an integral part of the life we have known here that we cannot even imagine eliminating it, we have some right to expect that under some circumstances the same kind of thing will exist in the next world.

The implication at least is that you will know the people that you love. That is one of the questions that people have asked me over and over again, Will I know him? I have no certainty about these things other than the faith that has come to me, and the inferences and the revelations that have been granted to the fellowship of Christians through the years but, on the basis of all those things, I am perfectly sure that in some way, not understood by us at present, you will know him.

In the story of the walk to Emmaus, in which the disciples overtake their risen Master and do not recognize him because, though he is in some physical form, apparently it is not the body they were accustomed to and therefore they think he is a stranger, there is a real clue to this mystery. During the course of their walk with him, and their talking with him and listening to him, and finally having supper with him, "their eyes were opened, and they knew him." They knew him because they loved him, and if that can happen in this world, I for one don't quite see how life in another world could be worth living if it didn't happen there.

The person you love, therefore, doesn't simply exist in God's presence, but he lives a real, recognizable life. It was in this spirit, and in the light of this faith that the young Benjamin Franklin, who at that time was a printer in Philadelphia, wrote an epitaph that was later put up on his grave, and this is what he wrote:

> The Body of
> B Franklin Printer,
> (Like the Cover of an old Book
> Its Contents torn out
> And stript of its Lettering & Gilding)
> Lies here, Food for Worms.
> But the Work shall not be lost;
> For it will, (as he believ'd) appear once more,
> In a new and more elegant Edition
> Revised and corrected,
> By the Author.

Some people want to know more than what I have tried to tell them in answer to their questions; they want to know when all this is going to happen, how it is going to happen, what about all the other people we are going to meet if we meet people we know in the other world, will it go on forever, what about my sins? On the whole, when Christians have tried to answer this kind of curiosity, they have usually floundered. Saint Paul, you know, when he tried to describe in detail the nature of the General Resurrection, did not come out very well. You feel the frail vessel of this thought begin to sink before it is barely launched. Christ, on the other hand, through his evangelist and interpreter, Saint John, came out so much better when he said, "In my father's house are many mansions; if it were not so, I would have told you. I go to prepare a place for you; that where I am, there ye may be also." No details in that, no time schedule; simply, "where I am, there ye may be also."

Jesus himself never talked much about life after death, never attempted to give any map or locale in which it was lived. What he did was to immerse people in the love of God, here and now, and try to help them take up the task when death came their way, and leave the future to him. That seems to me to be the wise and sound way for us to travel; we have the two great affirmations, the two things that mean most. As Phillips Brooks put it in one of his great sermons, *Standing Before God*, "All we need to know is that the dead are, and that they are with God. All beside these two things we can most willingly leave undiscovered."

In an eastern university there is a tomb of a man and woman who were both professors of astronomy in that university, and the inscription on their tomb is this: *We have loved the stars too dearly to be fearful of the night.* That is wonderful as it is, but if you change just one word it could be the inscription for many a Christian life: We have loved God too dearly to be fearful of the night.

O God, who art the Lord of Death as well as Life, help us to face these mysteries unafraid, in the assurance and confidence that comes to us from our Lord Jesus Christ, knowing that wherever he is, we will be also. Amen.

The Will of God

❧

A LITTLE OVER a month ago, a young man twenty-four years old came from the Midwest to a Boston hospital for a serious operation on his heart. He was born a "blue baby"; there was a deformity in the circulatory system of the blood so that there was not sufficient oxygen to give the baby the strength he needed. At that time surgery had not yet developed the operation by which babies born with that deformity are cured. This little boy, however, survived the handicap; he went through high school, and he got himself a job. He lived on a bare margin of energy; he had no surplus strength, and when he discovered that an operation had been developed for the remedy of this condition, he was determined that he should have it. He got himself here and in one of our hospitals where one of the great surgeons performs that operation. They told him ahead of time that he was not a good risk; to begin with, he was a little too old. He said, "I want to live, but I'm not afraid to die. And if I do live, I want to live a full, normal life."

The operation was successful, and, while he was in a very weak condition and while the shock was very great, at the end of the first week the doctors said that they thought he would make the grade. But at the end of the second week he died. One person, when he heard the news, said, "That is the will of God, we must resign ourselves to it." Another person said "That is not the will of God." And still a third person said, "The will of God has nothing to do with it at all; it just happened; it worked out that way."

There are three entirely different judgments, or interpretations, of the selfsame event. They all revolve around some notion of the will of God. Religious people talk a lot about the will of God, and I have been wondering how much they mean by it, and what they understand by it. And what I propose to do tonight, quite simply, is to expand your thinking about the will of God and perhaps clarify it by taking each one of these three points of view and stating it as clearly as I can without making any judgment upon it until the end.

I

Take the last person first. He says, "The will of God hasn't anything to do with the situation at all; things just work out that way." He would go on to say that the death of the young man can be explained by a scientific understanding of the causes. We do not understand the causes because we do not know enough about anatomy and surgery, but if we did, we would understand that given the situation, and the circumstances, and the boy's condition, and the operation and the risks involved, one cause led directly to another and brought about the boy's death. And that's all there is to it. He might go on to say that it's just like a machine—some machines break down sooner than others. Why? Because in the making of the machine there has been some careless accident which has resulted in a flaw or weakness. Nobody planned it; you can't say that anybody deliberately willed that this machine was to go to pieces before the others. It just happened. It worked out that way and that's all there is to it.

This person might be quite willing to admit that in human life we don't get anywhere without will power. He would certainly admit the fact that there never was an educated man or woman without the will to be educated. Nor was there ever a good person without the will to be good. Or a successful man or woman without the will to be successful. Certainly, there never was a recovered alcholic without the will to recover. He would very likely be willing to admit there never was a building built, or a book written, or a poem conceived without the will to write and build and create.

Will, as we see it in human beings, is desire plus determination. We all have it. We all have within us desires for certain things, we want this or that. Added to that desire is, in varying degrees, the determination to fulfill that desire. And those two things together make what we call the will of a man. And this person whose point of view we are considering would surely be perfectly ready to admit that in human life will power is back of everything, and if people did not have wills they would not have houses or churches or governments or great plays or families or anything else.

But, he goes on to say that *beyond* human life, that is, in those forces and factors which control human life from without, there is nothing comparable to that will. Things happen and no one knows why, and no one cares. If you understood the process well enough, you might be able to trace the cause, but to try to find an element of intelligent willing, according to this point of view, is absolutely hopeless and doomed to failure. Therefore he says, "This death of a young man was not willed at all in the sense that we use the word *will*. It happened. We don't know why and we never shall know why."

II

Now look at the first person, who said, "The death of the boy was the will of God, and his family and the people who loved him must resign themselves to that will." This person disagrees violently with the man we have just been considering. He says that all life is an expression of will. A book is the expression of the man who wrote it, the publisher who published it, the salesman who sells it. It is a composition of human wills. And he would go further and say that in fact everything that happens, happens because not only within human life is there this thing called human will, but beyond it, and over it and above it is a Superior Will that he calls the will of God. And everything, according to him, happens because God wills it. The emphasis there is on the word *everything*. Everything happens because God directly wills it so.

In other words, according to this point of view, God's will is supreme. No dictator ever assumed more totalitarian authority than a person like this attributes to the will of God. If the heart of a rose is eaten by a worm, God willed it. And if a fresh young life is snuffed out by an accident, God willed it. He will go on to say that some things God wills we like, like getting well after we've been sick, or making a comeback after we've had reverses; we like that. Then, other things that

God wills we don't like, like dying when we're young, or being failures when we want to be successes, but nevertheless, God wills them all, and our place is to accept His will, and to bow before the inscrutability of it. He might, if pressed, be willing to admit that in human experience once again it is not like that, that we see no evidence of such a supreme will.

For instance, a father lights a fire in the fireplace. In one sense he is the master of the fire; he willed it in the first place, and if he willed to put it out, he could put it out. If his little child, unbeknown to him, should begin to play with the fire, and be seriously burned, or if obeying its own law, a spark from the fire flew out and caught the dress of his little girl and set it afire, nobody would think of saying that the father willed the burning of the child. The father willed the fire, to be sure, but the burning of the child was the result of other factors which entered into the picture, which are the result of independent creatures having wills of their own. The child had his will, and the fire had its way and will. And this person would be forced to admit that in human experience things work that way.

But, he would go on to say, in the larger realm this is not so. In the great realm of the cosmic universe there is no place for these secondary wills. God's will is supreme; nothing that man can do can thwart it or block it or withstand it, and therefore the death of this boy is the will of God, and we bow ourselves before that inscrutable will.

III

Now, last of all, look at the second man, the man who said, "No, this particular death is not the will of God. I will not believe that God willed the death of this young person." He will not say, you will note, that there is no such thing as the will of God; he would agree with the man we have just been talking about in that, and not the first man. He believes that over us all there is a Superior Will and that the life we live is the manifestation of that will, that purpose. But he thinks that God's will can be temporarily thwarted by the independent wills of His creatures. For instance, he might point to the fact that for centuries human slavery was accepted by most people as a normal convention of society.

211

Certainly, that was not the will of God, as we understand God, that one man should be enslaved to another. The situation prevailed because the independent, that is, the relatively independent wills of God's creatures for the time being thwarted the will of God. Or, he might point to the much greater evil of war; certainly you cannot say that war as we know it is the will of God. It may be the judgment of God, but you cannot say that God wills the bombing of innocent citizens of great cities. That comes about because independent creatures with relatively independent wills of their own, for the time being, block and thwart the will of God.

To his way of thinking, what God wants is the fulfillment of life in love. *What God wants is the fulfillment of life in love.* As he understands God from his own observations, from his own inner experience, from what he learns in Jesus, from the Christian fellowship, God is a God of life. He is the Creator God, and what He wants above all else is the fulfillment of each one of the things He makes. If He makes a flower, His will is that that flower completely unfold itself and reveal its ultimate beauty, and then fade away. If it is a human life, what God wants is that that life unfold and develop until all its potentialities stand revealed, and then that it disappear into other realms.

Apparently Jesus believed this. He said to the people of his time, "It is not the will of your Father that one of these little ones should perish." His will is that they should live, and if they perish, they perish because contrary wills enter into the picture and for the time being thwart His will. And so this person would say, "God did not will the death of that boy. God wanted him to live, just as He wants everybody else to live his life out until all his powers are revealed and all his potentialities reach their maximum—that is what He wanted." But because He has created the world with a series of independent, relatively free wills, that in this case did not happen. We don't know why. The boy wanted to have the operation when he was eighteen but his parents refused to give permission. Perhaps if they had, he would have lived. Perhaps there is something in the surgical technique that has not yet reached full development and will be perfected in the future. There are all sorts of reasons why in this case the will of God was not carried out.

So as this person looks at the picture he says to himself something like this, "We are not resigned to that young man's death; we are aroused by it! We want to make the operation more skillful, we want more doctors to investigate this particular kind of surgery so that in the future people suffering from this particular kind of deformity will not die but live, as God wants them to live." And this person would go on to say, in spite of what some people may assume from what he has already said, that God is not at the mercy of His creatures because they can temporarily thwart His will. *In the long run, His will prevails.* Look at the cross of Christ, a classic example. God did not want Jesus to die, he wanted him to live. God did not want men to crucify Jesus, He wanted them to follow him. But when jealousy and envy and betrayal and denial and all those human evils entered into the picture because of men's free independent wills, and made it apparent that the only thing that Jesus could do was to die, and when he responded to that situation in such a way as to make that death one of the open doors into the great mysteries of life, then God could take even that act which thwarted His will and use it for His own purpose.

How He takes such a thing as the death of this young man is beyond us, and certainly we do not presume to say. But we believe in all these instances where the will of God, which is the will of fulfillment of life in love, is thwarted by the independent wills of His creatures, we believe that in the long run, in ways not now understandable to us, His will prevails.

There are the three people. From a Christian point of view the person who said that the will of God hasn't anything to do with it is completely mistaken. The second one who says that the will of God is responsible because the will of God brings everything to pass is on the right track, but misguided. And the third one who says that the will of God is mighty and holy and over and above everything but in this particular case, the death of the young man is not directly traceable to that will, is in our Christian judgment, right.

The sum and substance of it for you is that you think about these things. I am not here to tell you what to think; I am here to encourage you to think. Let me commend to you the proposition that there is a higher will with which your will is often in conflict and never will your life be what you want it to be and what it can be until you bring your-self to say, "Not my will, but thine, be done."

O God, as we think about these great matters, make up for the insufficiency and inadequacy of our thinking. Help us to face the facts of existence. Show us the shallowness of interpretations which avoid the reality of thy will. And once we see that there is a will greater than ours, then give us the grace and the grit to do it. Amen.

When Titus Comes

"God gave us comfort, as soon as Titus came." II Corinthians 7:7 (Knox)

I HAVE PREACHED this sermon many times before but not in this particular form. This time it grows out of a personal experience of my own. By and large, I think it is wise for preachers to steer clear of their personal experiences, especially in sermons. But sometimes an experience that comes to one man is so common to others that others may profit by it. This particular experience of mine is one of those and we can use it as a springboard for this sermon.

I left after the morning service last Sunday for a short holiday. I felt that my reserves were lower than they ought to be and that I needed refreshment. When I got to New York, I began to look for that refreshment. I looked for it in solitude and rest and did not find it in any great abundance. I looked for it in people who were friends but who had no association with the things that concern me all the rest of the year and, to my surprise, I did not find it there. Then I went to lunch with one of the members of the staff of a man who was once Rector of this church and I had a chance to see him for a while and talk about the things that concern us both and I began to feel the refreshment coming. And then, in the evening I had dinner and a long talk with one of the great people I know, a person who is greatly dedicated to life, a person infinitely superior to me, with a broad experience of life and a deep understanding of its problems and possibilities. As we spent the evening together, sharing the interests we have in common and also some of our problems that we have in common, I felt the energies beginning to revive. And when I walked home that night, that Wednesday night in January that was like a night in June, I was refreshed. I thought of the line I have noticed often in Knox's translation of Paul's Second Epistle to the Corinthians: "God gave us comfort, as soon as Titus came." So much for my own experience. Let it take us into the heart of one of life's greatest mysteries.

I

There are times in every man's life when he needs help and no one ever described those times better than Paul did. In this very letter, just before the line that I have already read, he writes: "All was conflict without, all was anxiety within." He is drawing the picture of a person who is in a state of confusion inside and out. He is like a man standing in the middle of Times Square. As he watches the traffic which thickens round him he has the sense that he cannot cope with it, and the more he feels that he cannot cope with it, the more he is frightened by it and the more he is frightened by it the less able is he to cope with it. All is conflict without, all is anxiety within. He needs the help of someone who can get him safely across the Square. Or, to put it another way, he is like a man living in an area of low pressure. The clouds are too close, the ceiling is hung too low. Life is more than he can handle, his burdens are heavier than he can swing gracefully. Life is too much for him and he needs help. His own powers are no longer adequate to his own problems.

Paul could describe those times in a man's life because he had been through them so often. Sometimes we are likely to forget when we read the great passages in the Pauline epistles that Paul was one of the most turbulent characters in Christian history. He was in conflict without constantly, with the elements, with the weather, with the sea, with the authorities; always getting in trouble, with the churches that he started and the troublesome people that he found in the churches always making complaints against him. Then, he had conflicts within. He suffered from some kind of nervous disorder which humiliated him and which plagued him to the end of his days. So, to find Paul himself in such a predicament takes some of the fear out of it and gives us confidence. There are times in every man's life, in your life and my life, and in Paul's life, when we are in trouble and we need help.

II

We can go on to say that when a man needs help there is always help to be had. No one knew that any better than Paul did. In all the perils of his travelling he had the help he needed. He was beaten, he was stoned, he was shipwrecked, he was robbed, he was nearly starved, and in all those experiences he had the sustaining help of God that he needed so that he could survive them—not only survive them but transcend them gloriously and magnificently and be a sign and a symbol for us of the transcendent power of the human spirit. When he asked God to relieve him, as he did on more than one occasion, of the disorder within that plagued him so incessantly, the answer that God gave to his prayer was, "My grace is sufficient for thee." Paul found that grace was sufficient, so that in this very letter in the same passage he could write that "there is One who never fails to comfort those who are brought low." *There is One who never fails to comfort those who are brought low.* Write that down in your memory. If it is true that there are times when a man needs help, it is also true that there is always help to be had.

As a matter of fact, and Paul knew this better than most of us, the very time when you need help most is the time when you are most likely to get it. You know very well that a doctor cannot really help a person until the person is so sick that he wants help. I know that a clergyman cannot help a person in any kind of situation until that person gets to the point where he says, I cannot handle this by myself. Can you help me? God cannot help you until you want it, and you will not always want it until you need it desperately, until the time comes when all your defenses are down and your pride is gone, your false hopes and ambitions are left behind. Then, when you need help the most and want it most desperately, then help comes. And it always comes. Put that down too, in your memory: when you need help the most, help is nearest to you.

But remember this, and this is one of the things that I learned in my experience, help always comes from above, never from below. Paul did not talk about help in general; he said, There is One who never fails to help and that One is God. Now, there is always the temptation that comes to most of us, when we are in a tight place in life and feel that life is more than we can manage, to look for help down below—take a drink, compromise with your highest standards, have a fling, take time off from the strenuous strain of life as you live it normally. Unfortunately, that temptation is aggravated by the fact that relief does come that way, but not help. Temporary relief is relatively easy to find, and it often comes the easy way. But real help never comes from beneath; help always comes from above. Remember this, among other things, you can never get up by going down; you can never find help in a family situation by digging down into the lower levels of your life and burrowing in the secret places of your lower self. If you want help, there is help to be had but it will come from the upper regions of your life, the better part of you, from the best people that you have known, not from the playboys, the irresponsibles, the indulgers; the most dependable things that you have stood for, not for the shaky things that sometimes you hoped would be substantial. Yes, when a man really needs help, there is always help to be had for when he needs it, he is in a position to receive it if he is willing to take it from above and not from beneath.

III

Come one step further now in this story of humanity when it is in need of help, looking for help from above, and see that the help of God often comes in the shape of a person. "God gave us comfort, *as soon as Titus came.*" Anyone who has any imagination can picture that scene, especially if you know anything about Titus and the relationship that Paul had with him. Titus was a Gentile convert, probably Paul himself had converted him, and when you remember that the one thing Paul wanted to do above all others was to win people to Christ, you can easily see how this young Gentile whom Paul had won to the Christian way of life had more than a passing interest for him. But he was not only a convert, he proceeded to be a partner of Paul. He, together with Timothy, travelled around the country with Paul and helped him in the building of his churches. He must have been one of those people with whom Paul had some unique, sympathetic understanding, and I imagine that Paul was not an easy person to work for and not easily understood. But Titus apparently was one of those younger men that sometimes come into an older man's life who did understand him, who could see all the richness of Paul's character, who could see the resplendent fruit of the internal conflict that had been resolved in Christ. Titus appreciated Paul and he did everything in the world that he could for Paul, and on the other side, we read this in another passage from the pen of Paul, and you can almost feel the unexpressed affection of the older for the younger man: "I went to Troas, but still I had no peace of mind, because I had not yet seen my brother Titus."

In other words, Titus meant a great deal to Paul, so that when Titus came and met Paul after a long absence, the very fact that he was there was enough to begin to revive Paul's life and to resolve the conflict without and quiet the anxiety within. Just to talk with him, just to see him, just to know that he was there was enough, but there was more than that, for Titus brought with him good news. Paul had worked very hard with the Corinthian church and had hoped that they would be welded together into one of the great Christian churches in that area. But they had been difficult people and he had been going through a period of misunderstanding with them. Being a pastor myself and knowing how much I count on the affection of the people, their support, their loyalty, their understanding, I can imagine what it meant to Paul when he heard by letters and by reports that the members of the church in Corinth were turning away from him and following other leaders. They had turned around and followed somebody else and it cut him to the quick, and with his temper and with all the impulsiveness that Paul had, he wrote them a stern letter which he probably regretted afterward. And it was after that letter was sent that he sat there waiting for Titus—"conflict without, anxiety within," a man in need of help—and when Titus came, he had the news that all was well with the Corinthians. They had forgiven Paul the letter, they loved him, they sent him their best wishes, and they were there ready to do anything he wanted done. The reassurance of the news that Titus brought went further to revive the spirit that had been flagging for so long, for the human spirit cannot permanently thrive without a modest amount of re-assurance that he is wanted and that he is useful.

There was something even more than that; it was not only the personal presence of Titus, not only the news that he brought, but it was something that came from God, that is the way Paul described it, some help that was more than could be comprehended by any one person, or conveyed by that person alone, something that was more than the good news that he brought, some help that began to coagulate his life once more and make the wheels go smoothly. It was a help that was like the grace of God. "God gave us comfort, as soon as Titus came."

So, how wonderful it is that people, people like you and me, can be channels of God's power. When God wanted to rescue Francis Thompson, one of the great religious poets of this century, from the gutters of London and from the drug habit, He did it not by an angel or by some abstract idea, He did it by Wilfred Meynell who went right down into the gutters and picked him up, stood over him, and watched him for months until he was made well. When God wants to help you, He may very likely do it not through an idea, perhaps not even through a prayer; He may do it through some person who comes into your life, some person that you know and respect and honor, some person who is able to bring down the help from above. As that person comes into your life, the power of God that helps you will stream through him and you will say, This help does not come from him, but through him.

When God wanted to save the world, it is not surprising that he chose a man, and we might paraphrase this line from St. Paul's Epistle so that it reads, God gave us comfort, as soon as Jesus came. In other words, the God we know is a specific God; He does not work in abstractions, He does not work in terms that our minds only can comprehend, He gets hold of things and people and uses them as channels, as ways of communication to reach people and make them well. That is the kind of a God we know, the God who is willing to help us always when we want help and who helps us in some concrete human form. Thank God for the Tituses you have known!

That, then, is the end of the story, the fruit of my own experience, and I hope that it may be a help to you. When the time comes when you feel that your water levels are lower than they ought to be and that the ceiling of life is unusually low, you will remember Paul, the spiritual giant in exactly the same position, waiting for Titus, all conflict without, all anxiety within. Then you may remember Titus arriving and in his person communicating to Paul the help that comes only from above, never from below. After that, having been helped yourself, you will want to be another Titus as you go about your life and work, realizing that you, too, may be a human channel through which the great and mighty God who is the source of all power and might can reach into some life and lift the low ceilings and raise up the low spirits and revive the hearts that have been flagging. "God gave us comfort, as soon as Titus came!"

We thank thee, O God, for all the people in our lives through whom thy power and love and strength have come to us; open our eyes to the fact that when we need help there is always help available; take away our pride and our suspicions and our fears until we stand before thee in all our naked reality, waiting only upon thee, knowing that in some human shape our help will finally come to us, through Jesus Christ our Lord. Amen.

The Curiosity of Man and
the Sociability of God

❦

ONE OF THE THINGS that we know about truth is that you can't
hide it, nor will it be hidden—not permanently. If you want any proof
of that, ask a child to keep something a secret. He will do the best he can,
but sooner or later he will blurt it out. Or, bury a treasure in some secret place where you think that no one can possibly find it. Sooner or
later someone is almost sure to find it. Guard the truth of atomic energy
with all the devices that the intelligence of the secret service agents can
think of. Sooner or later, every nation on the face of the earth will
know it.

One reason for this is that man is naturally *curious*. I am using that
word now not in what we have come to call its "pejorative" sense; that
is, not to denote that unpleasant impulse in a man to pry into things that
are none of his business. I am using it in the sense of man's natural in-
quisitiveness, his wanting to know, his unwillingness to settle down in
ignorance. He is curious, and anything that looks like a secret excites his
curiosity instantly. If you want to arouse a person's curiosity about your
whereabouts, one of the most certain ways of doing it is to tell him that
you are not giving your address to anyone. He will be all the more curious as to where you are.

This is the first reason why the truth cannot long be hid: man is
naturally, incurably curious.

The other reason is that truth is naturally "sociable." You don't ordinarily use that word to describe truth. By it I mean to say that the truth
longs to be known, does not enjoy solitude, being isolated, untouchable,

remote from human understanding. It is not aggressive in declaring itself, at least, not often; neither is it coy, hiding itself in a corner.

The truth about the sun and the stars didn't impose itself upon the human race in the early days of its childhood. Men were left to look at the sun and the stars and see them as they appeared to be—lights, windows in heaven. But when man grew up and began to ask questions, the truth about the sun and the stars did not withhold itself. It went out to meet man's inquiring, curious mind. The stars did not keep their distance from the earth a secret, nor did the sun withhold the fact that it stood still while the earth turned around it.

This may seem far removed from the Christian religion, and even farther from the story of the Wise Men to which we turn back every year in the dead of winter, in the season called Epiphany. Actually, this is precisely what the story is saying to me this year, and I shall pass it on to you in the hope that it will speak to you likewise.

The Wise Men were astrologers, and there is this paradoxical fact about them: they concentrated on the stars because they were curious about the world. They weren't interested in the stars in the same way that the modern astronomer is, they were not trying to find out more about the stars themselves; they were trying to find out something about the world they lived in, what would happen to it, and when. It wasn't having a very good time of it, but they had heard from several sources that someone would come who would set it to rights. When would he come? Where would he come? How would he come? They had that insatiable thirst for the truth that made them restless until they found the answers to these questions.

Beyond their immediate questions, there must have been others like these: What makes the world go around? Not everyone wanted to know, not everyone always does, but they wanted to know, and some always do. And what is life all about? If it means anything, what does it mean? Not everybody wanted to know that, but they wanted to know it, and there are some who always want to know it. And this craving for truth, what we have called their incurable curiosity, kept them searching, looking, sweeping the skies every night for some sign of the birth of the man they were looking for. In the stars there was a celestial language that they knew, understood, and read diligently.

There is something of that searching instinct in every human being. That is one of those generalities that I make with fear and trembling, but nevertheless, I am willing to make it. At least potentially, there is something of that searching instinct in every human being. Not everyone, of course, is searching for the same thing. There are some who are seriously searching for the truth about the nature of the physical universe, like the men who are studying the rocks that have been brought back from the moon. I am looking for other things, as you may be, but I admire the men and women who are constantly exploring the physical universe, how it came to be what it is.

Some are searching for the truth about themselves. Why do they do the things that they do? What makes them "tick," as the saying used to go? Why are they fearful when there is no reason to be afraid? Why does their temper flare up when they are not able to control it? And others are searching for the truth about the stock market, whether it is going up or down, and when it may conceivably hit the bottom. Still others are searching for the solution to practical problems, problems of transportation, population, transformation. They are studying the changes that are taking place in society, changes sometimes for the better and sometimes for the worse.

Not everyone is searching with the same intensity, not by any means. Some are so dedicated to their search that they are not aware of anything else, and some search occasionally, when it is convenient, and when they can spare the time from their other activities. And, of course, some are too tired to search at all; they have come to a standstill; they take life as it comes, and ask no questions.

Right now the company of the curious is unusually large. The young have swelled it. They always are perhaps more curious than people are when they get older, particularly the young now. And also the ranks of this particular company have been filled out by some of the older generation who have caught the enthusiasm of their offspring.

But especially the young are looking for answers. They realize that there is a vacuum at the very center of our society. They are looking for something to fill it. They are asking questions like these (at least, I think they are as I listen to them and read about them): What are the really important things in life? Is the hierarchy of values that we have inherited the best one, or is it upside down? How can we get out of the trap of war and poverty? It doesn't seem possible that we are destined as human beings to go on generation after generation caught in this web of slaughter and hunger. What do we do about the past? Do we reject it as one vast mistake, or do we listen to it, learn from it? We certainly do not idolize it, and yet may we not lean on it in order to stand more upright in the future?

And why do we do anything at all? What's the point of it all? What is the meaning of this great round of existence that goes on generation after generation? Not only what is the meaning, but what is the means? Granted that we glimpse the meaning, what is the means by which we bring it into reality?

So, while we watch the Wise Men set out to cross the desert, following a star, we see once again how curious men can be, and also how serious they can be about their curiosity. That is one side of a story that has two sides.

What they were looking for, they found. It wasn't easy. It never is. Any search that amounts to anything is likely to be a long and arduous one. It wasn't easy to find the North Pole, and it wasn't easy to get to the moon, and it isn't easy to find the best way to handle the frictions that exist in a family. It is never easy. It was a long journey, beset, as most other journeys are, by disappointments and inconveniences, and near the end of it, Herod the King tried to use them for his own nefarious purposes. That was the most intolerable thing of all about the journey.

But they found the newborn King of the Jews. He was not exactly what they expected to find. They expected a baby, because they were looking for someone just born. "Where is he that is born King of the Jews?" they asked; so the fact that he was a baby didn't surprise them. It was the surroundings in which they found him that were surprising; to say the least, a trifle plain for royalty!

Isn't it true that in human affairs, that is, in the drama of life as we know it, greatness is seldom obvious, at least at the beginning? When you run down a list of the people who were great—whether it be Mozart, or Shakespeare, or Keats—whoever it is, their greatness was not plain to be seen, not at the beginning. You go to the place where they were born—Keats over a livery stable, Mozart in a small second-floor apartment in Salzburg, and you say, Well, this isn't exactly the place that I was expecting to find, or that I would have chosen for the birth of a genius. Greatness is seldom obvious; it is more likely to be obscure in the beginning.

On a larger scale, it happens that truth is never exactly what you expect to find. (I say "never," but that is a word that you should never use!). Perhaps to be accurate we should say that truth is not often what you expect to find. We expect, for instance—at least a great many of us do—happiness to open the doors of life. When we get into the midstream of life, we discover that it isn't happiness that opens the door; it is suffering that leads the way to greater understanding and fulfillment. We expect freedom to answer all our problems. When we are young, we think that when we once get free of the family, free of all the ties that hold us so tightly, then we will be ourselves. But when we get there, we find that it is not being free, it is being bound that fulfills us, bound to something or someone great enough to deserve our service, and in that very service find our real freedom.

In the age in which we are now living, and there have been other times similar to ours, we expect the body to be the source of our satisfaction. In the Christian tradition the body has been, by and large, denigrated (though not always). Now the body is being liberated, and we expect the body to be the source of our satisfaction, our deepest satisfaction. But when we give the body its full due and its longest leash, we realize that it isn't the body—it's the life in the body, it's the spirit, the mind, whatever you want to call it, the imagination, the person in the body, that is the ultimate satisfaction.

We are tempted to expect the powerful to save us, the mighty to raise us up. It's the weak who save the strong. Think about that. It's the weak who in the long run save the strong.

There is always something surprising about the truth when we find it, but the most surprising thing of all is that the truth wants to be known, that it is there to be found; that it is reaching out to those who seek it. Granted that the Wise Men made a long and arduous journey; yet when they got there, the baby was there. It wasn't a wild goose chase. It wasn't exactly what they expected to find, but there was the baby, to be worshipped. The journey had been long and arduous, but there he was to be seen and known.

In recent years we have heard a great deal about the God who hides Himself. I wish I knew how many sermons had been preached in the last twenty years on the text, "Verily, thou art a God who hidest thyself" (Isaiah 45:15). And you can see why. God indeed is wrapped in mystery. So is every human being. You are sitting beside another person; you will never know everything there is to know about him. There will always be something about him that is beyond the reach of your understanding, even though that person be your husband or your wife. But you don't have to know everything there is to know about a person in order to enjoy the pleasure of his company, to enter into communication with him, and to share his life.

Likewise, you don't have to know everything there is to know about God before you enter into His presence, realize His existence, feel His undergirding strength, and share His life. God is not a show-off, but he shows Himself. He is always showing Himself. You say, I can't see Him, I don't see Him; I see no sign of Him in the ward of a mental hospital. I say, if you don't see Him, you may be looking in the wrong place, or you may be in the wrong position to see Him. On your knees is the best position. That is where the Wise Men were when they finally came to the baby. They had to get on their knees, not only because they wanted to worship Him, but because He was so small; they had to get close to the ground to see Him.

Early in my ministry I often told a story about a group of Americans who were approaching the coast of Japan for the first time. Suddenly, one of them caught the sight of the snow-capped mountain Fujiyama and exclaimed about its beauty. Others rushed to the deck to see the sight, and as they stood there awestruck, one women said, "I don't see it." The person next to her said, "Madam, look up higher." She was looking at the eye level of the horizon; when she looked up higher, she too saw it. As I told the story, the implication was that if you don't see God, look up higher. Look above the sticks and stones; look at the stars.

Without rejecting that, I am now turning in another direction. I turn to the poet Tom Boggs who published an anthology of lyrics in 1938. As an introduction to each section, he wrote a few lines of his own. This was in 1938, mind you, and it says something to me now that it didn't say then.

> Not with those who sing but those
> who pass without a word:
> not with the scarlet prelate
> but with the huddled herd!
> God, I feel, will likelier be
> found in hell's dim company;
> passing, with assuaging hand,
> the cup to every lip there damned.

In other words, I should be more likely to say to people today, If you can't see God, you may be looking too high. Perhaps you ought to look down, closer to the earth, where people are living, and suffering, and sometimes behaving magnificently.

As the Wise Men turn to leave they say to us, You have the capacity to be curious, exercise it fully. God has shown Himself, is showing Himself. Look for Him. See Him. Enjoy Him. The curiosity of man and the sociability of God: two inseparable sides of one truth.

We thank thee, O God, for the remembrance of things past, for the stories in which events that happened long ago are brought back to our memory. They remind us of the curiosity in our own nature and the approachability of thyself. Help us to look for thee in the right places and to recognize thee when we see thee, high or low; near, far, beside us, within us. Amen.

The Rebirth of a Man

༽

O N T H E T W E N T Y - F I F T H of January, we celebrated a remarkable event—the rebirth of a man. It happened almost two thousand years ago and the man to whom it happened was a man named Paul. It is interesting to notice, just in passing, that on December 25 we celebrate the birth of a baby, and on January 25 we celebrate the rebirth of a man. It is at that latter event that I would like you to look today, and upon which I hope you will concentrate your attention, not only because of the significance of the event itself but also because of the implications of it for us.

Let me tell once again, quite briefly, the story that is so familiar to most of you. Paul was a young Jew, probably in his early thirties. He was born in a fairly large cosmopolitan city of the Roman Empire, Tarsus, up on the shore of Asia Minor just before it curves around to come down the Mediterranean to the Levant. It was a commercial center of considerable size and it was the seat of a great university. His family was not poor; neither was it rich, but it enjoyed the privileges of Roman citizenship. His father and mother were conservative, however, as conservative as the city was cosmopolitan, for they were Orthodox Jews, which meant, of course, that Paul as a boy never mingled freely with the other boys of the city who were from a Greek and Roman background.

He was highly intelligent, his mind was quick and keen, and he was scrupulously conscientious. At a time when other young men are likely to be careless about some things, Paul was meticulously careful. He was religious by nature and by temperament, the way some people are. He had a feeling for the things of religion, we might say. He was torn, however, between the perfect and the possible. He longed to reach perfection and yet was well aware that the possibilities of his human nature kept him far from perfection, and this was something that so disturbed him that he had no inner peace whatsoever, and no real religious satisfaction.

He went to Jerusalem, the way many of our young men would go off to college, I suppose, to do graduate work, and there he studied his religion further under the instruction of Gamaliel. While he was in Jerusalem he ran into something completely unexpected. He found there a little group of people who were just as religious as he was, there was no question about that, and just as good as he was, only in a different way. But these people were radiantly happy. They glowed with an inner life and light; they were free, they were natural, they were spontaneous. There was no strain or tension about anything that they did. They had found the peace of God that passes all understanding. These people were the followers of another young Jew, about Paul's age, named Jesus.

Paul turned instantly and instinctively against them. Why? When a person who thinks it is a sin to have a good time sees other people having a good time, he either joins them, with a guilty conscience, or persecutes them. He almost never ignores them. And when Paul saw these people finding what he longed for and yet could never find, having what he would like to have and yet never had, he could not possibly join them—that would only accentuate the guilt he already had. He certainly could not ignore them. He persecuted them. He made life just as difficult for them as he possibly could.

One day on the way from Jerusalem to Damascus something happened to Paul. Exactly what happened we shall never know. How we wish we might! There are three accounts of what happened written by St. Luke, the author of Acts. He describes it always in the same way but with variation in detail. It was a blinding light that struck Paul down flat on the road, and a voice that he identified as the voice of Jesus. All that the voice said to him was to go into the city and it would be told him what he must do. The friends who were with him knew that something had happened, but they weren't quite sure what it was.

When Paul himself described what happened all he said was that there came a time when he "saw" Christ, saw him obviously with the inner eye of his understanding, saw the significance, saw the meaning of what happened to Christ and in Christ. It was like the light of the glory of God in the face of a human being suddenly shining in the heart of a man. It was like coming out of darkness into light.

Whatever happened—and certainly we would be the last to try to probe too far into that very sacred precinct—whatever happened, the tension under which Paul had been living broke. It was as though spring had come to the frozen rivers of the north, and the ice jams were finally broken, so that the waters of life could flow freely.

He was not a completely different person; he had the same mind, very much the same temperament, was susceptible to some of the same weaknesses and sins, but his life was integrated around a different center, and directed in a completely different channel, and he went off, moving confidently in the peace of God, to become the man who was later described as "the man who turned the world upside down." It was the rebirth of a human being.

You can see why, I hope, that every year on the twenty-fifth of January we celebrate this event. We do it because of the significance of the event itself and also because it reminds us of some things that we cannot afford to forget, and the first is this. *It reminds us that life can be lost before it is ever really lived.*

There are many unhappy people in the world, many more than you and I suspect. They learn to hide their unhappiness behind brave facades, and to live with it as well as they can. The reason, often, for their unhappiness is that life has never unfolded the way they had every right to believe it would. There are all sorts of reasons for this, and I shall not presume to mention all of them, but just a few of them, so as to suggest to you the kind of thing I mean. A long illness in childhood may fill a life with so many fears that it is partially crippled always. A frail nervous system may stand in the way of the full expression of the possibilities of a human life. A home where there is no love can do to a life what an early frost does to a garden. A disappointment can smoulder in a person's inner life long after the embers have burned out. An unhappy marriage can go on and on like a wound, hidden but open. A life can be locked up by inhibitions and frustrations so that the real person never has a chance to come out.

In other words, the whole story of St. Paul's rebirth reminds us of the fact that there is no guarantee—a rather sobering fact, I admit—that every life will unfold easily and naturally, and inevitably. As a matter of fact, the life of a human being is something like beauty imprisoned in a marble block; it does not often come out by itself; it has to be hammered out, sometimes painfully beaten out.

Listen to this, written by a man thirty-two years old, just about the age of Paul when this happened. "I am now the most miserable man living. If what I feel were equally distributed to the whole human family, there would not be one cheerful face on earth. Whether I shall ever be better I cannot tell; I awfully forbode I shall not." Abraham Lincoln wrote that when he was thirty-two, and he must have known that there was a chance, at least, that life might be lost before it was ever really lived.

Now, a second thing that this whole story reminds us of is that *life can be saved long after it seems to have been lost*. In other words, unexpected and radical changes do take place in people. Life is not as set and final as we sometimes think it is, and human nature is not as unsusceptible to change as we sometimes fear it is.

When you think of these sudden and unexpected changes, radical changes that have taken place in people, you are likely to think of the people that all the world knows about, a person like Pascal, for example. He died in 1662 and when he died, sewn between the inner and the outer cloth of his coat was a piece of paper on which he had written, under a cross surrounded by the rays of the rising sun, the year of his conversion—1654. Under it in great capital letters, FIRE. And then in exclamations, "I know! I feel! Joy! Peace!" He knew the very hour when he became sure of God—"from about half past ten at night till about half past twelve." There was a change in a man's life that was radical, unexpected, and complete.

But I should like also to think of some of the people who are not in any of the textbooks or the history books, because sometimes it is very easy for us to think of this as happening only to famous people, in classical examples, like St. Francis and John Wesley. Take, for instance, a young man who was born and raised in a religious family, a perfectly normal religious family. He, like St. Paul, was highly educated, very intelligent, and successful in his business when he started out. From the very beginning he rebelled; he rebelled against the family, and he rebelled against religion. He went about with unmistakable signs of cynicism on his face that no one could miss, and it was as plain as day that he was restless and dissatisfied. You felt that his real life was not fully released. Then his work sent him to the Far East. When he came back he had an entirely different expression on his face. If you asked him about it, all he would say was, "Something happened to me out there. Do not ask me to go into the details, but something happened to me out there, which completely changed my life." A sudden, unexpected, radical change took place.

In a very different realm—and I move into this realm only because of one phrase that I think may throw some light on what we are thinking about, and because I know that Americans are intensely interested in baseball, and especially Bostonians, and that many of them are interested in the Red Sox—the same thing can happen. Last spring, on May 13, there was an article in the *Boston Herald* announcing that the Red Sox had come back home. It then went on to say this: "For a team of what training camp experts dubbed as 'mediocre standpats,' the 1957 Red Sox show signs of defying the league." Whether or not that optimism was fulfilled or not, I dare not say, but this is the line that interests me particularly, and so often you find things like this in places where they were never meant or expected to mean what you find in them: "Williams [Ted Williams] has shown unexpected spring greatness. He has shaken off the seemingly inevitable injury." I wrote that down when I read it, not because I am particularly interested in baseball, because I am not, but because of that line I began to think of other people I have known who have shown unexpected spring greatness; a person like Paul, at the very peak of his life, when his life might have been lost before it had ever been lived, suddenly shows unexpected yet unmistakable spring greatness, and the seemingly permanent damage to his inner life was repaired completely.

233

I do not know about you, but I know there are some people in this congregation now listening to me who at some time will show those same signs of spring greatness. Don't forget that, when you are tempted to think that you must go on forever as you are, that the pattern is fixed and can never be changed.

The last thing that this event in the life of Paul reminds us of is that *nothing can save life but love*. I am not going to make any attempt to define the word *love* because I have done it so many times in so many other sermons. You know that it is not the common kind of thing that you think of when you use the word easily and lightly. The fact is that goodness is not enough. Paul was irreproachably good, and he came from a family that could never be suspected of doing anything that wasn't good. But Paul did not know much about love, about being included, about being cared for, about being understood, about allowances being made when he fell short. He did not know much about giving himself to other people who fell far short of the grandeur of God. He did not know much about this sort of thing. And how did he find out? The cross of Christ was the thing that made the love of God real to Paul. You ask how, and why? I do not know how or why. I only know that this dramatic, vivid, powerful event broke through the hard shell of Paul's outer life. In the cross, the love of God reached the innermost life of Paul for the first time. The blocks of guilt were completely removed.

The most we can say, all we need to say, is that this is the only thing that ever breaks the jams in life. Do you know anything else? If a family gets in a jam, not because its standards are too low and too lax as many of our families today, but because they are too high, because they really expect too much of their children so that there is alienation between the children and their parents, is there anything that can break that jam, but what we call love?

Individuals in the world today are not suffering on the whole, I think, from the same thing that was bothering Paul; they are not suffering so much from guilt, as from meaninglessness. Goodness by itself will never be enough to set those lives free. The only thing that can do it is the love that will not let them go, so that they *feel* as well as *know* that their lives count and mean something, in a world that means something, to a God who means everything. And the only way that most people are going to feel and know that love is through you! You are the only voice that Christ has, you are the only hands, the only heart, the only channel he has to express what was in him so completely and so intensely.

Woodrow Wilson was a complicated person. In the second term of his law school training in Virginia he had a nervous breakdown, and during that period he wrote, "How can a man with a weak body ever arrive anywhere?" Later he married a wonderful girl, and this is what he wrote to her: "You are the only person in the world with whom I do not have to act a part. To whom I do not have to deal out confidences cautiously. . . . My salvation is in being loved." Does anybody know anything about any other means of salvation?

So, as January 25 comes around every year, remember that it marks one of the most significant things that has happened and can happen in the world, the rebirth of a human being; remember that life can be lost before it is ever really lived, but that it can be saved even after it seems to have been completely and utterly lost, and that nothing can save it but love, and that love is never so strong and so powerful as it is in Christ Jesus.

O God, as we grope our way out of darkness into light, help us to find that which will release our lives so that we can be fully ourselves and fully thine. Help us to gather together the loose ends of life and integrate them into Christ Jesus, so that in us he may live again to save the lives of others. Amen.

235

The Depth That Is in Christ

ॐ

O NE OF THE MOST interesting things about our use of words is the way we often use the same word to mean quite different things. Take the word *deep*, for instance. If you say that a well is *deep*, you are saying that the distance, or the space, between the top of the well and the bottom of the well is great. But if, on the other hand, you say that a book is *deep*, you are not talking about space or distance at all. You are saying that the book is not easy, light reading, that the meaning of the book is not likely to be grasped by the casual reader who will not take time enough to read it carefully and thoughtfully.

The same thing is true of the same word in its substantive form. If you speak about the *depth* of the sea, you are talking about a distance in space that can be measured. But if you say of a portrait, That portrait has *depth*, you are not talking about space or distance; you are saying that the artist who painted the portrait has not only caught the features of the person he painted and made a good likeness of him, he has gone far beyond that. He has caught the quality of that particular person's inner life and revealed it in a way no candid camera ever could. The portrait, in other words, has *depth*.

This is one of the many examples of the way we elevate words. The word *deep* was used originally in reference to space, but we now use it to describe spiritual qualities and attitudes.

Speaking of portraits brings us a little closer to the subject of our thought today. There are four authentic portraits of Jesus. Very early in its life the Christian community chose from among many portraits of Jesus four and said, These four are the authentic portraits of our Lord and Master; upon these we put the sign of our approval. The artists, if we may refer to them as such, were called Matthew, Mark, Luke, and John. Each artist painted the same figure, and the figure is always unmistakably the same in each of the four portraits, but each one approached that figure from a peculiar, personal angle of vision.

Mark, for example, as he sketched the portrait of Jesus, sketched it rapidly, in bold strokes, and caught to an extraordinary degree the power of Jesus. The figure that you see in Mark's portrait is like a rushing, mighty wind. Matthew, on the other hand, standing in a different position, looking at the same figure from a slighty different angle, caught the authority of Jesus. His portrait is sterner, more severe. The word of Jesus is law, and it is not for you to choose whether you obey it or not; you disobey it to your doom. And if you are not there when your name is called, the door is closed, period. This, you see, is a quite different accent in the character of Jesus.

Luke caught the compassion of Jesus. He traced the more delicate strains of Christ's understanding and love for people who were out of bounds, beyond the pale. He painted the portrait of the One who came primarily to seek and to save the lost.

John caught something else, something that the others appreciated but not with the same intensity. He caught the more elusive quality that we have called *depth*. His portrait is a portrait of the same figure, with all the power, authority, and compassion of the others; but his portrait has a depth that the others do not have. His drawing is of a young man, a Jew who lived in Galilee and suffered under Pontius Pilate, but beyond that and through that you see Someone who was in the world from the very beginning; He made the world, and without Him was not anything made that was made. You may not understand at once what the artist means; you may not know exactly what he is trying to show you, but you know that you are facing a portrait that has depth.

That is what I should like you to look at this morning, and with these two things especially in mind. As you look at this portrait you may appreciate more than you have before the unique contribution of St. John to our knowledge of Christ, and also, as you look at it, you yourself may perceive more clearly and enter more fully than you have before into the depth that is in Christ Jesus.

237

You do not appreciate the depth of anything the first time you see it. You have to live with it. That is true of a place. A tourist in Boston sees the city and he gets a rough impression of what the city is like. He is likely to be impressed by the peculiarities of the city. He sees, if he is in the right place, the old brick sidewalks, the colonial houses, the Wren-like spires. He sees the low skyline which is strange to Americans who have grown up among skyscrapers. And if he goes downtown, he sees the narrow, crooked streets. But he does not grasp the depth of Boston, he does not know what Boston is really like, not in one visit. You have to live in it for that. You have to breathe its air, love its bricks, know its people, and be saturated with its atmosphere before you can say that you begin to sense this other element, this element of depth, in the city of Boston.

If that is true of a place it is certainly far more true of a person. The first time you meet a person you see a great deal. You see what he looks like; you get a general impression of the kind of person he is. You have a feeling about him, whether you trust him or distrust him. You see the way he walks and you hear the way he talks; you observe the way he carries himself, the way he behaves. But you do not get the depth of a person simply by seeing him once. You have to live with him, be near him, over a long period of time, before you appreciate his real quality.

St. John the Evangelist caught the depth of Christ because he had lived with him so long. We do not know exactly who St. John was, and as long as people read the New Testament his identity will be a moot question. There is no way of telling precisely, beyond the shadow of a doubt, who wrote the Fourth Gospel, but the tradition is that he was an old man, and everything in the Gospel confirms that tradition, for the picture that John gives us of Christ could only be drawn by someone who not only had lived with him as a companion, walking with him over the dusty roads of Galilee, but who in some way lived *in* him the way a man's body lives in the air. So John lived in Christ decade after decade. He walked in his light through all the dark ways of his own personal existence. He gloried in his love, and came to see that among all the traits that compose the character of Christ this is the essential one, and that the one thing that would distinguish the disciples of this Man is their love for each other. He gloried in this love, he lived in it, he breathed it the way we breathe air. He lived on his life the way we live on meat and drink. What he wrote, therefore, was the fruit of this lifelong association.

His portrait may not have as accurate an outline as the other three. I personally think that it does not; other people think differently. But accuracy of outline is not what John is concerned with; profundity, depth, is his concern. His portrait leads us toward a new appreciation of the depth that was in Christ; none of the others has it to the same degree, though in none is it entirely absent.

Perhaps we should say in passing that this is the only way you will get to know the real depth of Christ. You may be thinking to yourself as you listen to me talk that this is something quite beyond you, that you never even thought about entering into this sort of an experience and see no possibility of it. Perhaps not. But this much is certain—the only way you can ever have anything approaching it is to live with Christ. You can see almost at a glance the photographic image of Jesus. He was born in Bethlehem; brought up in a plain, simple family in Nazareth; a carpenter by trade; the friend of sinners by nature; he healed the sick, taught the people, preached about the Kingdom of God, was put to death because he was too good to live. You do not need to linger long to see that much.

But you will never appreciate the depth of Christ on any such casual acquaintance as that. To do that you must live with him, think about him, do your work—whatever it is—for his sake; try to be more and more like him even though you realize that you can never come anywhere near him, but try nevertheless to be more and more like him in your character and in your nature, in your sensitiveness to the needs of men and your willingness to try to meet them. A glance at him now and then will give you no more idea of what he is really like than one reading of Hamlet will give you any idea of the true grandeur of that play.

When you once see the depth of anything you are almost bound to describe it in symbolic language, simply because there is no other language available.

I shall give you an illustration that comes very close to some of us and that will show you what I mean. A group of men were sitting around a table discussing the possibility of life on Mars. In that group were the late philosopher Alfred North Whitehead and our parishioner and friend Mark Howe. After the learned men had discussed the possibility of life on Mars, Whitehead stood up and said, "Whether there be life on Mars or not, I do not know; but if there should be life on Mars, I nominate Mark Howe as the man to be sent there to represent the human race at its best."

Do you see what I mean by symbolic language? All the facts and figures about Mark Howe in *Who's Who* could not begin to give you the sense of depth that that symbolic language gives you. It may not be true in a literal sense, but it is true in a far deeper sense, and even if you never knew the man you would know that here is a person of real significance.

This is essentially what John did in his portrait of Christ. The others told the facts, and perhaps told them more accurately and in more perfect chronological order than he did. The others called Jesus the Messiah, which was a good, familiar Hebrew title, coming right up out of the land and soil. There was nothing symbolic about it; it was no more poetic than the title of our President. It was the name of the person who would deliver the nation from the enemy. John kept it, but he went further than that.

He said that Jesus is the Bread of life. His life is to a man's soul what bread is to a man's body. He is not one of the luxuries of life; he is one of the necessities. Without him, without his life and love, your life will wither away. Jesus is the Light of the world, not like the light of the sun that as it rises puts to flight the darkness; he is more like a searchlight that sends a shaft of light through the darkness driving it back further and further on either side so you can find your way through the night. John knew that because he had walked in that light.

Jesus, John said, is the Fountain of living water. He is not one of the wells that runs dry. There is in him inexhaustible energy and sustenance for the people who come to him to drink of the living water of life. He is the Resurrection and the Life. He can raise people from the dead. He can take a life that is withering away and bring it back so that it flowers again. He is the Way, the Truth, and the Life.

Think of all these words that he uses, so basic, so elementary, so simple; nothing national or local about them; words that people of every race, culture, and nationality can understand because they are universal words—words like way, truth, life, bread, light, and water.

John did not stop there. He went on to say that Jesus is the Good Shepherd. He is the Love of God looking for you, searching for you because he cares for you, wanting to draw you back into his flock, not against your will but because you wish to come home. He is the Vine; we are the branches. He is the life and we as a branch, if we are cut off from him, are lifeless. He is in the Father and the Father is in him, and he and the Father are one.

Do you see how the depth is growing? You may be beyond your depth at this point, but follow me. The climax he reached in the beginning, in the very first chapter of his Gospel, when he said, Jesus, the local carpenter of Nazareth who died on Calvary, is the Word of God—the express purpose, intention, and will of God—made flesh. You cannot go much deeper than that.

John then took the facts about Jesus and used them to fill out and give flesh to these great themes; he rearranged them to suit his purpose, included what would amplify it, and left out what would not. And as you read his Gospel you begin to get a glimpse of the depth that one man found in Christ.

What about you? I cannot end without saying a word about you. You represent every sort of person at every stage of religious development. Some of the younger ones, though not only the younger ones, older ones too, constantly say to me, I can't understand the divinity of Christ, and I don't really believe it. My suggestion to you is that you change your approach. Instead of beginning with a proposition about the nature of Christ, begin with John's Gospel and try to see the depth that is in Christ. If you go far enough, you will come to the depth which is the ground of all being, namely, God.

This matter, then, will not be a matter of intellectual assent. It will be your response to someone you have encountered, someone you have seen, someone you know, and you will be able to say, I do not understand the various formulations that men have made about the nature of Christ, but I know that there is in the Christ a depth that is so profound that it goes right down to the bottom of all things, namely, to God Himself.

Then with this portrait in your hands, you can go your way, trying to live with Jesus so that more and more, every day of your life, you will be able to say, He and the Father are one, and through him and in him I see God; and for me, he *is* God; apart from him I can do nothing.

Let us pause in silence a moment before this Portrait of Christ which is far greater than we can wholly grasp, yet which we can appreciate and respond to with all our being.

O God show us the Christ who is the way, the truth, and the life, in whom all thy fullness dwelleth; that we, going through dark and perilous waters, may know thee in him; we ask this through him, and in his spirit. Amen.

Help in Time of Trouble

%

In one of the sermons earlier this fall we began by pointing out that one of the things we know about human beings is that they have ideals which they never completely realize, and in the sermon we tried to see how God wants us to behave in that difficult and often frustrating situation.

There is another thing that we know about ourselves as human beings and that is that we constantly get into trouble. All kinds of trouble —major and minor troubles, physical and moral troubles, personal and public troubles; financial troubles—we borrow money that we are not able to pay back, we do not have the money we need to live on from day to day; domestic troubles—there is friction in that very place where above all others there should be peace; nervous and emotional troubles —disturbances in the very core of our being, disturbances that are the most difficult of all to reach. And then, of course, there are the troubles we have with our bodies which are constantly getting out of tune, out of order, and at times cease to function altogether.

Sometimes we have no one to blame but ourselves for the trouble we get into. We drink too much, we drive too fast, we crash into a tree. We bring that trouble on ourselves and we have no one but ourselves to blame for it. A great many of our troubles are like that. But sometimes the trouble comes through no fault of our own. We happen to live in a city—Worcester, for example—that is hit for the first time in modern history by a tornado, and our home is swept away. We are in no sense to blame for that trouble, and there are scores of troubles like that which come to us through no fault of our own. When the great wave of the world's travail breaks upon the shore of human life, we are sometimes

243

swept away by it as it recedes. It is no fault of ours, we cannot blame ourselves for it.

But whatever the nature of the trouble may be, or whatever the cause of it may be, the *fact* of the trouble remains. Job put it in a single sentence which by its very brevity and bluntness is powerful: "Man that is born of a woman is full of trouble." Indeed it is so, and we all know it. Amen!

We also know this about ourselves. When we get into trouble, we cry for help. Some are more reluctant than others. Some are brought up to believe that they should rely on themselves alone, that they should not be dependent on anyone, nor beholden to anyone. And some are very loath to let anybody know that they need help, that they are faced with something that they cannot handle themselves; they wouldn't let anyone know for the world. They are too proud to ask for help. But when the trouble reaches a certain point, only a few are too proud to ask for help. When the trouble reaches the point where it is beyond all the resources that a man has with which to meet it, then proud or not, self-reliant or not, he reaches out a hand and asks for help.

If the air carried every voice aloud, think of the cries for help with which it would be filled—women crying for help to save their children, men crying for help as they go down on sinking ships, as they are trapped in burning planes, caught in a net of lies, laid low by a fatal disease, lost in the labyrinthine ways of life.

When we get in trouble, we cry for help and when we cry, most of us eventually cry to God. In some cases we do it because we are in almost daily communication with God; we are in the habit of referring everything that happens to us to Him, and so it is the most natural thing in the world when we are in trouble to turn to Him and ask for His help. In other cases, we turn to God simply because we are so desperate. There is no one else to turn to. We know that we ourselves do not have the necessary resources, and we cannot see them in any of our friends. We sometimes feel as though we were locked up in a room alone by ourselves, facing a situation which we are not adequate to meet, and we cry out to whatever God there may be because there is no one else to cry to.

We may not think of God at all when things are going well. We may not pay any attention to Him when the sun is bright, and our lives are moving along smoothly, and we can get along on our own power. This shames us a little. It is natural that it should. It is like calling on a friend when you need him after you have passed him by without notice for months. We may not even believe in God. We may have come through the process of reason to a point where we can see no rational justification for believing that there is a God. Yet when trouble comes, trouble that is too much for us, we turn instinctively, almost impulsively, to God and ask Him to help us, and we cry with all the people down through the ages: "Lord, hear my prayer; and let my cry come unto thee."

These things we know. We also know (here some of you may not be able to follow me, your experience may not be the same as mine) that when we get into trouble and ask God for help, we get it. Help of one kind or another, that is. Sometimes the help comes directly and immediately as though God were answering at the moment our plea for help is uttered. For instance, a man was once in panic. He was in circumstances which he could not control and his irrational fears got the better of him. No one around could help him, he could not help himself, and he finally cried out to God for help. He prayed thus to God in Christ: "As the wind ceased when thou didst step into the boat beside thy friends who were afraid, come now into my life and calm the troubled waters. But if this be not thy will, and if my fears cannot be taken away, then help me to take them quietly, and in them find a new faith." The circumstances did not change, he did not change, but almost instantly the troubled waters began to grow calmer and in a little while his fears had subsided, like a storm that goes over and is gone, and he was able to move about as a free man. He asked for help; he got the help he asked for immediately, directly.

At other times the help comes indirectly through a person. Another man was facing a rather serious personal problem. He had thought a great deal about it and the more he thought about it, the more insoluble it seemed. He did everything that he knew how to do to find his way through it. It involved a human relationship which was precious to him and, therefore, he dared not take it lightly. The more he thought about it, the more the problem grew until it was out of all proportion to its real significance, yet no solution was forthcoming. Finally, he asked God to show him the way. Nothing happened for a long time, but he kept asking God every day to show him the way through the dark woods of this human situation and to give him the wisdom to handle it well. Then, one day he was on a train and met a man whom he knew but didn't see often; he hadn't seen him for several years. The man knew nothing about the problem, never did, never will know anything about it, but in the meeting and in the conversation that took place, the solution of the problem emerged. The help that he asked for came. It did not come directly, or immediately; and when it came, it came through a person who was not at all aware of being one of God's ministering angels, and probably would not like to have been called that!

At still other times the help we get is not the help we asked for. A child, for instance, is stricken with a serious handicap and it looks as though all his life would be ruined by this unfair limitation. His parents know that they cannot do anything about it, nor can any of the doctors do anything to change the situation. They turn to God instinctively and ask for His help. They ask that the handicap be removed. Time goes by, and the handicap is not removed, but the child learns almost miraculously to handle his handicap, and to handle it in such a way that it transfigures his life, and gives it a nobility and significance which otherwise it might never have had. The help was given, but in this case was not at all the help that was asked for.

So it happens over and over again. Sometimes we ask to be spared from something that we cannot bear to face. We are not spared, but we are given the strength to endure it. We ask for wings, and we are given a yoke. We ask to be rid of the thorns that are pressing upon our brows, and we are given the grace to wear them for a crown.

We must reckon, however, with this fact. There are times when no help comes, directly or indirectly, from God Himself or from Him through another person, the help we ask for or some other kind of help. No help comes. When then? Think of it first in terms of the help one man asks from another. A friend of yours is in trouble and he asks you for money. You decide, after looking at all the circumstances in the situation, not to give him the money; not because you do not want to help him, but because you know that if you give him the money, it will hurt him, for the very thing that he has to do is to learn how to stand up to the trouble he is in and take the responsibility for his own actions. If you make it easy for him and give him the money he needs, you simply help him postpone the fatal day when he must stand himself before his responsibilities, and this will only make it harder for him in the end. It is one of the hardest decisions, incidentally, that a person ever has to make—that to help someone he loves would hurt him.

I am sure that there are times when God feels the same way with us; that there are times when God withholds His help from us for the same reason, because to give us His help would be ultimately to hurt us. He knows that what we need most is to wrestle with the enemy ourselves, to take responsibility for the things which we have always been able to slip out of. Like as a parent knows that it will not help his child to do his homework *for* him, even so our Father above knows that there are times when it will only hurt us if He helps us. Later on, years later, we come to see that help did come, even in those times when it seemed not to come, but that the help was hidden in the trouble itself!

These are things we know about life, from our own experience; we get into trouble invariably, sooner or later, some more than others; when we get into trouble, we ask for help; eventually, if not at first, we ask God for it; and when we ask for it, we get it.

These facts of human experience bring certain things into plain view. Let me try to focus them for you, if I can, make them as sharp as I can so that you will be able to take them into your own consciousness.

The first thing that is made plain is that there will *never* be a time when you are completely free from trouble, never! Though there will be times when your troubles are at a minimum, there will never be a time when you can say, I am immune to the trouble of the world. No matter how well-off you are, your material wealth will never make you secure against trouble. No matter how good you are, you will never be spared because you are good. As a matter of fact, the better you are, the more sensitive you will be to the things that will hurt you most. So this we might as well settle with in the beginning—there will never be a time when we will be completely free from trouble.

Second, there will *eventually* come a time when you will be in trouble that you cannot handle by yourself alone. I am sure of that. There will eventually come a time when you will be in some kind of trouble that you cannot handle by yourself alone. When that time comes, don't hesitate to ask for help. Don't be too proud. You have nothing to be proud of; everything you have and are was given to you originally and all that you have done was to cultivate it. Don't stand on your dignity. To be sure, you want to do everything that you can to help yourself first; but if, after you have done everything you know how to do to help yourself, you are still helpless, then don't hesitate to ask for help.

And may I say this to you? Don't be ashamed to ask God. Even though you have not paid much attention to Him when times were better, don't be ashamed to turn to Him. Remember that the God who made you makes allowance for all your little weaknesses; He never makes excuses for you, neither will He ever exclude you from His love and care, never. Don't hesitate, don't be ashamed to turn to Him. And remember, you will be in good company. You will be in the company of Paul the Apostle, who turned to God for help when he wanted to get rid of a physical affliction that he felt was impeding his work preaching the Gospel around the world. He did not get the help he wanted, but he got a greater help—he was given the grace of God which was more than sufficient for all his weakness. And you will be in the company of Jesus himself, who when he was in the garden asked God to spare him the death that he saw waiting for him. He was not spared, but he was given the strength to go through it in such a way that he took the sting out of death forever, for everyone.

The third thing that this brings into view is that you will not get help unless you admit you need it, want it, and ask for it. You know that from your own personal experience. You cannot really give any help to a friend, even though you see that the friend is in a bad way, unless the friend asks you for it, wants it. If he is closed up, so that no one sees what is going on inside him—or at least he thinks no one sees it—if he is never willing to admit that he is in a bad way and, therefore, never in a position to ask you to help him, you can stand there with everything you possess ready to give him, and yet not be able to give a single thing because he hasn't asked you for it. So God cannot really help us until we reach the point at which we are willing to admit that we need the help, and have the humility to ask for it. It is only then that God is able to give us the things which He is so ready to give.

Fourth, and most important of all, if you ask God for it and get it, that experience will be the greatest assurance you will ever have of the reality of God. There will be times in your life, in some cases many times, when God is not real and, in spite of everything you can do yourself, you will not be able to feel that God is a present fact, that He is there. You will search the natural world to find some intimation of His presence and all you will meet is the blind and heartless face of the sky. You will search through all the proofs for God's existence that the mind of man has been ingenious enough to devise, and they will be hollow and empty as a shell. You will come to church with all the sincerity in the world, looking for God and yet not finding Him; open the Bible, and not find Him. Then you will remember this: *When I was in trouble, I called upon the Lord, and He heard me.*

Then you will know.

O God, we are surrounded by so many disturbing things that sometimes we know not how to face them. Help us always to remember that when we need help, ask for help, are humble enough to receive help, help of one kind or another is always forthcoming. Thou, O God, art the Helper of the helpless, and when we have the humility to recognize our helplessness, then in the help that we are given, we find the reassurance of thy presence. Amen.

Why Can't We Do It?

❧

I<small>F YOU HAD TO CHOOSE</small> one word to describe the mood of people in this part of the world—the prevailing mood, that is—what would it be? My word is *frustration*. Frustration is purpose minus power; and a frustrated person is a person who has the will but cannot find the way.

It goes without saying that there is always a certain amount of frustration in life. No man alive, so far as I know, can honestly say that he has never run into a dead-end street, or come up against a blank wall. A man with no frustrations at all is either a man who aims so low that he can't possibly miss, or a man who always misses but never knows it or believes it. So much for the frustrations of life in general.

Today, frustration is a national epidemic. We want things that we cannot bring to pass; we don't know how to do it, we are incapable, impotent. We want to stop the war, but we can't. We want to keep our cities clean, safe, habitable, but for the most part we can't. We have tried every known means, but the obstacles are so great, the bureaucratic obstructions and political graft so enormous, that we never succeed in doing it. We want to stop inflation; we can't, we don't know how. We want to renew the church, make it once again a center of life where people find renewal for themselves and their children; but in most cases we can't. We want to stop the violence, the crime in our cities, and in the villages as far as that goes; we want to control the drug traffic. We try, we use every means known to man, but so far we have not been able to do it. We are frustrated.

There are some, to be sure, who escape this national epidemic of frustration. There are those too small to care about anything; naturally, they escape it. And others, only a few, too great to be daunted by anything; and they soar above it. Still others who are clever enough (and devilish enough) to exploit it and make a "fortune" on it. Most of us are in none of these groups. We are not too small to care at all, and not great enough to soar above it. We are frustrated every way we turn; we have the will but we cannot find the way. We Christians turn, almost in desperation, to the New Testament.

An incident in the Gospels (St. Matthew 17:14–21; St. Mark 9:14–29) points the way and sheds light on this particular condition of ours.

Briefly, this is what happened. Jesus and his friends had just come down from the hills. They had been through one of those experiences that come only once in a lifetime, the experience that they called *transfiguration*. And after it was over, they came down from the hills. Dr. Halford Luccock, in his exposition of St. Mark's Gospel, makes the comment that normally when we say a person is "going downhill" we say something detrimental, at least not flattering, about him. But, he said, in the case of Jesus it is true that in one sense he was always going downhill, from the mountain tops of exhilaration, transfiguration, and vision down into the valley where people were suffering, and where the need was great. So, he and his three friends came down from the hill.

Immediately, they ran into a crowd of agitated men, among whom he recognized the other nine disciples. They were involved in a heated discussion, one of the favorite indoor and outdoor sports of church people: discussion. They linger to discuss the situation when they might be doing something.

It soon appeared what they were discussing. One man ran out of the crowd toward Jesus and told him about his boy. He was an epileptic, the seizures were severe. In some cases they were so severe that he al-almost died. He had brought him, after trying everything else, to the disciples hoping that they could cure him. And he had good reason to think that they might because they had gone out on a healing mission and had healed a great many people. But they couldn't; they didn't.

Jesus said to the father, Bring him here. So the father brought his son, a grown boy, into the presence of Jesus, whereupon he had one of his seizures right there on the spot. Jesus said to the father, How long has he been like this? The father said, Since he was a child. The father went on to say, But if you can do anything, please take pity and help us. And Jesus said to him, If *I* can do anything? If *you* can, you're the one who must do it, for all things are possible to him who believes. The man said, I do believe; help me to believe more. Or, in the familiar version of the King James Bible, "I believe; help thou mine unbelief."

Jesus cured the boy. As the demon, or whatever you wish to call the evil spirit that took possession of his body, left him, he was prostrate. The people thought he was dead. And Jesus, characteristically, reached down and took him by the hand, and lifted him up, and gave him back to his father.

After it was all over, and they went home, the disciples asked Jesus (I wish we could hear the tone of their voices), Why couldn't we do it? Why couldn't we do it? And he said, This sort of thing takes prayer.

Now, that's the incident, told very briefly. It is bound to raise a great many questions, especially in a twentieth century congregation of intelligent people, especially two. The first question is, Did Jesus actually cure the boy? The disease was so serious and the cure was so sudden. I am not going into that question now; I have done it a hundred times before. I shall simply suggest an answer to it by asking another question: Have you ever known any great person, any really great person, past or present, who did not do things that to you, at the time, seemed miraculous in the sense that they surpassed your understanding? I never have. Incidentally, as you told the story to your friends, have you never made it a little taller?

The second question is, Is it true that all things are possible to the person who believes? Certainly it is not literally true; it would be nonsense if it were. But let me once again point to the answer by asking another question, How far would the Wright brothers have gotten with their flying machine if they had sat around concentrating, day after day, on the ifs, ands, and buts, of the situation? They would have gotten nowhere, surely not off the ground.

But set aside those questions for the time being, and concentrate on two facts. The first is that the disciples were frustrated: "Why couldn't we do it?" So was the father in the beginning; and so, we might say, was Jesus when he looked upon his helpless disciples, knowing that they should have been able to do it. The second fact is that Jesus said that the reason they couldn't do it was that they didn't have what it takes, namely, prayer. They could *say* a prayer, just as well as you or I can. But they didn't have the inner resources that come to a person who lives with God.

As I hear him speak to us now he is saying this: Many of the things you want, the things you want to do, require a basic training that you do not have. Not you as individuals, but you as a people do not have either the basic training or the habitual practice without which you cannot do these things. It is an irresistible temptation to think about that, at least it is to me, and to take it to heart.

No one, surely, has to tell us that to achieve anything that amounts to much a certain basic training is an absolute requirement. No one of us could go to the moon today simply because none of us has the basic training required. Not many of us could plan or construct the John Hancock Building next door, even if we wanted to, because we do not have the basic training either in engineering or architecture. I couldn't try a case in court, or take out an appendix, or play the Emperor Concerto; and most of you couldn't preach a sermon—for the same reason. So that is perfectly plain; we all take that for granted.

The extraordinary thing is that someone *does* have to tell us that we as a people lack the basic training required to move the mountains we are trying to move. Training in things like these: telling the truth; being honest. Two secretaries are discussing their clothes. One tells the other how much she paid for a dress. The other says, Do you pay for your clothes? She said, Why, certainly. The other girl said, I just take mine! Training in seeing through the vanity of money, not the power of money because it is great, but the vanity, the emptiness of money, as an object of supreme concern. Caring about the way things look. Where this training starts I don't know, but it must start somewhere early in life, in the home. If a young person cared, he wouldn't enter Copley Square by walking through the planting along Boylston Street and St. James Avenue when he could perfectly well go in by the pavement. And he wouldn't leave his empty beer cans for someone else to pick up.

Yesterday I went to see one of our little giants. She has been in the hospital since October; she's radiant. She is eighty-four. She was sitting up in a chair when I arrived at two o'clock and had just turned on the Metropolitan Opera, *Il Trovatore*. She is a great opera lover; for some reason or other she thinks I am not, so she turned it off. After we had talked a little while, I said, "Turn it on!" So she did, and a soprano was singing full tilt. She knew exactly who it was and what role she was singing. I saw some buttons on the top and said, "Turn it up, let's hear it, I want to hear the voice in full force." And it filled the room where we were sitting. "Oh," she said, "you can't do that! Think about the other people." That's the result of basic training in thinking about other people.

We lack the basic training in accepting what we have been given before we take it back and try to change it; our body, our temperament, our nervous system, the fact that we are no longer young. Accepting it, before we take it back and try to change it. Respecting life, beginning with your own body—knowing that it is one of the most wonderful, mysterious, beautiful things that God ever made, and that there are only three things you can do with it: worship it, wreck it, or respect it. And then, respecting all other growing things—every plant and flower, every bird and beast, every star and shell; and all other growing people.

We lack the basic training in giving up some things for the sake of greater things. No one ever had his heart set on something great who didn't know that in order to achieve it he would have to close many doors along the way. If he didn't know that he must have been a fool. Controlling passions. We all have them; without them we would be uninteresting, dull, lifeless. But they have to be controlled, channeled. Rage, lust, the desire for loot. These are passions as common as water, but without a dam or a channel, like the water in a river, they can ravage a whole countryside.

Living under authority, the authority of the moral order of God, knowing that you cannot do anything that you want to do—that's another required item in the basic training of every human being. Learning how to care and not to care, how to sit still, learning how to be quiet inside, when everything is racing full steam ahead outside you. Knowing that if you do nothing, nothing will happen. But if you do something, what happens will not necessarily be the result of what you do.

You have to think that over. It is one of the things I am more sure of than almost anything else in the world; that if I sit around and do nothing, nothing will happen. If I do the things that I can do, something will happen, but nine times out of ten what happens is not the direct result of what I was doing; it is something else. In other words, there is something beyond me that is bringing things to pass.

And the last thing on my list is basic training in knowing when to give in. "The courage to change the things that can be changed; and the serenity to accept the things that cannot be changed; and the wisdom to know one from the other" (Reinhold Niebuhr).

There is always the danger in every sermon of too many loose ends, and there are a great many in this one. But there are two that are not loose. The first is this: Jesus did not answer the frustrated disciples by saying, You couldn't cure that boy because you are not divine; I am. He didn't say that at all. He said, You couldn't do it because at this point you haven't got what it takes; you haven't the basic training, the habitual practice, you haven't the inner strength that it takes to do wonders. You *can* have it, but at present you haven't got it.

And the other loose end that I want to tie into this is that our people in the U.S.A., in the year 1971, generally speaking, haven't the basic training to do wonders. They can do financial wonders because they have lived for so many years so close to money; they know every one of its tricks. They can do scientific wonders because they have lived for so long so close to technology. They can do mechanical wonders because they have lived for so long so close to machines. But when it comes to moral, spiritual wonders they haven't been living very close to those things, to God.

I know it sounds vague, and is too general to be practiced. Just one vignette to suggest what we, with the disciples, lack. Dr. Harry Emerson Fosdick once told about a woman in her early middle years. She was left a widow with five children and very little money. Never once did I see her distraught to the point of giving up, one of her sons said.

She saw them all through college. One son was the president of a great railway system. Another was the president of a state university. Another was distinguished in medical research. And the two daughters were happily married. At her funeral, at the age of ninety-six, the son who was the president of the university said to Dr. Fosdick, "No one could understand her who did not understand her prayer-life. It was a strong, sustaining force. Her resource came from an unfailing, inward companionship." That is what Jesus was talking about when he said that this kind of thing can be done only by prayer, only by that kind of inner companionship with God.

Fix thou our steps, O Lord, that we stagger not at the uneven motion of the world, but go steadily on our way, neither censuring our journey for the weather we meet, nor turning aside for anything that befalls us. Amen.

A Case of Skepticism Overcome

⚘

"Can any good thing come out of Nazareth?" John 1:46

W E BEGIN with a case of skepticism. It occurs in the first chapter of John's Gospel when Philip finds Nathaniel and tells him, "We have found him of whom Moses and the prophets did write, Jesus of Nazareth, the son of Joseph." Nathaniel's reply was, "Can any good thing come out of Nazareth?" It was not so much that he did not believe in Jesus—he had not even seen him yet—as it was that he did not believe in Nazareth. He simply could not believe that this human situation of ours could produce anyone who could become the Saviour of the world. There is skepticism that is profound indeed.

Our hearts and minds go out to Nathaniel, for we too are suffering from a bad case of skepticism. We look at this wretched world of ours and we say to ourselves, Can any good thing come out of that? Or we look at this human nature that we all share with its wickedness and weakness and we say, Is it conceivable that any supremely good thing can come out of that? Men and women have always had their doubts about one thing or another. Sometimes they have doubted the reality of God, sometimes the value of a moral principle, but their current doubt goes much further than that. People are now doubting the value of existence itself. They are wondering whether the world has any future. The more carefully they look at the whole bedraggled scene of human life they say despairingly, Can any good thing come out of that?

Well, we turn back to Nathaniel and we find that in his case his skepticism was overcome. For when he asked Philip the question "Can any good come out of Nazareth?" Philip answered, "Come and see." What he saw dispelled his doubts forever. We turn, therefore, on this last Sunday of the old year to this case of skepticism overcome in the hope that we may find in it the cure for our own skepticism.

Let us now take our stand with Nathaniel and look at Nazareth as he might have seen it. Using the best wits that we have and all our knowledge of the past we might ask the question, What can we reasonably expect to come out of that town? Well, it was a town that had no prominence at all in the past. It was never mentioned in the Old Testament or in any of the books of Jewish history. Apparently it had never made any great contribution to the life of humanity. Beyond that it had no prominence in the present. It was off the main road. It was just a small town with all the typical characteristics of small-town life. But if we look more carefully at the people who lived there, we see people that live on every main street of every town in the world. When one of their native sons grew up and showed evidence of tremendous power, they would not have any faith in him whatever and because he touched one of the sore spots of their self-interest, they drove him out of the town and attempted to lynch him. Well, we say with Nathaniel, what good thing can come out of a town like that, with all of its main-street narrowness, with all of its refusal to make great responses to great things, what good thing can come out of a town like that? On the basis of all our reasonable predictions, not much. And yet, the fact is that out of Nazareth, right off its main street, came Jesus of Nazareth, right out of that town with all its restrictions and limitations came the flower of the human race. So we come to the first point in the cure for our skepticism: there is always an unpredictable element in human history. After we have made all our predictions and all our calculations of what we *might expect*, history does not by any means always go that way.

We are told on very reliable authority that this planet of ours was once wrapped in a solid sheet of ice. Suppose there could have been a human mind suspended somewhere out there in the Milky Way observing this ice-sheathed planet. He might have said to himself, Well, nothing more will ever come from that. There will never be another green thing growing there, never another bird singing; there will never be a living creature there, for all life has been frozen. That is the end.

And yet, we know that history did not go that way for there came one of those unpredictable moments when the ice began to melt and the trees began to grow and the fields were green and the birds sang and human beings stood up erect, aspiring after great things. It was the unpredictable element in human history. That gave the lie to the pessimists.

Or to come nearer to our own time, look at a shoemaker's family, and with all our common sense we might say to ourselves, Can any great thing come out of that shoemaker's family? It has not many opportunities; it has not much background. Oh, there is not a chance in the world that any great thing can come out of that family! Well, that is the way it appeared, but, as a matter of fact, the one who wrote the lines:

> Was this the face that launched a thousand ships
> And burnt the topless towers of Ilium?

came out of that shoemaker's family—Christopher Marlowe.

Or we might turn again to a woolen merchant's family and say, Surely there is no possibility of anything great coming out of that limited family. That is the way it may have looked on the surface, but the Bard of Avon came out of that woolen merchant's shop,—*Macbeth, Hamlet, Othello, Lear, Midsummer Night's Dream*—all those wonders came out of that woolen merchant's shop. A livery stable—can anything good come out of that? Well, John Keats came out of it. A midwestern town in the United States of America with all the things in it that arouse the satire of our current novelists—can any great thing come out of that? Well, Dwight Eisenhower came out of that with a character that is about as straight as any character that we have seen on our stage in recent times. The unpredictable element in human history.

Coming to our own time, we look at the towns that we know. *Life* magazine took pictures of one of them, Indianapolis, as a typical town in the United States of America. And what do we see? We see a hairdressers' convention, a meeting of women of the Order of Moose, we see the children's courts, we see the shops and factories closed because of strikes and unemployment. We see the jammed movie houses and great crowds of children in a cheering section at a high school football game.

And we say, Well, if that is typical of the towns of this country with all its shallowness and its tawdriness, can any good thing come out of that? The Christmas warning is this: do not be too sure. Do not be too positive in your predictions, for just when you think you have made the most careful, foolproof predictions history surpasses your wildest hopes and exceeds your greatest dreams. And out of Nazareth Jesus comes.

Look again at this town of Nazareth and imagine how it has over and over again choked the spirit of its young people. How many people do you suppose born in that town grew up with every ambition in the world to do something big? And then the conventions and the restraints of the town began to close in upon them and the opposition grew and the spirit of the young person was smitten and finally faded into oblivion. That probably happened over and over again. Nazareth choked the spirit of its sons and yet there came along a person whose spirit was not choked by Nazareth so much as it was challenged by Nazareth. When Jesus grew up, it was those very limitations of the people which challenged him to his greatness. It was the very fact that their minds were small and their spirits were meager—that was the thing that challenged the young Jesus to go out into the world to do something to let life loose and to free the people from the inhibitions and the restrictions and the restraints that had been crippling their lives. That brings us to the second point in our cure for skepticism: there is an unexpected resiliency in the human spirit.

To be sure, adverse circumstances do choke some spirits, but they challenge other spirits and make them great. Of course, as we look at the slums of our great industrial cities we hang our heads in shame, realizing how many youthful spirits have been practically strangled by the poverty and the disease and all the lack of opportunity of those slums. But those same slums challenged the spirit of Jane Addams, Jacob Reese, Lillian Wald, and a whole army of their followers, and just because of those adverse circumstances, those spirits grew big and strong because they had the resilience of the human spirit. We cannot afford to make any conclusions about our time and its possibilities and its prospects leaving out that quality of human life at its best. I think there are some signs that it is already at work.

A CASE OF SKEPTICISM OVERCOME

The man who writes the first page of the *New Yorker* magazine is one of the most astute observers of contemporary life, at least in my judgment. He describes walking up Fifth Avenue and looking in one of the big shop windows just before Christmas. In most of the shops he finds nothing but the sales aspect of Christmas demonstrated, but in one shop he finds a great processional of children, all colors under the sun, all nations, all races, all revolving around one central child, The Child, the Christ Child. He said, "I could not help pausing to watch the passers-by and to see the gleam in their eye as they saw this great international, interracial picture in terms of childhood. And I saw the joy on the faces of the Negroes as they saw their little black children in the processional." Then he goes on to say this, "There has not been a Christmas like this since the first Christmas. The fear, the suffering, the awe, the strange new life that nobody understands yet, all the traditional characteristics of Christmas are this year in reverse. Instead of the warm grate and the happy child in most parts of the world, the cold room and the starveling. The soldiers of today return to their homes to find people groping toward something which still has no name but which keeps turning up—in department store windows and in every other sort of wistful human display. It is the theme concealed in the victory, justice among men of all races, a world in which children of whatever country are warm and unafraid."

Sometimes it does look as though this old world had come to the end of its rope. But so long as there are human spirits that refuse to be confined, who, the more they are squelched, the stronger they grow, so long as there are minds that quicken to the pulse beat of a new idea, so long as a few young people can get excited about a new world order, the Nathaniels of the day, the skeptics,—are overcome.

We must take one more brief look at Nazareth before we bring this sermon to a close. We have tried to look at the town with all its assets and liabilities. We have tried to make allowance for the resilient human spirit that transcends and transforms its environment. But certainly there is something else. We could never draw the picture of Christmas if we left God out. If you will allow me to think of it in terms that you may think are old-fashioned because they are pictorial, think of God looking down on this world with all its tribulations. There is a little town just like all the rest, all the gossips on main street, all the things that hold life back, and yet as He looked at it He said to Himself: If I can find one good home, one good father and mother, I can fashion me something there that will be an instrument to redeem the world. He chose the home of Joseph and Mary and He put His own life into their son Jesus. So as through the mind of Jesus God expressed His thoughts to humanity, and as through His lips we heard the words of God, there in that typical scene God came to work out His purpose for humanity.

The world must indeed look dark to people who have no belief in any such kind of a God who is constantly planning and plotting and working his purpose out through the Nazareths of the world to make them better, nobler places. The God we believe in is the God who can take such action, who can pick up the fragments of humanity and re-assemble them into something good and redirect the course of human history along lines we never dreamed of. We might call all this the Christmas cure for our skepticism. "Can any good thing come out of Nazareth?" Well, sometimes we sincerely doubt it. But at Christmas we remember that Jesus did come out of Nazareth, like a perfect flower out of very poor soil. Let that unpredicted fact of history warn us against the thought that the world is exhausted. He came out of Nazareth, hurt by it, challenged by it, rose magnificently above it. No Nazareth can be lost so long as the human spirit can soar like that. He came because God had not lost track of His universe. In His own way and in His own time, He was setting it to rights.

"Can any good thing come out of Nazareth?" Before you answer— "Come and see."

Help us, O God, as we face the perplexing circumstances of this world to re-member always the power of the human spirit to rise above whatever circum-stances beset it and so triumph over things here below that we finally reach the great truths of eternal life. Amen.

Revelation at Midnight

&

THIS SERMON BEGAN on the platform of the Union Station in Baltimore last Friday night about eleven-thirty. I had been the chaplain for the Hood Conference for church workers from the Third Province, about four hundred of them, which had been meeting in Frederick, Maryland, for a week. I had celebrated the Holy Communion every morning, and preached every night, and conducted a class in preaching for the clergy at noon. I had been taken back to Baltimore by friends after my last service, and I was waiting for the Federal, the night train from Washington to Boston, to bring me back home. I was tired.

The platform was dreary, unusually dreary. At their best, railroad platforms are not the most attractive places in the world. It was dimly lit with that half-light that you expect to find in the nether-regions, neither bright enough to make them beautiful nor dark enough to blot out their ugliness. It was hot, hotter than it is here now, a great deal hotter. It was humid; and it was late, and the train was late. There was almost no sound; in a strange way, whatever noise there was seemed to be muffled by the heat.

The people and, considering the time of night, there were many of them, were drooping with the heat; most of them were carelessly dressed, at least they looked that way to me; and some were vulgarly dressed, almost slovenly. Some of them looked as if they didn't quite know where they were going. They probably did know, but they gave the appearance of moving aimlessly through the heat haze, drifting through life. They looked as if they didn't know where they were going, or quite why, or as if they cared much whether they went north or south. The whole scene was, to my eyes at least, dingy, dreary, sooty, grimy, and pointless. I thought to myself, I suppose this is what many people think the modern world is like—half-lit, industrial, mechanical, impersonal, on the move constantly so that nobody has any roots, and, by and large, meaningless.

Then down one of those long flights of stairs that descend from the waiting room to the tracks came a young couple carrying a small child. I noticed them as they were coming down the stairs and I could not take my eyes off them. The wife had on a dark dress and carried a suitcase. The man was carrying the child, and he was dressed in white from head to foot, white shoes, white suit, white shirt. When he passed me, I could see something that confirmed what I suspected. I could see just a part of a stethoscope sticking out of his pocket, and I knew then that he was a resident or an interne in one of the Baltimore hospitals and was coming to the train to put his wife and baby on it for the north. I continued to watch them.

There wasn't anything particularly unusual about them, and I suppose they would perish if they ever thought that they were being used as the centerpiece of this sermon. They were quiet, but everybody was quiet. They said very little to each other. If they felt the heat, they gave no indication of it. They looked as cool as a person would look on an autumn day. If they were tired, they gave no sign of it. They looked as fresh as anybody could possibly look. You had the feeling that they knew exactly what they were doing, and where they were going, and they conveyed to anybody who looked at them the supreme fact that they cared enormously about each other.

Still I couldn't help watching them and as I looked at them, it was the man's white suit that first held my eye. It was whiter than almost anything I have ever seen; there wasn't a wrinkle or a crease in it anywhere. And I thought as I stood there—you know how you look at things like that and see things far beyond them as your mind begins to wander off in all directions—I thought of the attempt of the writer of the Gospels to describe the whiteness of the Lord's garments when he was transfigured. "His raiment became shining, exceeding white as snow; so as no fuller on earth can white them." The man's suit was shining and white, by contrast. Everything else was so dark. And yet the strange thing was that, at least to me, instead of making everything else look darker and dingier, by comparison, it made everything else look brighter.

Then he put the child down on the platform. He was just old enough to walk; he looked as if he had just accomplished that feat. He had on a little blue suit and pale, red sandals. I shall see them for years; that soft, terra-cotta red, the only spot of color in that whole dingy scene. A tiny boy with blond hair, blue suit, and red shoes. The train was late so his father took him by the hand and in a kind of absolute communion of the spirit they walked up and down the whole length of the platform of the Union Station. They might have been walking in the sun, on the most beautiful beach in the world. And as they went farther and farther away from me, and then came closer again, what I saw began to enlarge in its proportions. The man in the white suit seemed to grow taller, and the child smaller. There they were, the big man and the tiny child, walking together in the midst of the infernal engines that might snuff out life at any moment, without the slightest sign of fear. There they were, walking up and down the platform, tenderness and trust hand in hand. The train finally arrived and we all got aboard. The man put his wife and child in the same car that I was in, and that was the end.

My mood was entirely different than it was when I went down to the platform. And when I put myself to rest, I couldn't get this image out of my mind. I began to think of all sorts of things, and the first thing I thought of was this: there *is* something in the world besides violence and cruelty. There *is* something in the world besides ugliness and vulgarity, besides meaninglessness and chaos. So often we get the impression that the modern world is nothing but violence and brutality. We get that impression, of course, because there is a great deal of violence and brutality in the world no matter how you look at it, and some of us, at certain periods of our lives, are almost completely surrounded by it. Another reason why we get this impression is that the young intellectuals tell us that we are living in the most violent and brutal time that ever existed, and the modern artists repeat the grand refrain. So we believe it.

Modern music is dissonant and hard to listen to. Modern poetry is harsh, the lines are gnarled; they seldom sing; nothing sings. The modern theater is brutal and vulgar; modern painting, by and large, is violent, distorted, and conveys the sense of the utter meaninglessness of life, the fact that the world is gradually going to pieces and nobody knows what to do about it. Modern building is angular and graceless. When we uneducated laymen say to modern artists, "Why is this? Why is art like this? We understand what you mean, but why is it that we don't want to look at it, that we don't enjoy it?" They say to us right away, "The reason is that we live in a world of violence, brutality and meaninglessness; this is what the artist sees; this is what the artist is dutybound to express." The implication is that there is nothing else to see or express. I am bold to say that there is; that the fault lies not in the world, but in the artist. It is not the world that is twisted out of any recognizable shape; it is the man. It is the artist who creates order out of a disordered world, and this he cannot do if he is disordered himself.

There have always been brutality *and* beauty in the world. There have always been violence *and* tenderness in the world, chaos *and* order in the world. Always there are the two now, and there have always been the two. I suppose it is idle to make any comparisons and I should not want to put myself under the judgment of the historians by trying to do it, but I would guess that if anything, England in the age of Elizabeth I was infinitely more violent and brutal than the England of Elizabeth II, and that the hill towns of Italy were more thickly infested with disease, poverty, and bloodshed when St. Francis was alive than any comparable towns are now. In other words, what I am saying is that, in spite of the fact that our age is one of those peculiarly distraught ages of revolution, it is not so peculiar as some people make it out to be. And my judgment for what it is worth—and I am not speaking now as a prophet or even a priest of the church, I am speaking as a private individual—my judgment is that it is the people that are different. It is the people who are disorganized inside themselves, not the world. It is the people of our time, the artists, the interpreters of life, who are not often willing to stop and look at the beauty and the order that is right in front of their eyes.

There are families going to pieces, husbands disloyal to wives. But there are wonderful families like the one I saw. There are hundreds of people who cannot communicate with each other, who never break through into the lives of the people they know. But there are other people who are in wonderful communication, in communion with the people whom they know and love. There are people who are totally tied up in the net of competitive and acquisitive modern business, but there are men like this man, who probably had just come from the ward of some hospital, standing day and night by the beds of people in pain. There are hundreds of people like that. There is something in the world today besides violence and brutality; the trouble is not many people pay much attention to it.

Did you read the article in this week's *Time* about Robert Frost? He was given three degrees in England last week, one at Oxford, one at Cambridge, and one at the University of Dublin. At the age of eighty-three this great tribute was given to Frost by the people who first appreciated him. I was amused by one of the things that *Time* said about him as he went up and down England making his quips. An English Bishop went up to him, I hesitate to think which one, but probably a formal, pompous one, and said that one day he would see the light. Mr. Frost replied, "Oh, I see the light. I just don't pay much attention to it." In this little episode I am all on Mr. Frost's side. On the other hand, the remark can be interpreted another way. I think that there are a great many people in the world who see the light; they just don't seem to pay much attention to it. They would rather look in the dark corners, at the rubbish.

I remember Thomas Hardy's poem that he wrote in 1915 during the war, upon his recollection of the great phrase in the book of the prophet Jeremiah, "the breaking of nations." Thomas Hardy wrote:

> Only a man harrowing clods
>   In a slow silent walk
> With an old horse that stumbles and nods
>   Half asleep as they stalk.
>
> Only thin smoke without flame
>   From the heaps of couch-grass;

Yet this will go onward the same
Though Dynasties pass.

Yonder a maid and her wight
Come whispering by;
War's annals will cloud into night
Ere their story die.

This is one thing I thought about.

I went further than that. I said to myself—and this is hard to put into words, but I shall try to do it—this is the real thing. Not these two particular people and this particular child, but what they are. This is the real thing. This is what makes everything else go. All else besides, the surroundings and the dreary setting, are incidental to this, the everlasting caring, the life going out from one generation to another, the mother and the father reaching out to take the new child into the difficult and dangerous world, taking the shocks and giving themselves, spending themselves for this new life to be brought up, to have everything that it can possibly have. This is it. This is what life is meant to be. This is what life really is. This is the life that I live for. The tenderness and the trust.

How can it be? How can you say that? you ask. Nothing is creative in the surroundings, in the ugliness, in the listlessness. But in this there is something creative. The little family transfigures the whole scene. Everything else in it depends upon them. They are what make the world go round.

The good and evil in the world are sometimes likened to the black and white squares on the checkerboard. We cannot deny that the black and white squares are there. The question that each of us has to ask is this, "Are they white squares on a black board, or black squares on a white board?" You can see what I mean without my going any further into it. Is the black the basic thing? Is the evil, the meaninglessness, the ugliness, the basic thing? Or is the white, upon which splotches of evil, and ugliness, and meaninglessness have been thrown, the basic thing? Christianity says that the board is white. You can't prove it, but every once in a while you *see* something that tells you that it is so. That is what

I saw. It wasn't an argument; a theologian could never have convinced me if I had been skeptical at that moment that this is so, but I saw something and what I saw said to me, This is it! This is what makes the world go round. All the rest is secondary. Put your trust in this.

One thing more I said to myself. This is the way God speaks to men in the Bible, this is what the Bible means by revelation. In the Bible God speaks to people directly, in concrete events, in situations, in people, and in things. Things happen and this is what it means. This is a sample and this is why I am telling you all this, because it may illuminate the meaning of the revelation that God makes of Himself in the Bible.

This is what happened to Moses as he was taking care of his father-in-law's sheep. He had run away from home because he had gotten in trouble with his own people. He was forced almost against his will over into a strange part of the desert and suddenly he saw a bush that seemed almost on fire and yet it didn't burn. Just an ordinary bush, but Moses said, I will stop and look at this, "I will turn aside and see this great sight." And as he looked at it, he began to think: This is beyond me, this is mystery, this is holy; I will take off my shoes; this is God; this is the ground of existence; this is the meaning of life; I had better go back to my own place, and do the thing that I am called to do. This is God speaking to Moses out of the burning bush.

Isaiah went into the Temple. Everything in the political scene was collapsing and crashing to the ground. The King had died and everybody was distressed, thinking that the end of all things had come. Isaiah stopped to look at the Temple. He had seen it a thousand times and everybody else was seeing it along with him, but suddenly he saw something that was above and beyond the current scene, something that outlasted the political careers of the various monarchs, something that was above the mortal judgment of man, and God spoke to Isaiah in the crashing chorus of the seraphim and cherubim while he stood in the Temple. He saw also the Lord, high and lifted up.

Hundreds of other illustrations come to mind and there is a great temptation to give more but I shall not, simply this one which is the climax and the point of the whole sermon. Years later these same people, these people of the Temple, people from this background, people accustomed to this kind of revelation, stopped to look at a man die on a cross. They had seen hundreds of others, but this one was different. He didn't deserve to die. He died as he lived, outgoing, generous with love, love that no one had ever seen before and, when they stopped to look at him and to think about it, they said, This is it! This is the love of God. This is the thing that is at the heart of all this world of events that we don't understand. This is the thing that makes the world go round. The outpouring of a man's love took them off into the realms of the cosmic and they said, This is the love of God, taking the most ugly thing in the world and making it good. This is why there is a world, this is why you were made, why I was made. They took that one incident. They couldn't take their eyes off of it. It was a revelation to them of the meaning of every other thing in life.

How did they know? How did they know God was speaking to them in that event? How did I know that God was speaking to me in this particular little incident on the platform in the station? How do you know whether God is really speaking to you in incidents like these? Well, in one way you do not know *how* you know, and you could never tell anybody else. The only thing you can say is what the blind man said one time when people asked him how he knew that Jesus was good. He said, "One thing I know, that, whereas I was blind, now I see." Do you see? I hope you do.

Open our eyes, O God, to the heaven that lies about us wherein they walk who having been born to the new life serve thee with the clearer vision and the greater joy. Amen.

The Friend of Sinners

W E BEGIN AGAIN TODAY with the New Testament, with the story of one of the most dramatic dinner parties ever held. The circumstances which surround the party show very clearly that it was held almost two thousand years ago and yet the repercussions of it have continued to this very day. The host was a man named Simon. He was a pillar of the church. His conduct was impeccable. The guest of honor was a young man of Nazareth named Jesus, not yet very well known, but a teacher concerned chiefly with the coming of the Kingdom of God. There was, however, a rumor about him growing day by day that he was a "friend of sinners." It was about the worst thing that could have been said about him, comparable to saying in our time that a man is a "fellow-traveler."

At any rate, the guests gathered and the dinner was under way. Oriental houses were normally open to the street so that people who were not invited might come in and stand in back of the guests as they reclined at the table. On this occasion there was at least one uninvited guest. She was a woman not only from the street but "of the streets." She stood directly behind Jesus, apparently intending to anoint his feet with oil, which again was a custom perfectly familiar to people in those days. As she began to do it, before she scarcely had a chance to do it, her eyes filled with tears. She was overcome with emotion so that she ended by kneeling at the feet of Jesus, washing his feet with her tears and wiping them with her hair. The host was dumbfounded, not so much because the woman did it but because Jesus accepted it. The host was shocked because Jesus was not shocked!

After this extravagant act Jesus went on to say to the host, because he could read his mind and knew what was going on inside of that brain of his, "This woman has been far more gracious to me than you were, and I say to you that 'her sins, which were many, are forgiven, for she loved much.' " The rumor was confirmed. He was a friend of sinners! And the question that I think went round and round in the mind of good, respectable Simon (and if we could free ourselves from all our pretenses and prejudices would go through the minds of a great many people here) is this, Why would a man like Jesus befriend people like that? That is the question I want to look into with you today for reasons which may appear more obvious as we go on, and certainly at the conclusion of the sermon.

I

First of all, Jesus had a very different idea of sin than Simon did. Simon had the idea he was brought up on. It was the popular idea of the day and of his people and was altogether acceptable. It had the antiquity of the ages behind it, and it was as clear as daylight. It was something like this: there is a law. That law has been given to us by our father Moses. It was given to him by God, and in that law is revealed the will of God. Everybody knows what the law is. Hence, when a person breaks the law, his act is a sin and he himself is a sinner. You see, that is quite simple, and it is easy that way to reckon up on a balance sheet who is a sinner and who is not because you can tell what the score is, how many laws have been broken and how many have been obeyed.

In this particular case, of course, it was extremely simple for there were ten basic laws, the Ten Commandments. To them were added some six hundred or so other laws that interpreted the basic laws, but in this case we are concerned only with these ten basic laws, one of which happened to do with sexual behavior. For some reason or other, both in Judaism and in current Americanism, that law outranks all the others, both in the frequency of its violation and in the severity with which the offender is condemned. A man may break every other rule with impunity, but woe to the man that breaks that one! Here was a woman who had broken it, flaunted the breaking of it. Therefore, she was a sinner and as far as Simon was concerned, the case was closed. There was no room for argument; there was no doubt in the case whatsoever.

Now Jesus had an idea of sin that went much deeper than that. In the mind of Jesus, if we dare to paraphrase what was in that divine mind, sin was not primarily the violation of a law but the climate and disposition of a man's whole being, of which the breaking of a rule was only the sign and the symptom. It was not, therefore, so easy for Jesus to know exactly who was a sinner and who was not because it was something inside the person. You could not always tell by observing a person's external behavior whether he were a sinner or whether he were not.

He had known in his short life, just as you have, many people like Simon, upright people, pillars of the church, observers of all the rules, keepers of all the conventions, those who never transgressed any of the rules of society by so much as an iota, models of conformity, but who were wrapped up in themselves, proud of their achievements, censorious of other less fortunate people. He knew other people also like the woman who had broken some of the rules of society, who had not, for one reason or another, been able to keep within the patterns of conventional life and yet who were generous, kind-hearted, large in their outlooks, bountiful in their giving of life and love to all humanity. And Jesus, with that idea of sin, found those people often more responsive to God than the ones who were more morally correct! Jesus was a friend of sinners because he knew that you could not detect sin by looking at the outside of a man. He knew that the sinners around him were likely to be more humble before God than their proud, respectable neighbors. God had an infinitely better chance to penetrate the frail covering of the woman's sin than he had to make a dent in Simon's conventional goodness.

II

Furthermore, in pursuing this question we can put this down, that Jesus had a deeper understanding of human nature than Simon did. Simon was brought up, again quite simply and in the popular notion of the day, to think that sinners were wicked. Everybody, according to Simon and his father and mother and his teachers, everybody, so the teaching went, knew what the rules were. They knew what was expected of them. If they deliberately chose to break the rules and go out and defy the code of humanity and of God, they were sinners and they deserved to be punished. They were wicked. There was nothing more to be said.

Once again, Jesus' understanding of human nature went deeper than that. Here it is not possible, I think, to quote chapter and verse, and I should be the first one to warn anyone against trying to make Jesus into a modern psychologist, but I do think that the total picture of Jesus that we see in the Gospels is one whose understanding of human nature went deeper than that of Simon. In other words, Jesus knew that the ordinary man is not always deliberately wicked, whereas he is often desperately weak.

When he was accused, as he was over and over again by his enemies, that he was a friend of sinners, that he consorted with these people who were the outcasts of society, he said, Why, these people are sick and when a doctor comes, he goes to the sick people; he doesn't go to the well people. And may that not be a clue to Jesus' attitude toward a great many of the sinners that he had to do with, that in reality they were sick? He knew by instinct that the reason some of them did the things that they did was that their lives were so empty that they had to fill them up with interests that proved to be devilish. He probably knew that the woman before him had a history that was not completely revealed there at the dinner party. He had the wits and the discernment to see behind the woman's life and to wonder what kind of childhood she had, what man may have disappointed her, disillusioned her, and turned her in the direction in which she was walking. Why was it that she was behaving like this?

Jesus was not satisfied to look at sinners of this kind and say that they were wicked, for he knew that all too often some of them were not nearly so wicked as they were weak. They needed help, understanding, intelligent care. The psychiatrists have followed the path that Jesus opened. The best psychiatrists never judge a man until they know why he has done what he did. If a wife goes to one of them and says, My husband is a problem which I cannot cope with; he behaves in such a way as to make life miserable both for me and for him and I cannot stand it any longer, the good psychologist will begin to try to discover, if he can, by one way or another, what it is in the life of that man, either at home or in the office, which makes him behave that way. Perhaps his eccentricities are not appreciated at home. It may be that his comforts are ignored and all the little things that make a man feel secure at home neglected. It may be that he is behaving this way simply because nobody is understanding him or giving him the love that he needs. It may not be. Psychiatrists often go too far so that they relieve men and women of their obligations and moral responsibilities, I am willing to admit that. But what I am saying is, and I say this with all gratitude and congratulations to them, that by and large they are going in the right direction. They are in the direction of the Friend of Sinners. Understanding, not censure, is what a sinner needs.

III

Finally, Jesus had a different attitude toward this particular sinner, or any other sinner, than Simon did. We are not surprised to find that Simon wanted above everything else to get rid of the woman. She had broken the laws; he wanted to protect himself and his household and his society against the likes of her and he wanted to punish her in the bargain, and, I suppose, get some satisfaction for himself. (We will not go into that here: what kind of satisfaction we get by seeing people punished for doing the things that we might have liked to do ourselves!) But however that may be, Simon's attitude toward the woman was to want to get rid of her.

Jesus wanted to help her. I can imagine Jesus saying something like this to himself, This is not this woman's real self. Nobody when he is himself behaves this way, for the thing she is doing can never satisfy that which is deep in her and that which is best in her. It is only a last resort as a way out of an empty life that has no meaning. And to confirm him in that there were signs that the woman was being stirred, that something had been awakened in her by him. Hence, this outpouring of affection and penitence. She had heard from people that there was a man coming who was a friend of sinners, who understood them and did not censure. She had never heard of that before so she came prepared to give something of herself and she discovered when she came into the presence of Jesus that love was crowding out something that had been in her life before because something larger and greater and infinitely more satisfying was about to take the place of the baser thing.

Jesus saw that happening and it thrilled him. He wanted to give that new life that was beginning to come up from beneath every encouragement. He could not say for sure whether she would ever go back to her old life. Nobody ever can. But he knew that at the moment she saw something better and that buried down underneath all the filth of the years was that which is pure in the human soul; Jesus wanted to give that every chance and encouragement, and so he went out to her with all his understanding and love and affection and protectiveness, defending her against the rigidity and hypocrisy of Simon as though he wanted to say to her, Now, woman, here is your chance! Keep going, stay on this track! Your sins are forgiven! The past is over! Go on, go forward! Your faith has saved you!

Surely Jesus was not casual about moral weakness, but curative. No one could ever suppose he condoned what the woman had been doing if only because it led to so few fruits in life. What he was doing by his understanding was attempting to cure the life and change the pattern and lift it into something better.

Henry Commager, the great professor of history at Columbia, has written a new book called *The American Mind* which is filled with phrases which once you read you never will forget. And one of them comes in the chapter in which he is describing what happened to religion in this country in the nineteenth century, and this is one of the illuminating phrases: "Puritanism curdled into censoriousness." And it has. Our puritan tradition, fine as it is, has in more cases than we like to think curdled into censoriousness. There are too many Simons among us, right here in Christian congregations, with an attitude toward sin like a scoreboard in which they check up the rules broken or not broken, with an understanding of human nature that is so shallow that it is not worthy of any educated man, let alone a Christian. We need in our world, and I always hesitate to say that we need things because that is so easy to say, but I am saying this to you because I mean it right here, we need in our church, shall I say, less judging and more understanding, less berating and more befriending. We need people who see through the shallowness of Simon and have caught a glimpse of the glory of Jesus, the Friend of Sinners.

During the past week there has been in our papers an instance of the thing that I am talking about and I bring it to you in conclusion as dramatic an incident as the dinner party we began with. A young man twenty-nine years old, a veteran of the last world war, went up to a police officer in New York and said, "I have just murdered a woman," and he took the officer to the apartment where the woman's body was. He had been living with her for a month. He had a wife and a child in New England. They sent for his wife. When she went to New York to talk to her husband and to the authorities this is what she said: "He is a sick war veteran in need of hospital care. It was not his nature to live a life like that, and I shall stand by him to the end."

So, reverberating down the arches of the years come the words of Jesus that have cheered men's hearts and minds. "Her sins, which are many, are forgiven, for she loved much." Jesus, the Friend of Sinners.

Moderate us, O God, in our judgments of others; make us stop and think twice before we censure them without knowing the circumstances of their lives; fill us with the spirit of understanding that was in Jesus that in our Christian communities everywhere people will look upon us as those who understand more deeply than others do and find there the peace that comes to those whose sins have been forgiven. Amen.

A God to Pray To

❧

ONE OF THE THINGS that we know about Jesus beyond the shadow of a doubt is that he prayed. The record is unmistakable. At the beginning of his ministry, when crowds pursued him everywhere he went, it is written that after he had healed many of their infirmities he withdrew himself into the wilderness, and prayed. Not long after, when the forces of opposition had begun to gather, and he could feel the danger of their threatening power, it is written that he went up into a mountain to pray, and spent the whole night in prayer to God.

And again, on a day when he had been with the multitude, teaching them and feeding them, his energy spent, it is written that, while he was praying by himself, the disciples approached him. And finally on the last night, the darkest night of his life, he went into the Garden of Gethsemane, and it is written that he went off by himself and falling on his knees, prayed, "Father, take this cup away from me. Nevertheless, not my will but thine be done." The fact that he prayed is incontrovertible.

Before we go any further, however, we must try to answer a question that some of you, many of you perhaps, will almost certainly ask. You will say, the church teaches that Jesus is God. If prayer is an activity which involves both God and a man—how then could Jesus pray? Why did he pray? If Jesus was God, when he prayed was he not simply talking to himself, and does not this make a mockery of prayer?

There are two things to be said about that. The first is this, and I can say it quite dogmatically: the church has never said—never, that is, in the mainstream of its great tradition—that Jesus is God. The church has always said that Jesus is God *incarnate in a man*. His first followers called him the Son of God, not the Father, but the Son who has a unique rela-

278

tionship with the Father. They called him the Word of God, the Image of the invisible God. St. Paul said that God was *in him* reconciling the world unto himself, and the church has rediscovered this truth about him over and over again. When it came time to put all these insights into the nature of Jesus on paper so that they could be passed on to future generations, the Council of Chalcedon finally made the statement that Jesus is "perfect man and perfect God." It was wise enough not to try to explain the mystery, but to let it stand by itself, expressing as it did the inexplicable experience of those who were closest to him, that there was something about him before which they stood in awe and reverence as they fell down on their knees before the Almighty God, and that there was also something about him that was human, as human as you and I.

The second thing that I have to say in answer to your question is more particularly my own contribution. Not everyone would say the same thing. When you ask if Jesus was God how could he pray, you are beginning at the wrong end, and this is a bad habit to fall into, whether it has to do with questions like this or questions that are not religious at all. The place to begin is with the facts, not with the conclusions that have been drawn from the facts, or the theories that have been made about the facts. Knowing that Jesus *did* pray, and believing that God was in him, what does that reveal about man and God? That is the question.

Think of it this way. If you had been living in England in 1945, when George VI was still the king—one of the most beloved of all the British monarchs—if you had read in the paper that George VI was seen alone, unescorted and unguarded walking down the Strand, and that he went into Simpsons to have lunch at a table filled with other men who were lunching there, the question that you should have asked was not, If that man were king, how could he do such a thing? The proper question would have been, Knowing that he *did* such a thing, what kind of king do we have?

In other words, you begin with the fact, and the fact determines and illuminates the conclusion. We know that Jesus prayed. We know that in the crises of his life he had a book to go by—guidelines, the accumulated wisdom of the race, through which the word of God spoke to him in a unique authority; we know that he also had a few close, intimate friends to turn to. We also know that, in addition to these things, and surpassing them all, he had a God to pray to. Of all the resources of his inner life, this was undoubtedly the greatest.

This is the resource we all need. If I could speak with each one of you individually, I am almost certain you would say, This is what I want, this is what I need. Some of you have it, some of you do not have it at all, I am afraid, and none of you has it to the degree to which you would like to have it, and you feel in this particular area of your life an unusual kind of poverty, of undernourishment.

First, then, may we think about prayer in its broad, general character, before we begin to think of it in its more specific expression. When a man prays, he is responding to the presence of God. There are hundreds of definitions of prayer. Everyone, I suppose, who has ever prayed with any intensity at all, has tried to tell other people what it is. I have made my own definitions, accenting first one phase of prayer and then another, down through the years. None of them, of course, includes the whole of what prayer is but, as I thought about it this time, this is what kept coming to my mind: when a man prays, he is responding to the presence of God.

Now when a man comes into the room, and for the sake of our illustration we shall assume that he is a man of some stature, you respond to his presence. You do not simply sit there and do nothing. First, you rise out of respect, you greet him in one way or another, by shaking hands with him, by telling him how glad you are to see him. Then you may ask about himself, what he has been doing, how he is, about his family; you listen to him, you listen to him as he tells you about his life, and his world, and what he has been doing. You listen to him and you pay close attention to what he says. And then, if he is the kind of person that I have assumed, he will ask you about yourself, and you will tell him about the dark days as well as the bright, the difficulties that you may have had, the successes and the trials, and, as you tell him, he will listen. Then you may be in a position to ask him for something that you need, or tell him about the things you want most.

You will all, I think, agree with this, that if you ignore him completely when he comes into the room, it means one of two things: either you are not aware of his presence—you are deaf or dumb or both—or you are so preoccupied with what you are doing that you are not even conscious of the fact that he is in the room; or, you think that his presence is not worth noticing. Let him come and let him go.

You see to what this is leading, I am sure. It is so simple that you could talk about it to a child; but, of course, it is not so simple when you begin to do it. If God is present here, there, and everywhere, but especially in certain places where you feel that He is present, you respond to His presence, you do something, you stand up or, in the case of God, you are more likely to kneel, because you realize that you are a creature in the presence of the Creator, a derived object in the presence of Him from whom all life is derived, the maker of the sun and the stars. So you kneel in His presence. You greet Him. You say something which indicates your gladness and which expresses in feeble language what you may think about Him. Even though you may not always act as though you thought it, at your best you think it.

Then you listen to Him as he tells you about Himself and His plans for the world; what He has done, what He is doing, where He is at work particularly at the moment, what He wants you to do, and where. And then, you tell Him about yourself, about the things that are on your mind, the questions that perplex you, the responsibilities you are trying to carry, fearful that you haven't the energy necessary to carry them. And then, before you leave Him, you ask Him for the things you need. This is natural, the most natural thing in the world for a man to do, so that a man praying (and this I would say was true whether the man be a Christian or a Jew or a Mohammedan, any man who is sincerely praying) is a man in the presence of Someone other than himself, and the Someone is the One in whom he lives and moves and has his being.

Prayer is an acknowledgment of the presence, in the first place. It is also an indication of the man's own need. And that need (this is very important, and I know that some of you will not feel the truth of it at the moment but, if you don't, I hope you will when you think about it later on), that need is not for what the other person can give him, although we do need specific things and need them desperately; the primary need is not for what the other person can give, but rather for the other person himself.

"Yea, though I walk through the valley of the shadow of death, I will fear no evil." Why? Because there are no evils there? Not at all! Because Thou art with me. It is the person himself, who gives himself to the man who meets him, who acknowledges his presence, and who thereupon opens himself to his life.

Jesus, in his human situation, was always aware of the Father's presence, uniquely so. As I have said so many times, he was aware of it so intensely because no other man has been in the same relationship with the Father. He, therefore, did not have to seek God out as we sometimes deliberately do, coming into the church, or into our own room, where we can close the doors and shut out the noise of the world, in order to get into a position of quietness where we can be aware of God's presence. He was aware of it all the time, and he was also aware all the time of his dependence upon the Father. This runs like a thread through all the Gospels, especially the Fourth Gospel. "Of mine own self, I can do nothing. It is not I who speak, it is the One who sent me. I am here to do the will of him who sent me."

As he prayed, God gave him Himself, His life, His energy, His vitality, His love, and it was this that steadied him, not only in the crises of his life, when he needed it most, but all along through the ordinary ways of every quiet day.

We said a moment ago that if a man does not pray, it means either that he thinks God's presence is not worth noticing, or that he is not aware of it. Which group are you in? Perhaps some of you are in neither group. I hope so. I think not many are in the first group, not many here would dare to say, or even think, that they were well aware of the presence of God in the world but that they did not think that it was worth noticing. I do not believe there are many like that here. I think most of you would say honestly, the trouble with me is that I am not aware of the presence of God much of the time. There are too many things that make me immune to it, and I live in a world of so many responsibilities that I don't have time to be aware of God's presence. The bricks on the street cut me off from the earth and the tall buildings that go up to the sky shut out the stars, and these things which have always been an invitation to God's presence are largely absent from my life. I go along from day to day, aware of each day's pleasures, its needs, and its lengthening shadows; but that's about all.

I am sure many of you would say, I am not aware very often of God's presence; I beg blindly in prayer, because there come times when I need things desperately, and I have no other place to go but to my knees, but I do not often pray in the sense in which we have been thinking about it. Is there anything in Jesus' experience that can help me, help you?

For one thing, when you pray, try to think of God and not of yourself. Stop and ask yourself, the next time you say your prayers, Who, am I thinking of, myself, what I need, what I want? Stop. Think of God. How to think of Him? Think of Him as Father and, if you cannot because of some emotional block or some intellectual difficulty think of Him as your own father, think of him as the Father of our Lord Jesus Christ. You know him and you can think of God as his father.

A very intelligent and aware young man, just beginning to enter into the early years of his young manhood, was going to college. He lived with his aunt. She happened to be one of those rare, unusual people who knew God. She never talked much about Him, but no one could know her without being aware of His presence. The boy lived with her, for he was away from home. He adored her. As he plunged deeper and deeper into the things that every college student is exposed to, he said one time, with a wistful smile on his face, "You know, the God of the stars baffles me; I don't know what I think about Him. But I know Aunt Mary's God, and I love Him." Sometimes the only way that we can really come face to face with God is through another person, and never so clearly as through Jesus Christ, our Lord.

One other suggestion. Make your prayers brief, but frequent. Remember the Lord's Prayer in that original account of it in St. Luke's Gospel; remember how brief it is. It addresses God first with one word only, *Father*. Then there are two words of greeting, you might say. *May your name be hallowed.* May your name always be remembered and treated with respect. And may your kingdom come, your will be done.

And then three requests: for bread, the necessities of life; for forgiveness; and for protection in time of temptation. That is all.

To be sure, Jesus spent all night in prayer with God, and you too, may do the same thing sometimes, but at the stage at which most of you now are, I believe that you would do better to pray briefly and frequently, constantly reminding yourself of the presence of God everywhere, whether it be in a church like this that speaks to us of God, or in the drab streets of the city.

One final suggestion: Don't keep your eye on the results. That is fatal. Remember, prayer is not a method of persuasion; it is an act of devotion. All of you would probably say yes to that but I hear people talk about prayer all the time as though they thought of it as a means of persuasion. Consequently, prayer can often deteriorate into pressure and, when it does, it becomes blasphemous, the pressure of one man or one group of men on the Almighty! Remember this. Prayer is not telling God what you want, although you do this in prayer. It is not telling God what to do, and putting yourself in the way of receiving the strength he is willing and glad to give you to do it.

As you think about the resources of your own inner life, listen to this. "And when Jesus was at the place, he said to them, Pray that ye enter not into temptation. And he was withdrawn from them about a stone's cast, and kneeled down, and prayed, Saying, Father, if thou be willing, remove this cup from me: nevertheless not my will, but thine, be done. And there appeared an angel unto him from heaven, strengthening him."

Open our hearts and minds to thyself, O Father of all men. May we never be so preoccupied with other things that we are blind to thy presence. Give us the grace to know thee and to see thee, to reveal ourselves to thee and to accept from thee the things which thou art ready to give us, in the name of our Lord, thy Son, Jesus Christ. Amen.

The Water Levels of Life

N OT LONG AFTER I became the Rector of Trinity Church, the Senior Warden gave me a list of the Vestry committees and the names of the men who served on them. I remember that the first one, as you might imagine, was the Finance Committee. Then there was the Budget Committee, and the Buildings and Grounds Committee; there was a Music Committee at that time, and a Nominating Committee; another was called the Long-Range Planning Committee; there was a Committee on Ushering, and a Committee on Trinity Camp. Then, at the end of the list, there was the Committee in Charge of Water Levels.

I was on familiar ground until I got to that point. I had been the Rector of a church before I came to Boston, and I was familiar with all the committees but the last one. I said to one of the men, "What in the world is the Committee in Charge of Water Levels?" He explained it to me briefly. This is the Back Bay, he said. It was once a real bay, and where we now stand was water. In the nineteenth century, around the middle of it, the Bostonians had the imagination and the ingenuity to fill in the bay. It was an enormous undertaking. All the city around Trinity Church is made land and the water is only a few feet under the sidewalk.

Trinity Church was built in 1877 and it rests on 4,500 wooden piles. You know as well as I do that wood does not rot so long as it is kept in water. Once let the air get to it, and it is the end of the wood. The Committee in Charge of Water Levels, therefore, is responsible for seeing that the water is kept at a level high enough to protect the piles and keep them from rotting. In the cellar of the church there are wells. They look like manholes, and every week someone takes the reading of the water level.

There have been times when the water level has fallen. There have been times even since I have been the Rector that this has happened. When the I.B.M. Building was built across the street, for instance, the water had to be pumped out of the area so that the concrete barge upon which the building stands could be built, so the I.B.M. directors, by grace, pumped back into the foundations of Trinity Church the water that was needed to keep the water level high enough to protect the wooden piles. If the water level ever falls below a certain point and stays there, this building would fall to the ground. That is the sum and substance of it, and that is why the Committee in Charge of Water Levels is so important.

This, as you may guess, is by way of an allegory; not a parable, but an allegory. The wooden piles are the foundations upon which our society is built; hidden, but nevertheless without which we would have no society at all. You can see that, can't you? The water is the moral and spiritual environment which keeps the foundations from rotting. If the level of our moral and spiritual life falls below a certain point, the foundations of our society will begin to crumble and the structures that we have built, no matter how magnificent they may be, will eventually fall.

My question is, If we could take readings of these water levels—these water levels of our moral and spiritual life—what would they be? There is no possible way to do it, so your guess is as good as mine, but I have a feeling that the level is at the present moment too low for safety. Obviously my reading is based upon my own experience, and upon my limited observation and reading. I do not know enough people to make a dogmatic statement, but it seems to me that the water level is dangerously low.

Begin with our homes. What do you think about the water level there? They are long on freedom and short on discipline; long, as I have observed them, on standards of living and short on standards of value. They are long on independence and short on happiness. I am amazed, as I go to see people in their homes, how few are really happy homes. The people are often either bored or discontented with their lot, and some are so oppressed by the emptiness of life that there is nothing that gives them any sparkle at all. I know that there are many homes not like this, of course, and I see hundreds of them, but there are too many that are.

Our schools are long on technical training and short, by and large, on those basic disciplines which give a person not only an education but a character. Don't shrink from the word *character*. Whatever you want to call it, it is the stuff that a man is made of, and it is what makes him able to meet the situations which he has to face in life. Our schools, by and large, with many exceptions of course, are well prepared to give him an education which provides him with a certain amount of knowledge, but not those basic disciplines which help him build a mature character so that he can handle well whatever happens to him.

Our hospitals are sometimes long on scientific research but short on the human approach to the patient. Our business houses are long on promotion and public relations. They can create an image to their liking about almost anything, and I admire their cleverness in doing it. Too often, however, they are short on what we call integrity. They can create an image but they never ask very seriously what the image is about, or whether it is true, or whether it really represents what they are trying to sell. They are long on expense accounts and short on public service.

Industry is long on the rights of labor, short on the responsibility of labor to the public, and the privilege of labor to make something well. Perhaps I am biased about this, and perhaps it is because I do not see enough people, but it seems to me increasingly plain that there are fewer and fewer people in our country who rejoice in making something well just for the sake of making it. In other words, we are long on cleverness, but short on craftsmanship.

We must not exempt the church from our examination. What about the water levels of our churches? Again, of course, we can make only general statements, recognizing that there are hundreds of exceptions, but our churches, by and large, are long on organization and buildings and machinery, and short on vision and vitality.

Allowing for the exceptions, I wonder if you agree that this is a fair reading. You may not; I do not know. From your point of view you may think that it is too austere a reading, that it is not as bad as this. I hope it is not. I don't think that I see it as I do simply because I am a

287

minister, although of course I cannot step out of my skin and be someone else. But if it is anything like a fair reading, if you agree that while the water level may not be quite so low as I have made it out to be, nevertheless it is too low for comfort—if that is true, what can we do about it? How can we raise the water level?

I must tell you right in the beginning that I do not know how. I do not know the answer, but I know that you cannot do it the way we raise the water level of the church. When the water level goes down here we pump water into the basement. We cannot do the same thing to the foundations of society. I know that we cannot raise the level of our society by force. It cannot be done. I know from experience, if my own intelligence did not tell me, that you cannot *make* people decent and honest and concerned. You cannot dun people into goodness, you can only draw them.

Neither the church nor any other institution can put on a campaign to raise the moral and spiritual level of our society. I had a letter recently from a man who was complaining about the quality of entertainment on television and in the moving-picture houses, and he went on at length about the violence and cruelty and immorality to which thousands of young people are exposed, all of which I agree with. Although I never see them, I see the advertisements and it sounded as though he was probably right. He wanted me to start a campaign to bring pressure to bear on television and on Hollywood to stop these pictures. If the Roman Catholic Church, with all its power, has not been able to bring this to pass up to this point, there is not much chance that one Rector of Trinity Church, Boston, or in any other church, will do it. You never raise the level of people's inner lives that way. I know that.

But I know from history, and from my own experience, that a relatively few people can do a great deal indirectly, if not directly. I know my own temptation when I think about these things is to say, What can I do, only one person, to resist such a tide as this? I am helpless. When I stop to think about it, I know that I can do a great deal more than I am likely to think I can.

Never underestimate the power of a woman, someone once said. Never doubt the power of one determined, dedicated individual. One of the people whom I follow closely is a professor of history in Cambridge University, England. His name is Herbert Butterfield, and in one of his books written several years ago there is this paragraph. Let me tell you ahead of time, to avoid any misunderstanding, that he is a layman in the Methodist Church, and all of his writing must be read in the light of his deep Christian faith. Near the beginning of his book, *Christianity, Diplomacy and War*, he writes, "A comparatively small number of Communists, possessing initially no measurable degree of power, achieved in the thirty years after 1917 such a transformation of the globe as has rarely been equalled in magnitude or in thoroughness or in extent. They achieved far more than all the armies of the Kaiser and the Tsar, or the British and Austro-Hungarian Empires, and of the United States, put together. . . . All those people who are driven to pessimism and paralysis by the idea that nothing can be effected on this earth save by numbers and power, may take comfort, therefore, from this exhilarating example." And then comes this line, "Given the required intensity and intenseness, a comparatively few Christians could alter the course of history as powerfully as the Communists have done."

It is worth remembering, especially when you feel hopelessly outnumbered, that many of the great things in the world have been started by relatively few people. How many people came over on the *Mayflower*? Since this was one of the breeding grounds of the democratic experiment, it is worth knowing how many people were involved in that particular chapter of its story. There were about a hundred. And how many signed the Mayflower Compact? *Forty-one!*

I don't know whether any of you have had any experience with Alcoholics Anonymous. You must have heard about it; you may have been a member of it. That group has saved more individuals from hell than any other group that I know anything about. Do you know how it started? One man started it: Bill Wilson. One man! Of course there were many influences in his life, all converging together at one strategic point. But that does not alter the fact that one man started the movement that has saved thousands from alcoholic hell.

How many people started the Christian movement? A handful. You can almost count then on two hands. So when you are depressed by the magnitude of the undertaking in contrast with the microscopic forces marshalled to attack it, don't withdraw into a shell and say, I can't do anything because I am only one person, or there are only two or three of us. Where two or three are gathered together, anything can happen.

One final thing I know and that is that if the level of our moral and spiritual life is raised, it will be done by people who are not trying to do it. That may not make much sense to you at the moment, but if you stop to think about it you will see, I think, that the people who have often made the biggest dents on the world for good have invariably been engaged in doing something else. Most of the historians say that John Wesley saved England from a violent industrial revolution. He had no idea that he was doing it; he was drawing people to the Mercy Seat. St. Paul, historians say, changed the course of western Europe. He had no idea he was doing it. He was going up and down the civilized world preaching Christ crucified.

In the long run the people who lift the level of this world are the ones who have their eyes on something beyond the immediate thing in hand; they are not the reformers, they are not the do-gooders, almost never. They are the people who are lit by a light from another world, which shines without their knowing it, and they do, often quite unconsciously, something that changes the climate of the world they live in. Again, I quote Herbert Butterfield. "The profoundest effects on our civilization have been produced by people who were not thinking of affecting the course of human affairs at the mundane level; they have come as unanticipated by-products of lives that had really been intent on spiritual things."

One of my heroes is Louis Pasteur. In him were combined scientific genius and great spiritual depth. He said one time, "I wish every lecturer, on entering his class, asked himself in silent reflection, 'How can I today raise the minds and hearts of my students to a higher level?'" And he might have gone on to say, How can I do it without being either a prig or a prude? The only way that he could possibly do it is the way he did do it; that is, to be so steeped in the things that are good and true and beautiful that naturally, and without knowing it, he lifted the level of their lives.

What do you think about all this? I always tell the men in my preaching class at the theological school that sermons that end with questions are not good sermons. This is one of them. Its purpose has been to raise questions in your minds, and its hope is that you will make the right answers.

What do you think about all this? What do you think about the water level of your own life? What do you think your influence is on the lives of the people around you? Do you care whether our society stands or falls? Perhaps you don't. I think you do. Will you make yourself a committee of one to do something with yourself, so that wherever you go there may be a chance that the level of life is lifted, imperceptibly perhaps, but lifted, nonetheless?

Accept, O God, our concern for the world in which we live. Save us from self-righteousness and complacency. Take away all our pride and help us see ourselves as we really are, and then give us both the grace and the power to raise the level of our moral and spiritual way, that the good things we have built may stand secure. Amen.

Not One World, but Two

༝

"*And when he had sent the multitudes away, he went up into a mountain apart to pray: and when the evening was come, he was there alone.*"
St. Matthew 14:23

THE THEME of this sermon can be put in a single sentence: We live not in one world, but in two. And this is the text: "And when he had sent the multitudes away, he went up into a mountain apart to pray: and when the evening was come, he was there alone." In other words, the time came when Jesus deliberately separated himself from society, from both its demands and its delights, and chose the solitude and the silence of the mountains where he could be alone with God. His action, undoubtedly, was open to criticism then as it is certainly open to criticism now, and upon at least three grounds. Some people probably said then, as they would say now, From a human point of view, his action was unsympathetic. Here were people who craved his companionship and he deliberately deprived them of it for spiritual advantages which were personal and private. Some others might say that it was unhealthy from his own point of view. Having spent a long, arduous day with the crowds he would have done better to have gone home and had a good night's rest and restored his physical body. The most serious criticism would have come from those who said that his action was impractical and visionary. Jesus lived at a time when things were out of joint and there was much to be done. If he had any surplus time on his hands and any reserve energy, let him spend it down there with the people where he was needed. Think of the men and women he might have cured; think of the hearts he might have stirred and the consciences that he might have quickened; and the lives he might have changed if he had lingered there a little longer instead of separating himself and going apart into the mountain alone to pray.

Before we accept these criticisms, let us reconsider the action of Jesus in the light both of our own nature and our present predicament. First, our nature: We are built for two worlds. Look at yourself. It will be perfectly obvious certainly that you have a body which is built for this world of familiar material surroundings. You have lungs that are built for the air; you have eyes that are mysteriously and wondrously built for light, by which and through which you can perceive both things far away like the sky and things near like the stones and the grass under your feet; you have ears that are built for the sound waves by which you hear the thunder in the heavens and the voice of your loved ones; you have a digestive system that is built for food and all that means sustenance in life; you have limbs that are built for the globe and by which you can travel.

It is not so apparent to all people that we also have other things in our equipment which indicate that we are built also for another world. For instance, who is there in this church who has not at one time or another in his life looked at something that he has done and said to himself, That action is wrong from the ground up and I cannot rest until I right it. In other words, we have a conscience that is built not so much for earth or sky or sea, as it is for those invisible realities of the moral order. We have in varying degrees a desire for the truth. Clarence Darrow was a man who believed in no God and belonged to no church, but when he found a young man whom he believed to be unjustly convicted by a jury, he went to that man and said, I will give you my services free of charge, and he carried his case through court after court, giving hours of his time until finally he convinced the judge and jury that the man was innocent. There was a desire for truth in him as it is in us, something built not for these seats we are sitting upon so much as it is built for something that is written into the universe of spiritual values. We have loyalties that have no cash value whatever. We have far-reaching sympathies which outstrip time and space, and sometimes some of us make sacrifices for those we love that are founded on no rational basis, the food we eat, the house we live in, or the earth we travel. Not for one world, but for two are we built. That is the reason that Sir Thomas Browne was the first to describe a human being as an amphibious creature, and in our day Evelyn Underhill has put it in a very homely figure when she says, We all begin as tadpoles but we ought to end as frogs. At home in both elements, at home both on this wonderful earth and in the realm of the spirit. Not one world, but two.

I think it does not need very much elaboration to convince people that the great experiment of our time has been to try to live in one world. That experiment has been going on for several hundred years. There are good reasons for it. There have been great contributions from it. Men concentrated all their energy and their time and effort upon this material order of things and they plumbed it to its depths and scaled it to its heights and revealed such wonders as the heart and mind of man had not dared to dream of. But it has not all been good. What would you think, for instance, of a man who set about to build a house? He built it of the best material that money could buy; he had an architect who could arrange those materials in the most perfect form that man can achieve; he equipped it with everything modern and convenient; he furnished it with things that were not only comfortable but beautiful. Once it is built, he is so preoccupied by his industry downtown that he has not time to spend uptown in his home. No time to cultivate the relationships with his wife and children. He sends his children away to school if they interfere with his pleasures and luxuries, and divorces his wife if she fails to satisfy him. What kind of a home is that? And yet, is that not a parable of just about what we have been doing? Trying to build our home in one world, not two!

What would you think of a businessman who conducted his business on the sole principle that it was the profits that counted rather than the service which was rendered, who paid no heed to the people who worked for him or the people for whom he worked, and counted success in dollars and cents? A novel like *The Hucksters*, rough and crude as it is in spots, makes it perfectly apparent that that is what we have been doing in business. We have been doing it among the nations; we have built a heaven here for ourselves with the best buildings and all that makes life

294

pleasurable and delightful, and we do not care very much whether we make a hell for people in other countries.

That kind of a movement, that kind of an experiment, trying to live in one world when we are built in reality for two, has certain very definite tangible results which can be observed and tabulated. We see them when we find a man, for instance, who thinks that golf is more important than God. A man used to give one-tenth of his income and one-seventh of his time to the things that pertain to the spirit. Now according to the latest statistics, he gives practically none of his time and only a small fraction of his income. It is the boldest experiment of our time, to rewrite the experience of the ages until it reads, Not two worlds, but one world—this world, and you had better get as much out of it, have as good a time in it, as you can, because that is all there is, there isn't any more.

The folly of that experiment is revealed in all its terrible reality when we see and examine it in the light of Jesus. Jesus like us was built for two worlds and he lived fully in both. In the lines of Matthew's Gospel that I read as the text we get some indication of how he lived that two-fold life. He was greatly concerned with people. No one could read the Gospel and come away without knowing that there was a man who had a passion for the needs of mankind. You find him with crowds pressing around him so that he cannot tell who is touching him; you find him giving his time and his energy to teaching and instructing and healing and preaching, going about doing good, constantly, day after day. He was with the multitude. And then the time came when he sent them away and went apart into a mountain to pray. Most of us would not know what to do if we got there. But Jesus lived in a different age when, to be sure, it was easier, more natural, for him to do it than it is for us, and as we try to picture him there on the mountain in the solitude and the silence which were the gateways into the presence of God, we find him there feeding his spirit upon the things that last forever, getting his judgment lined up, getting his values straightened out, coming to the instinctive awareness that God is love, overcoming his doubts, wrestling with his temptations, strengthening all the moral and spiritual fibers of his being. So there is about the life of Jesus a wonderful rhythm like the rhythm of the tides. There is the great outgoing of the tide as it plunges out into the deeps. So he goes out into all the needs and cares of humanity. Then, just as surely, there is the incoming of the tide, as though it came in to rest upon all the seashores of the world, to regather its strength, and to recapture its power. So Jesus comes back from the multitude to the mountain, to rest, to pray, to think, to breathe deeply in the presence of God. Backward and forward, now engaged in all of the pressures of political and economic life and then completely separate and apart from those cares and tribulations. Mountains and multitudes —like two poles from which the life of Jesus was magnificently swung.

It is interesting to note that the single descriptive line in Matthew's Gospel comes like a link between two stories about Jesus. One is the story of the feeding of the five thousand, and the other one, coming after, is the story of the walking on the water. Whatever we may think about those stories as being literal transcripts of fact, which I for one do not believe them to be, they are, nevertheless, stories that could be circulated only of a man who had tremendous spiritual energy. He was the kind of man who with no matter how little equipment, only a few fish and a few loaves of bread, was able to meet the emergency. The kind of man who could go to his friend's rescue even though he had to walk on the water to do it. Whence comes such power? Is not the answer to that question found in the verse that links the two stories, "When he had sent the multitudes away, he went up into a mountain apart to pray."

When we think of the spiritual power of Jesus, it makes us only the more conscious of the greatest shortage of our time. The shortage of today, as we certainly know, is not a food shortage or a labor shortage, it is a simple shortage of spiritual energy, both the vision and the vitality to pursue the vision to the end. And the tragic spectacle of our time is the sight of giants in industry working and acting like pygmies in public affairs. In our homes, in our public offices, in our schools, in our churches even, everywhere we look, we see men who when they go to the cupboard to meet some great spiritual emergency find the cupboard is bare because they have put nothing in it for ever so long. Their loyalties do not stand up and their values do not ring true and their vitality is quickly and utterly exhausted.

What I want to say today is as simple as this. We can have the power when we recapture the rhythm. We can apply to the complicated problems of our day the same kind of spiritual energy, though to a less degree, that our Lord applied to the problems of his when we are willing to recapture that rhythm for which we are built. And I want to be the first to say that I know how difficult it is. We have neither the time nor the technique. Our lives have been so crowded with so many things that we have no time left to be alone or to be quiet. We are not like the shepherds in the agricultural days when they had all night with nothing to do but think about God. We have so many, many things to do that we do not do any of them very well. Our techniques are shabby because the church has been more thoughtful about its organizations and its properties and its fabrics than it has, I am afraid, of the inner lives and the awareness and the sensitiveness of the people. And so what are we going to do? We must make time for the things which are essential to life and we must develop those techniques without which we cannot live successfully in this world which is so much with us. That is our first task.

I am preaching on this theme, which is a familiar one to you and certainly has been preached on millions of times before, at the beginning of this season because I would like to set it before myself as well as before you as our goal during this year, as well as all the years to come. In this world that has lost its direction and lost its nerve and is bewilderingly trying to find some way out, we stand here in the church of God forever reminding people that we live not in one world, but in two. The church will then provide for them, as well and as diligently as it can, opportunities for solitude and for silence in which they can cultivate all those dormant capacities within them so that they may rise up with new spiritual energy and that they may go out from this place men and women who are giants in the spirit as well as in the industrial centers of our nation. That is the biggest contribution we can make. We cannot run the politics of the nation or the world, but we may be able to train some people in the stillness and quietness of life who can go out and inject into the political life of the world something that is good and great. Remember, then, this action of Jesus, so out of date, so jarring with our fast-keyed-up existence; "when he had sent the multitudes away, he went up into a mountain apart to pray: and when the evening was come, he was there alone." We are built not for one world, but for two. We have tried to live in one world only. The proud experiment has failed. We can recover the Power when we recapture the tidal rhythm of Jesus.

Help us to be still and know that thou art God. Give us both the will and the way to renew our spiritual resources, broaden our vision, and enlarge our concept of thy purpose for us so that we may grow daily, steadily, in spirit as well as in body, at home not only in this world of the flesh, but in the greater world of the Spirit. We ask this in the name of Jesus, our Lord. Amen.

When Things Do Not Go Well

❦

THE SERMON TODAY is about what you do at a crucial point in your life, namely, when things do *not* go well. When things are going well, when you are happy and healthy, successful and appreciated, you know what to do; you don't stop to think about it, though perhaps you should. But when they do *not* go well, or rather when they do not go the way you would like them to go, what do you do then? That is a crucial point in your life, and what you do then may be decisive for the rest of your life.

If you are a parent, what do you do when your daughter tells you that she is going to marry a man whom you don't like? You don't like him personally and, in your parental love and care, you don't think that he will make her a good husband. Or, when your daughter comes to you and tells you that she is going to divorce the husband she already has; or, when she comes and says to you that she is going to have a baby with no husband in sight—what do you do then?

What do you do when you lose your job and can't find another, and all the doors of life are suddenly closed, slammed in your face, shut tight? Or, when the doctor finds a lump and says that it must be removed *at once*? When someone who has been very close to you dies? When your son goes off to Vietnam with nothing but the call of duty? When someone you greatly love is mentally blank and there is no longer any communication at all between you and that person? What do you do then?

What you do then reveals the kind of person you are. Do you panic? Do you fold up in a state of paralysis? Do you withdraw from the situation in fear and trembling? Do you protest, and shake your fist in rage and say, Why does this happen to me? Or, do you pray? Do you do what the psalmist did who wrote, "When I was in trouble, I called on the Lord, and he heard me"? Or do you call up someone else and ask him to call upon the Lord?

These are all possibilities, but there is a more excellent way.

I

The first thing to do I have tried to do myself. I do not always succeed in doing it, but I try to do it, and I am convinced that it is right. The first thing to do is to sit down for a half hour and do nothing at all. Breathe deeply, until your body quiets down. You cannot sit absolutely still and do nothing; but you can sit still and do nothing if you think something. Say to yourself these four things, and if it would help you, you might have them written down.

1. There is nothing that can happen to me that has not happened to millions of others. Say to yourself, I am unique, I am a unique creature. There never before has been one like me and there never will be another. I am unique; but my trouble is not unique. To be sure, it comes to me in different ways, but it comes to everyone. In other words, you try to enter into the great company of people who have gone through similar valleys of trouble, and you shed once and for all the idea that you have been selected as a special target for life's worst blows.

If you have children and they are in a position to make you feel out of date, remember that Johann Sebastian Bach had two younger sons, and that they reached a point when they thought that their father was very old-fashioned. And, if you are a person who is depressed by the changes that you see going on in the world, and think to yourself, I belong to a different world; my world is gone, remember also that the same Johann Sebastian Bach preferred the clavichord to a new-fangled instrument called the "piano."

2. Then say this: I knew ahead of time that as a human being I ran the risk of something like this. One of the things that surprises me as I see people going through difficult times is that so many of them seem to be completely surprised that anything like this could happen. I try to say to them, Life means exposure to all sorts of things and, among other things,

it means exposure to all the four winds of misfortune. Those four winds blasting upon the lives of human beings come from the four corners of the earth: they are disappointment, disease, defeat, and death. And simply to be born means that you are exposed to each one of those four winds.

The winds do not often blow all the time, and they do not all blow at once. We can be thankful for that, but there is no shelter that will always protect you from them, no shelter at all, not even the crypt of the church. The crypt of this church has been designated as a fallout shelter in time of bombing, and perhaps there may be some degree of protection if we go there when the bombing starts. But for the kind of trouble that I am talking about, there is no protection, either in this part of the church or in the crypt.

Adverse winds are a part of life. To be sure, you can never be prepared for them, not in one sense. You are never ready for them; you are never waiting to welcome them, surely not if you are normal. But you can prepare yourself for the possibility that they may one day or another strike you.

3. Then go further and say to yourself, There are people who did their greatest work when they were blown by all four winds at once. John Keats, the English poet, is a perfect example. I have spoken about him a great many times this winter because it was in the early autumn that I read the Bate's Life, which is the great biography, written in 1963. Think now about John Keats as a young man and to what misfortunes he was exposed. When he was nine years old his father was killed; he fell from a horse. When he was ten his grandfather Jennings, his mother's father whom he adored, died. When he was fifteen, his mother died. When he was nineteen, his grandmother died. She was the last one to hold the family together and to provide a home. When he was twenty-two, his younger brother, George, married and left for these United States, and when he was twenty-three, his youngest brother, Tom, at the age of nineteen, died of tuberculosis.

Not long after Tom's death, John recognized symptoms of tuberculosis, his own fatal illness, in himself. At about the same time he fell desperately in love with Fanny Brawne, whom he could never marry because he didn't have the money and had nothing to look forward to but the prospect of almost certain death in the near future. At the same time his reputation among the literary people of the world was ruined by cruel reviews of his second book. Nevertheless, in two months in 1819, after all those things had happened, in two months he produced the five poems, including the great odes, which raised him to the highest ranks of English literature; and in six months of that year produced all the great poetry that he ever wrote.

Think of people like him and think how they were able to do great things when all the winds were against them. Think of William James, fascinating class after class of students by his lectures, brimming over with vitality, and at the end of every term saying that he was suffering from neurasthenia, that all his energy had been exhausted and that he was limp and could do no more.

If you are anything like myself, think of Pablo Casals, the veteran performer, the great musician, now having celebrated his ninetieth birthday, remember how he said, "Nerves and stage fright before playing have never left me throughout the whole of my career." But it did not stop him from playing. It may have helped him play more magnificently.

You may say, Well, to think of people like that depresses me. They are great and I am not. They can do it, but I can't. It is impossible. It simply makes me feel more inadequate than I did in the beginning. If thinking of people of that kind does do that to you, then I suppose the best thing is not to think about them, but I do not think it need do that. It doesn't do that to me, even though I recognize their superiority and the greatness which I know I do not have. When I try to enter into their lives and see what they do, I say to myself, "That he overwent; that also may I"—in some way, and to some degree. If he can do it so magnificently, then I can do it in my own small way.

4. The last thing you say to yourself is this: I do not know *how* I am going to handle this, but I know that I *can*. I know that from sources of which I am not conscious help will come, not necessarily the help I ask for, but help that I know nothing about will rise up in me, will appear suddenly from all sorts of unexpected places. If I wait quietly, that help will come. I do not know how it will come, I do not know how I am

going to handle it, but I know I can. I can do all things through Christ who strengtheneth me.

II

Then you are ready to pray. That is the next thing to do. Instead of praying *for* something, pray *about* it. In one sense, you have already been doing it. You have already been thinking about your situation in God's presence before you ask for anything. You have been draining off some of the bitterness in yourself. You have been looking at it not so much from the ground as from the sky. Things always look different from the side than they do from above and, if you can be quiet enough for a long enough time, you will begin to see the situation in which you find yourself and which you find so painful and threatening, not only from your point of view, which is naturally very important to you, but you will see it from another point of view, and it will look different.

Then ask God for what you want. If you want a job, ask Him for it. If you want help, ask Him for it. If you want to win some battle, perhaps some inner battle fought behind the closed doors of your life, ask Him to give you the victory. If you want to get out of a difficult situation, ask Him to help you get out of it. If you want your child to fall in love with a good Protestant, ask Him to move that child toward such a person.

And after you ask Him, then go to work on it yourself. If you want to be well, work with the forces of nature that will help to make you well. Don't work against them, let them work in you and with you. A clenched fist never produced anything but a blow. It is the open hand that is free to point to the unreachable stars, paint the unpaintable pictures, and heal the unhealable wounds.

If you want a job, go out and look for one. You probably will not find the one you are looking for, but if you don't look, you won't find any. They don't come looking for you until you go looking for them. If you want a friend, if you feel left alone in life, be a friend to someone. If you want to find the meaning of life (and a great many people now are saying that they do not see any meaning in life at all; this is one of our current moods, the meaninglessness of life), if you don't see any meaning and you want to find the meaning of life, begin to make some little corner of your life mean something.

You will not get what you want just for the asking. If you do nothing about it, nothing will happen. On the other hand, if you pray about it, you may get it, but you may not. You may get something even greater than what you asked for. You may get what I wish all of us could get, myself included, and that is a deeper rootage in things. One of the reasons why we are so likely to snap in heavy storms, the way trees do, is that our roots don't go deep enough. You may get a deeper rootage, and the deeper your rootage is, the greater your lifting power will be; that is, the deeper you go into the very nature of existence, the more realistic you are about life and suffering, joy and sorrow, death and defeat, the greater lifting power you will have when the time comes for you to raise some great burden that you would never choose, but which has been laid upon you.

I wonder if this is what Isaiah meant by "waiting "upon the Lord. I have never been absolutely sure what he meant, but I think that this may be partly what he meant when he wrote the famous lines in the fortieth chapter of his book. "They that wait upon the Lord shall renew their strength; they shall mount up with wings as eagles; they shall run, and not be weary, and they shall walk, and not faint."

When things do not go well, wait upon the Lord. Sit down. Stop fussing. Let the engine idle. Say those four things to yourself, say other things to yourself, so that you begin to see things from above; and then talk about it to the Lord. As you have waited upon Him, you are more than likely to find that you will not only have the strength to run but to walk, step by step, day by day, and not faint.

O God, when we move through the valley of suffering, sorrow and disappointment, help us to be quiet, to trust in the goodness of thy being and love; to wait upon thee; to do nothing quickly, rashly; and then to go forward, believing that all things will work together for good to those who love thee and try to do thy will. We ask this in the name of him who when things did not go well for him, thought about it, asked that the cup might be taken from him, and then said, thy will, not mine be done. Amen.

On Being Raised with Christ

🎜

"I F YE THEN BE RISEN with Christ, seek those things which are above, where Christ sitteth on the right hand of God" (Colossians 3:1).

You have heard that sentence every single year of your life if you have been at one of the Communion Services on Easter Day. I often wonder what it means to you when you hear it. I was only a little boy when I heard it for the first time. I was at the first Easter Service at six o'clock in the morning, with my mother and father. At that time, it didn't mean anything to me. In the first place, it was too short to make an impression. It is one of the shortest passages appointed to be read as the Epistle in the Prayer Book—four verses of Scripture, a single paragraph from a letter to people I didn't know, and had never heard of, the Colossians.

But strangely enough, even though the words didn't mean anything to me, I remembered them. I remembered them even more vividly than I did the words of the Gospel. My memory has never been good, but I can say those words in the middle of the night at any time—"If ye then be risen with Christ, seek those things which are above, where Christ sitteth on the right hand of God"—and I hear them as I heard them at the early morning service on those Easters when I was in church with my mother and father. I never heard them at any other time, and I imagine that the setting had something to do with it. The church was filled with flowers, the music was beautiful; it was a victory celebration, and I was aware of the fact that it was an important occasion. These first words of Scripture that were read in the service stayed in my mind.

Later I began to ask two questions about them. The first is, How can I be risen with Christ while I am still alive? Christ rose from the dead.

305

How can I be raised with him if I am not yet dead? The second question was, What are the things we are supposed to seek, and how can I ever hope to find them if they are so far above me as the heavens? "Seek those things which are *above*, where Christ sitteth on the right hand of God." How can I be risen with Christ while I am still alive, and what are the things that I am supposed to seek?

The answer to both questions begins with the understanding that St. Paul is using words figuratively, not literally. This is an old story to many of you; you do the same thing all the time. When you see someone who does a difficult thing and does it well, you say, He *rose* to the occasion. You are not suggesting that his feet left the ground. You are not making any reference to the level of his position, high or low. When a person is running on one cylinder, when he is limp, you sometimes say that he is more *dead* than alive. You are not implying that he is dead and buried, that he is a corpse walking about. You are simply using language in a figurative sense to say that he is dead on his feet. He is not taking things in, he is not functioning on all cylinders.

You also say about a man who refuses a shady proposition, He is *above* that; and if you see someone who is ecstatically happy, as you do once in a while even in this dark and gloomy world, you say, He is on *top* of the world. In neither case are you making any reference to the geographical location of the person, or to the level of his altitude. You are talking about things that are inside him, but you are using words that ordinarily describe things that are outside him.

Also, when you see a boy who is helpful to his father, as boys sometimes are even in this day and generation, you might say, He is his father's *right-hand* man, and you would be surprised if anyone thought you were talking about his father's own right hand.

What we do all the time the writers of the Bible did constantly. They used words in a figurative sense. When Isaiah was in the Temple in the year that the king died after a long reign, and people thought that everything had come to an end, he said, "I saw also the Lord sitting upon a throne, high and lifted up, and his train filled the temple." He would have been dumbfounded if anyone had come to him and said, Can you paint a picture of that? Will you tell me exactly what you saw? He didn't see anything with his eyes. He saw something with his imagination, his insight, and his intelligence. He "saw" the roof raised from the Temple, and in his imaginative mind he "saw" the fact that though the king was dead, the King of Kings was alive. Paul used language in the selfsame way.

This is a very elementary lesson and you might think that everyone had learned it by now, but they have not. I meet people again and again, people just as intelligent as you, who have not learned it, and when they come across passages like these in the Bible, they are absolutely misled because they have not learned that simple fact. Once you do learn it, you can see how you can be risen with Christ while you are still alive.

You can think of other experiences which point to the fact that there are people who raise other people to a different level. This is one of the most exciting things in human experience. Going back to the eighteenth century, there was Edmund Burke, British orator, writer, and statesman. Someone once wrote about him, "If one stood under a doorway to escape a passing shower with Edmund Burke, one went away with one's shoulders thrown back, with heart uplifted to face the realities and battles of life." You have known people like that. They may not be famous at all. Sometimes they are people who will never be heard of in the world, but when you are going through one of the passing showers of life you happen to meet them, and when you leave them you have been raised to a new level, and you can throw your shoulders back and face the realities and battles of life.

Coming to our own century, there was Alfred North Whitehead, one of the most extraordinary men of our time. Someone said that his life was written in three volumes: the first, Cambridge, England; the second, London; and the third, Cambridge, Massachusetts. All of us who live here praise God that his life did not end before the third volume was written. He came here to teach philosophy at Harvard. He was already an old man, but that third chapter of his life was one of the richest ones. A man, once a student of his, wrote that instead of allowing a student twenty minutes for a conference, he often gave him a whole afternoon or a whole evening. And then he added this revealing line: "From that inspiration a man comes back with a changed tone." Whitehead was a man, completely in the context of our human life, who could raise other human beings to a higher level.

Experiences like these are not entirely separated from Christ, not from Christ as I think of him, for every sign of vitality that has lifting power has only one source, Christ. But there are times when you are more explicitly aware of this than other times. Some things in your life stand out with a vividness that other things do not, and one of those things in my life happened to me the first year I was Rector of this church. After Easter I went to Nantucket. I did not go for the quietness of the island; I did not go to rest; I went to see someone. I went to see Dr. Will Gardner. I had never met him. He had been on the staff of this church for many years. He retired just before I came; I heard about him everywhere I went, and I wanted to see him. I was glad to be here, but the task was often bewildering and sometimes overwhelming. There were many things I didn't know. I knew the parish had a great history, but I was not quite sure what the future would be, and I thought to myself, I will go and see Dr. Will Gardner.

I cannot describe the impression that he made upon me. Some of you knew him and remember him well, and will understand what I mean when I say that he wasn't anything like Jesus, in one way. There was nothing Hebraic about him; he was a Yankee to the core. He had a wife and loved his home; he was old, with beautiful white hair. He had the gentleness, the kindness that we associate with Jesus, and people who didn't know him might think that he was too gentle and too kind. But if you did know him well, you knew that if you should try to purchase him for an unworthy purpose, you would be scorched by that same righteous indignation that was in Jesus. He was one of Christ's Men. I came back to Boston with "a changed tone"; everything looked different. I had been raised to a different level.

Now you may ask, It is all very well to see Christ in other people, but do we never see the Christ directly? I do. My experience may not be like yours, and there is no reason why it should be; and you must not feel guilty if it isn't because we are all different and we all respond to different things in different ways. I see Christ most vividly, the risen Christ, at the end of the Good Friday Service, even more than I do on Easter.

Easter says what I already know, and tells what has already been done. When you come to the end of the Three Hours, and have gone through the shame, and the pain, the humiliation and the sin, the suffering and the death, when you have gone all through that, there he stands in his regal simplicity, alone; beside him everything else fades away, and he claims the allegiance and love of the whole world.

There is a hymn written about 600 A.D. which puts in words what many feel on Good Friday but have never been able to express.

> The royal banners forward go,
> The cross shines forth in mystic glow,
> Where he, the Life, did death endure,
> And by that death did life procure.
>
> O Tree of grace, the conquering sign,
> Which doth in royal purple shine,
> Gone is thy shame: for lo, each bough
> Proclaims the Prince of Glory now.

When that happens, for the time being at least, you have been raised to another level of existence. At least for the time being the clouds of life that can be so thick and so frightening are below you instead of around you or on top of you, and you come away with "a changed tone."

That experience suggests the answer to the second question. Seek those things which are above—what things? Certainly not heavenly things as opposed to earthly things. Through the ages people have been misled about that. In the letter St. Paul goes on to say, "Set your affection on things above, not on things on the earth." Certainly, St. Paul could not have meant that I am to shun every material thing, everything in which the beauty and goodness of God is made manifest. Certainly, he could not have meant that I am to shun every human relationship without which life to me would not be worth living, shun it simply because it is an earthly relationship and not a heavenly one. Certainly, he could not have meant that I am to shun every silver dollar because it is money, and money is evil; or that I must shun every work of art and every feat of engineering genius, every flower, star, and stone. He could not have meant that. In Romans twelve and thirteen he makes it plain that he did not mean that.

What it means to me is that once you have been raised to a new level, your aim is different. In place of the word *seek*, the word *aim* may help you to see more clearly what it means. Your aim is different. You do not aim at the same things you aimed at before, or you do not aim at the same things in the same way.

For example, you do not aim at money as you did before. It is not because money is inherently evil, because it isn't; but you do not aim at it as an end in itself. When it becomes an end, it swallows you up, as it has swallowed up thousands of American human beings now who would do anything for a dollar. You aim at money, but you aim at it in a different way. You aim at it as a means to an end, the means to do things for yourself and for your family and for other people; if you do not have it, you let it go; unless you can get it without stealing it, without prostituting the newspaper you work for, or the advertising company you serve, or any of the other agencies in which you are engaged, you go without it.

You do not aim at happiness as you did before. That may sound strange to you because happiness is a good thing, and we want everyone to be happy if he can be; but we cannot be happy all the time in life, and the sooner we find it out, the better. And happiness is one of those things which by seeking we will never find. At the new level of our life we do not aim at happiness as we once did. Albert Camus in one of his journals suggested how the aim shifts. When he was only twenty-three, he said, "What I want now is not happiness, but awareness." At my best, I want that. I cannot be happy all the time, and I don't expect to be, but I would like to be more aware of more things and of more people, be more sensitive to what is going on around me, than I was before I had been raised to that new level of existence.

You do not aim at pleasing everyone the way you may have done before. This is one of the temptations that comes to every person in a position like mine; to every political leader, to everyone who is at the head of any institution. It is the beguiling temptation to please everyone.

Once you have been raised up to the new level, you do not aim at that. You aim at the courage to be yourself, not the self that *you* would like to be, but the self that you think *God* wants you to be, and you aim to be yourself without deliberately hurting anyone else. You would rather *be hurt* than hurt.

Also, more and more as you live on this level (and I am not suggesting that you live on it constantly because you do not; I don't and I don't imagine you do), you do not aim as you once did to be free of life's handicaps. There are times when you would like to shake them all off, all your physical liabilities, all the things which make life difficult for you, all the inconveniences in your work, all the opposition that you have to face, all the decisions you have to make. But you change your aim. You do not aim to be free of life's handicaps; you aim to handle them well, to meet them as well as you can when they come. A man with a temper knows that he will probably never be free of that handicap, but he aims to handle it well, and when he cannot prevent it from burning some innocent person, he has the grace to apologize. That is the best he can do. A woman with a memory failing as she grows older knows that she cannot be free of that handicap. She is not embarrassed about it, and when she is talking to you and cannot remember a name or a date or a fact, she laughs and says, "Oh, I can't remember anything any more!" That is what I mean by changing your aim, and when you change your aim, you yourself are changed.

One thing you must remember. The first verb in the sentence is passive. The correct translation is, If you have *been* raised with Christ. You cannot do it yourself. It is something that is done to you. All you can do is to put yourself in a position to be exposed to the lifting power. The second verb is active: *Seek.* That is something that you do; you must work on it. The tone will be changed, raised to a higher pitch; but to keep it from dropping, you will have to keep working on it. Begin the day by asking yourself the question, What was the tone of my life yesterday? If it was the C minor of despair and defeat and dejection, then say to yourself, The best thing for me to do today is to stand under the doorway with Jesus while these showers pass and let him change my tone to the D major of resurrection.

O God, let our hearts and minds be open to the truth and above all to the spirit of Jesus, that his life may renew our lives, and his way be more and more our way. When the clouds are thick and everything in life looks dark, help us to withdraw with him during the passing shower and be raised with him to a new being. Amen.

The Man Who Came by Night

☙

Nicodemus was a conservative Jew of considerable prominence. Seventy-one men sat on what we would call the Supreme Court of Jerusalem. It was the Sanhedrin. Its function was both legislative and judicial, and it heard both civil and religious cases. Its influence in local affairs was enormous, even during the hundred years of the Roman occupation. Nicodemus was one of those men. In other words, he was a Pillar of the Establishment.

He had heard, probably from his colleagues, about a young man up in Galilee; that he was a dangerous, radical sort of person and a possible troublemaker. He also heard that he did wonderful things for people in trouble, and that whenever he spoke, the crowds listened to him. To the credit of Nicodemus be it said that he wanted to see for himself. In other words, he was a conservative with an open mind. There are conservatives and liberals whose minds are like airtight compartments, but thank God there are also conservatives and liberals who have open minds. And Nicodemus was one of the conservatives whose mind was open; before he made a final judgment he wanted to see for himself, and he did not automatically exclude the possibility that he and his colleagues might be wrong.

The man from Galilee was in town, so Nicodemus went to see him, at night. Why did he go at night? Why didn't he go honestly in the daylight? Obviously, he didn't want to be seen by his colleagues in the company of Jesus. He was something like the man who visits a friend on the shady side of the street, but goes in by the back door.

There is something to be said for caution at this point. This was, after all, only an exploratory visit; he wanted to see for himself the man about whom he had heard so many things before he made any commitment to him, or before anyone else seeing him with him could spread the rumor that he was already committed to him. Jesus was a controversial figure, not only religiously but politically, and a certain amount of caution was in order, especially when it came to a person in the position that Nicodemus held. There is nothing new about "guilt by association."

This much can be said in favor of Nicodemus: he had the courage to meet Jesus face to face; he did not stand on the edge of the crowd so far away that he couldn't really see the look in his eye, or catch the tone of his voice. He made the move, and went to see him.

He was not only a conservative by nature; he was also courteous, and began the interview with a compliment. He said, Rabbi, we know that you are a teacher sent from God; no one could do the things which you have done if he weren't. It is interesting, by way of observation, that he did not ask any questions. He wasn't like the young man in the Synoptic Gospels who ran to Jesus and asked, What must I do that I'm not doing? He didn't open any such door as that; he just made a perfectly courteous, conventional approach to a controversial person. He was not flattering Jesus; he was showing him the courtesy of good manners. This is the approach of an open-minded conservative; reasonable, not fanatical; courteous, but cautious. It makes you think of a man paddling around in the shallow water at the beach to see whether the water is warm enough for him to make the plunge.

Jesus, on the other hand, wasted no time with formalities; he went straight to the point. He began to talk at once about the necessity of rebirth. The gist of what he said, if we dare to paraphrase it in the language that we speak today, is something like this: Nicodemus, if you're interested in what I am doing, if you're really interested, you might as well know from the very beginning that you've got to start from scratch. You can't inch your way into it. You can't make a few alterations here and there. You can't do it by making minor repairs or even major ones. You can't do it by amendments to the constitution. It must be a completely reconstructed life. You must be born again.

Nicodemus, like the woman at the well, took in a literal sense the words that Jesus used in a figurative sense. Nicodemus asked, How can a man be born when he is old? How can he go through that physical process again? And this is the place to point out a fact about the method of St. John in his Gospel. Nicodemus wasn't stupid; he wasn't as stupid as that. It is conceivable that the woman at the well might have been rather obtuse, but Nicodemus wasn't stupid enough to ask a question like that. His misunderstanding, as it is all through the dialogues in the Fourth Gospel, is a device which St. John uses to develop the theme, to get it moving along its way. Yet before we move on, we must remember that there are many who do just what Nicodemus did.

Many people in this congregation, for example, as I put the bread in their hand at the communion rail and say, "The body of our Lord Jesus Christ which was given for thee," later ask, How can that little piece of bread be the body of a person who lived two thousand years ago? And when they say in the creed, "I believe in Jesus Christ his only Son, our Lord," they ask, How can God have a Son? They are not stupid people, but they often fail to see that the literal meaning of a word is not always its only meaning. So, we are not too far removed from Nicodemus, not even the brightest among us.

Jesus went on to describe the kind of rebirth he meant. First, it was a birth by *water*, and it is reasonable to assume that he had in back of his mind the baptism of John the Baptist. It was a movement that everybody knew about and Nicodemus must have heard about it. It was a clean start, beginning with a frank recognition of mistakes made in the past, an open acknowledgment of them; and being washed in the River Jordan, muddy as it was, by the waters of forgiveness and starting a new life with a clean slate. A great many people do start that way. They see that they have made a mess of things; they acknowledge it, and they are given strength to begin again. They turn over a new leaf.

It was also a birth by *spirit*. You must be born of water and of the Spirit, Jesus said. In other words, it is something that happens to a person when something "comes over him." Nothing that he can see, nothing that he can predict, nothing that he can analyze or explain, at least not at the time. It just happens; suddenly he is a different man, a new person.

With his feeling for the beauty and imagery of poetry, Jesus said that it was like the wind. (Incidentally, the word in Greek for *wind* is the same as the word for *spirit*.) It's like the wind, he said, this new life. You know what the wind is; you hear it, you see what it does, but you don't see the wind itself. You don't know where it comes from, you don't know where it goes. This birth of the spirit is something like that. It is not a physical thing; it isn't repeating once again the physical process of birth; it's something that happens in a different realm.

Sometimes as another person observes it from the sidelines, it is not quite so invisible. Sometimes it is the result of another human being. Elizabeth Barrett was a famous poet, forty years old, an invalid since she was fifteen, living in a dark room. Suddenly, she got married, had a son, and began a new life. There is no secret as to what caused it. Robert Browning walked into her room!

Sometimes it is a book. An Anglican monk got hold of *The Phenomenon of Man* when Teilhard de Chardin first wrote it, and he said that once in a lifetime there is a book that shifts the ground you stand upon to such a slight degree that it changes your attitude toward everything; nothing ever again looks the same. And such a book was *The Phenomenon of Man* for that monk.

Sometimes it is an event. A young man was an alcoholic for a long time. Everything was done that could possibly be done; he tried, his wife tried, his family tried, without any success whatsoever. He was brilliant. His employers tried, they made every allowance. Then one day, because he lived in a state that did not take this sort of thing lightly, he was arrested for driving under the influence of liquor and was put in jail for six weeks. We all thought that that might be the end of him. He never has taken a drink since. It was years ago; he was reborn.

Whatever it is, one thing is certain about this rebirth: it is not contrived; it is not planned. It is nothing that you can set out to do. It is, in the words of the Bible, "from above," whatever that means. But you know what it means. It means something that happens to you; something that gets hold of you and does something to you; it is not the result of anything that you yourself do; it comes when you're not looking, from a source you cannot locate.

Then Nicodemus asked one of those stupid questions which I am sure was for the purpose of the dialogue. He said, How can these things be? Jesus was surprised. He said, I'm surprised at you, Nicodemus, that a man of your standing in the nation, of your intelligence and training should ask that question. This is a familiar sight in everyday life. I have used familiar words to describe it—birth, water, wind—all things that you know and see.

Jesus then went on to speak of things that Nicodemus might not be expected to understand. He then went down deep, or up high—whichever you prefer—to say what God did to make this new life possible. At that point Nicodemus dropped completely out of sight. The dialogue continues as a monologue by John, whom the spirit of Jesus uses as a mouthpiece. And John is speaking out of the depths of his own experience, else what is said makes no sense whatsoever.

He plunges right into the heart of the subject and says, "God so loved the world, that he gave his only Son to the end that all who believe in him should not die, but have everlasting life" (John 3:16). It is not customary for us to cite the chapter and verse of a key passage like that, but I shall never forget Henry Sloane Coffin toward the end of his life, when he was deploring the way the New Testament was being ripped apart by the new theologians and biblical critics. He raised his voice to its inimitable and piercing level and said, "Pretty soon everything will be gone; John 3:16, and all the rest, will be gone!" I didn't have any idea what John 3:16 was until I looked it up! It is the jewel for which the rest of the dialogue is merely the setting.

Remember that to the woman at the well Jesus said, *God is spirit*. To Nicodemus he says, *God loved the world and gave his Son*. The first is a statement about the nature of God; the second is a statement about the action of God. Both are important, but the second is more important; even in our earthly framework it is the second that makes the real difference. It is important to know that a man is good, but to know that a man is so good that he gave up his temporary pleasures for the sake of his family is more important. It is good to know that a man is a good ballplayer, but it is more important to know that at one particular point he gave up the game to save his son's life. To know that God is spirit is important; let no one ever underestimate it and try to put him in a box, or a building, or a system of thought. But to know that God loved so much that he gave Himself to save men from a living death, that is quite a different thing.

How in the world could John say a thing like that about God? How could anybody know anything like that about God? It is an obvious answer that comes to my mind, but I think it is the real answer. John could say it because he had seen it happen; it had happened to him. He saw Jesus live: it was no ordinary life. He saw Jesus die: it was no ordinary death. It did something to him; he felt in that death something that was deep in the nature of things: the desire, the will, to give, to spend, not for gain but for love. And this love, rooted in the common ground of earth, the earth of Calvary, that skull-shaped hill, set against the background of the sky in all its infinite implications, this love, for John, was the center of everything.

He came to see that God's nature is not only to be but to give, to love; and that man finds his life not only in existing from day to day—though thousands of people are trying to do that—not existing from day to day, but in responding to that love like an echo. You know how you call in a certain place and the call comes back from the rocks opposite you. That is the echo; it is the response that John makes, that you and I try feebly to make, to that kind of love. By trusting that love, by believing what we cannot prove. The consequence is new life; it is not "everlasting life." It is not life that goes on for ever and ever. It is "eternal life," and you know or feel the difference. It is difficut to put into words. It's life with a different quality. You know the difference between everlasting music, don't you?—it goes on and on and on until you almost go crazy—and eternal music that has something about it that is the very essence of all things. That was the life John had found.

He went on to say that whatever may be the final judgment on a man's life he brings upon himself. His judgment will be the response he makes to the light that he has seen. It may be the light of a Fact, which requires him to change all of his former assumptions. It may be the light of his conscience. It may be the light of the cross. Whatever the light may be, his response to it will be his judgment. If he withdraws from it, if he turns his back and runs away from it—denies the facts, drugs his conscience—he is lost. If he is drawn toward it, he finds life. But that is the subject of another sermon!

What happened to Nicodemus? Once in the Temple, later, Jesus was the center of an accusing multitude. Most of them were Pharisees as Nicodemus was. They were all condemning him and criticizing the police because they were so impressed by him that they didn't arrest him. One man stood up and said, "Does our law pass judgment on a man until we have first given him a hearing?" That man was Nicodemus, one sane voice in an ill-tempered crowd. The crowd dispersed.

And at the very end, Joseph of Arimethea, another Pharisee, asked permission to take the body of Jesus and give it decent burial. Nicodemus joined him. So there he is: Nicodemus, the sympathetic observer, the man who stood on the sidelines, the man who had the courage to go and see for himself, the man who did more than most of his colleagues; but for one reason or another never made the plunge. Do you see anything like yourself in Nicodemus? I do.

We thank thee, O God, for the people with open minds, who have been willing to listen, and see, and take risks. In our own time there are so many questions that we cannot answer, so many moves that we hardly know which one to make. Give us the open-mindedness, the willingness to listen; and then, if it be thy will, give us the courage and the grace to make the plunge. Amen.

Trust in Spite of Everything

"Though he slay me, yet will I trust in him." Job 13:15

THIS SERMON is addressed especially to troubled Christians who are asking themselves, either secretly or openly, the question: In a world like this, can we keep on trusting God? Such people have a natural inclination to trust God. Normally, they have begun life with a deep basic trust in the goodness, the rationality, and the dependability of God. They recognize very quickly that a man or a woman with a trust like that has a stability and also a serenity about his life that other people do not have. He is like a man driving in an automobile who has implicit trust in the driver. He need not worry about the traffic; he can enjoy the landscape. So a man who trusts in God need not be harassed by ultimate fears and doubts. He is not easily upset by defeat; he is not distracted by the worries and anxieties that lead other people off the track. We want that kind of trust, but some of us sometimes feel like a person who, when he sets out to sea, trusts the captain implicitly, but after the storm has raged so long, he begins to say to himself, How long can I trust the captain? He is at the mercy of the storm, the ship is sinking, and my child is overboard. Can I keep on trusting?

A great many serious-minded and thoughtful Christians are going through that dilemma right now. It seems as though our God is Himself at the mercy of impersonal drives and forces, that the ship of state and civilization is sinking and our children, our precious values and those things we love most, are overboard. In the face of those facts, how long can we keep on trusting God?

When we are in a mood like that, and I take it that all of us are at some time or other, we need to remember that there was once a man who kept on trusting God in spite of everything; who, when everything seemed to be against him, could say, "Though he slay me, yet will I trust in him." He is not the only one who has had that kind of trust in spite of everything, no matter what. Men and women in every generation have had that kind of trust. We want that trust. Our question is, Can we have it, honestly, realistically, without fooling ourselves? Is it perhaps only the nonsense of a stubborn man who refuses to face facts, or is it, perhaps, the seasoned wisdom of a man who knows God? This sermon is an attempt to set before you four considerations which may be foundations for that kind of trust. They are not geometrically or scientifically proven, for this kind of trust is not subject to that kind of reason. They are suggestions, intimations which, may I say, I have tried to work out myself as I ask the question that I set before you at the beginning of the sermon.

To begin with, things in the world are coming out just about as we expected they would. For example, the world, or at least a large part of it, is in economic chaos. That chaos is most explicitly observed in the economic disaster of Great Britain. That is exactly what perceiving people expected would happen. When the war first began, one prophetic soul made a statement something like this, To win the war is one thing, but whether or not the Western world will ever be able to recover itself economically is another thing. How tragically true his words turned out to be. We see all around us the present danger of scientific suicide, the possibility that the race may be destroyed by the very magic which we have so highly valued. It is just what some people expected would happen when, in our Western civilization, we put almost exclusive emphasis upon the material order of things and neglected, practically speaking, that spiritual realm of ends and values and moral purposes. We are now threatened with suicidal destruction by science! Yes, that is exactly what we expected to happen.

Again we see all around us a kind of tragic moral disintegration. There again is something which we might have expected to happen. You cannot dislocate the greater part of humanity, separate them from their homes and from all domestic and community responsibility, and subject them to all the techniques of terror and cruelty and brutality, and expect them to go on living with moral sensitiveness and awareness of all the finer realities of life. If there is moral disintegration after a global war, that is exactly what we expected would happen. We might say that all around us we see signs of general disorder, and I think that the younger people in this congregation, if not the older ones, will agree with me that the disorder is widespread and deep-seated. Just exactly what we might have expected to happen, for in 1923 Albert Schweitzer, from the edge of the African jungle, had the eyes to see it and the wits to write this: "It is clear now to everyone that the suicide of civilization is in progress. What yet remains of it is no longer safe. It is still standing, indeed, because it was not exposed to the destructive pressures which overwhelmed the rest, but, like the rest, it is built upon rubble, and the next landslide will very likely carry it away." The "next landslide" is now sliding full speed.

What does this do to our trust in God? For a great many people it tends to weaken it. I submit that in my case it confirms it. For example, if in a cold room you lighted a log fire, you would expect the room to be warm. If you put too many logs on, it might become too hot so that you would have to go outside, and if too many more logs were put on the fire, you might burn down the house. However uncomfortable you might be, such a course of events would never lead you to distrust the physical universe of chemical actions and reactions. But if you lighted a fire in the room and suddenly the temperature went down to zero, you would say in utter bewilderment, What kind of a universe is this where such an unpredictable thing can happen? I say that if we could have gone through this worldwide, colossal destruction of everything that is humanly valuable and dear to us, if we could have gone through it and come out with prosperity, and plenty, and happiness, and goodness, then we would say, What kind of a moral universe is this? What kind of a God can work that way, apparently going back on everything that He has revealed to us about Himself, breaking all His own moral laws? Oh, I for one, when I see these things, terrible as they are, coming out just about as we would expect them to in the light of what we know about God, I am prepared to say, "Though he slay me, yet will I trust in him," trust Him in spite of everything, for in Him there is an integrity that prevails even though to my hurt.

Then again, we point out as a second consideration that things are not always coming out the way we want them to. We do not need to elaborate on that for everyone knows that what we want in life and what we get are two very different matters. We want, for instance, peace and plenty and we seem to be getting strife and starvation in large parts of the world. We all want health and happiness, and a great many of us are getting pain and misery. We all want life and some of us are getting death. Those facts as some people observe them threaten to weaken their trust in God. Is it not true that to contemplate the fact that we do not always get what we want implies that our God has a will of His own? It may not always be our will; thank God that it is not. God has greater purposes than the mere comfort and even the happiness of a single generation of men. If we could only stretch our understanding and imagination of God just enough to glimpse His infinite purpose and some of the concerns that He has on His mind, not only the welfare of the human race but the glory of the furthest star; to appreciate His concern not only with our immediate comfort and happiness but with the total welfare of humanity that He has set before Himself! God has a will of His own, and as we see things coming out, not always as we want them, sometimes it seems to me as though God were saying to us, You cannot have everything you want, willy-nilly. You cannot have a world of peace and plenty, willy-nilly. You cannot have a family life that is good, willy-nilly. We worship the God who is the Creator of the universe and the Governor of it on His own terms, and I for one, if I should see signs that God suddenly became indulgent and said to us, You had a hard time; although you have not paid the price and measured up to the cost, nevertheless I will give you what you want just the same—I should begin to suspect a God like that. But so long as I see a God who has a will of His own, with great purposes that stretch out far beyond my own personal purposes, valuable as they are to me, I can say, "Though he slay me, yet will I trust in him."

Furthermore, there are some things that God has little if anything to do with directly. That is always a dangerous thing to say, especially in the presence of theologians, because it involves the question of the omnipotence of God. We grant that everything that we know ultimately depends upon God. Its existence is derived from Him, and yet there seem to be some things which God has given a life of their own and within certain limits lets them have their own way. For instance, there is a sense in which, of all men, Lincoln was responsible for the Civil War. He accepted it as a policy to bring about what he believed to be right. Yet no one, I think, could claim that Lincoln was personally responsible for every individual heartache and certainly not for the animosities and hatreds that prevailed long after the war was finished. Lincoln was responsible for the whole thing, but there were many details in the war for which he was not directly responsible. I think the same thing is true in some sense about God. He is responsible for everything that happens to us and yet, in His mysterious and loving wisdom, He has given us and other forms of life a share of His creative will, and He lets us go about our way to see what we can make of it. Sometimes we make a mess. We make planes that kill people. God is not responsible for that. We are responsible for the mismanagement of the power that He has given us. We are now in a seething cauldron of postwar hatred, fear, and strife. God is not responsible for that; we are. We have misused some of the precious rights and privileges that He in His generosity gave us and He is saying to us, at this time, You are in a mess, to be sure. Do not hold me responsible for it. You are in it because you thought you knew better than I. I am trusting you to get out of it. A God like that is worthy of our unqualified trust, trust in spite of everything.

Finally, there is nothing that God cannot do something with *in time*. We who have only a fraction of time in which to work out our lives are often understandably impatient. That was impressed upon me two weeks ago today when I stood as I have wanted for years to stand on the rim of the Grand Canyon. What a spectacle of God's creative power that is! He has been at it for six billion years! He has been working with man about six thousand. You may say to yourself, cynically, Well, He has had enough time to do better than He seems to have done. It is not for us to stand in judgment on the Almighty. The fact is that God works

His way slowly and that it is unfair for us to judge the outcome before He is anywhere near through. It would not be fair to judge *Hamlet* at the end of the third act, and neither is it fair for us to put a judgment on the trustworthiness of God when He is just about at the end of the first act of the human drama.

That may not relieve our own private little calamities and catastrophies, but it ought to enlarge us and equip us to face some of the facts of life with new vigor and a new trust. Sometimes in these sophisticated and cynical days we are likely to read with a trace of scorn the hymn of William Cowper. We cannot afford to do it.

> God moves in a mysterious way,
>   His wonders to perform;
> He plants his footsteps in the sea,
>   And rides upon the storm.
>
> Deep in unfathomable mines
>   Of never-failing skill;
> He treasures up his bright designs,
>   And works his sovereign will.

This, as you know, is not entirely a matter of the mind. (No one can rationalize himself into trusting God.) It involves all of a man. The great German theologian whom I quote so often, Baron von Hügel, had a pet dog. When William Temple was last in the United States, he told the story of that dog's end. It came to the time when the dog, after years of faithful companionship with the Baron, was no longer able to get around and the Baron took him to the veterinarian to have him put out of his misery. The Baron told William Temple that as the doctor was about ready to take away his life, the dog looked up at his master with a kind of implicit trust, doubting nothing, fearing nothing. The Baron said, "I knew then what Job meant when he said, 'Though he slay me, yet will I trust in him.'" That is the kind of trust that the Baron had. It is unqualified; it is unshakable; it is a trust in God, no matter what, in spite of everything!

O thou eternal God, whose ways are beyond our understanding, open our eyes to all the facts of life and then give us the heart and the courage to trust in thee in spite of everything so that we can ride the storms, survive the disasters, and find the peace that passeth all understanding. Amen.

The Story of the Iron Gate

T HIS IS A STORY about a gate. Unfortunately, it is not one of the golden gates that leads to paradise. It is an iron gate that leads to a prison. On one side of it were the dark cells of despairing men, and on the other, the enchanted life of the city. There it stood, shut, locked, forever closed, save when someone had a key to open it.

Inside the prison was Peter. Peter was only a fisherman, but he happened to be a follower of Jesus and as such he was an innovator. All innovators get themselves into trouble; Peter got himself into serious trouble and was imprisoned by the order of one no less than Herod. As far as Peter could see, and as far as his friends could see, there was no escape possible. Then, one night something totally unexpected happened. There was a light in the cell as if from nowhere. There seemed to be someone with Peter. He roused him out of his sleep.

"Get dressed," he said, "put on your shoes, wrap your cloak around you." Peter did so, and as he did his chains fell off. Then the strange visitor said, "Follow me," and they went through the halls of the prison, passing one guard after another. Peter may have thought to himself, "Well, they are just lackadaisical, careless guards; we can get by them, but what about the iron gate? How can we ever get past that?" Finally they came to the gate. It was severely, impenetrably closed; yet, when they actually approached it, it opened for them of its own accord! Now this is not a fairy story, but a miracle story, and I hope the difference will appear as the sermon proceeds.

There were at least two influences at work which may have had something to do with the opening of the gate. The first was the prayers of

327

Peter's friends. The story says that "there was a continual stream of prayer going up to God from the church on his behalf"—a continual stream of prayer going up from all the other people who were associated with him in the new resurrection movement. It certainly must have been reassuring to Peter to know that his friends had not forgotten him. There is hardly any other strength so sustaining in time of trouble as that—to know that hosts of people who care about you are lifting you up in their prayers.

But Peter must have said to himself, "It is all very well to have that reassuring strength, but what good can those prayers possibly do me under these particular circumstances?" He might have said, "What chance has a stream of prayer against a prison wall? You might as well match a butterfly with a bulldozer, or expect a zephyr to blow down a skyscraper as to expect a stream of invisible, intangible prayer-thought to have anything to do with, or make any impression upon, a prison wall." And yet, we know that in life spiritual forces are continually mastering material situations.

Take a man's body, for instance. That is just about as material as you can get. There is the body—free, flexible, mobile, expressive—then there creeps into the mind of that body fright. That is a spiritual thing. You cannot see it; you cannot touch it; and as that invisible wave of spiritual fright takes possession of the material body, what happens to it? The body is paralyzed. Even the chemical action of the body changes; the appetite goes, sleep disappears, and the man is good for nothing. On the other hand, suppose that same body is overtaken by faith. That, too, is a spiritual thing. You cannot see it, but it can make its way into a man's body and take control of it; and when that faith controls a man's body, then it begins to be free again, flexible, vital, workable, ready to do the man's bidding; and he goes out in the strength of that spiritual power and overcomes obstacles which hitherto he could not face, let alone surmount.

Think how ideas have often changed man's material world. In 1812 there was a small boy in a French village playing in his father's saddle-shop, and he put out both his eyes when he fell with an awl in his hand. He grew up a blind boy and when he became an adult he wrote to his father, "The blind are the loneliest people in the world. Only books can free the blind. But there are no books for the blind that are worth anything." That idea impressed itself upon his mind and kept working upon him until one time he saw a French army captain with a code of dots and dashes that were raised so that they could be read in the dark. He took his clue from that and in five years he printed a book that the blind could read. He was Louis Braille. The idea that was in his mind that only books could free the blind did free them, and did open their prison door. Here then is another instance in which spiritual forces master material situations.

Why, then, does it seem so strange, I wonder, to us modern people that a stream of prayer coming from sincere, devout people, rising up to God on behalf of someone whom they know to be good and honest and true, why does it seem strange to us that that great spiritual power and force could do something? The longer we live the more we believe from experience that prayer has power; and the more we appreciate what Martin Luther meant when he wrote that he would rather have an army against him than a hundred men and women praying. That is one of the influences that was very probably at work on the iron gate.

The other is the angel of the Lord, for the Bible describes the strange visitor in Peter's cell as an "angel." The Bible is full of angels, but we don't take them very seriously, or think much of them. We use them for decoration and we often speak of them figuratively, but we don't think of them (at least most of us don't) in the very real and literal way which a great many people all through the years, up to the present, have thought of them. As far as I can see, angels as they appear in the Bible are the personification of laws beyond the range of our present understanding. It is as if there were, beyond the horizon of this world in which we live, and the laws and principles of which we know and by which we operate, another infinitely greater world, of which this world is only a small, but exposed area. From time to time that other world breaks in upon this world; when that happens, we see strange and marvelous things. The angels are those who dwell in the margin of mystery by which our life is bounded; and from time to time they come into our world like unearthly visitors and then strange things come to pass.

329

If you want to put it in very earthly terms, think of the fact that for generations everybody believed that any object that was heavier than air was bound to fall to the ground. Gravity decreed its fall. Then the Wright brothers made an airplane that could remain aloft and make its way through the air. They did not violate the law of gravity, but they put into operation another law, the law of aerostatics. When that other law penetrated and modified the law that we already knew, then something unprecedented happened. People in Bible times would have said that an angel visited the earth.

To think of it in more purely personal terms, here is a man who has used up his reserve energy and he knows that he has come to the end of his resources. He is spent; he has overdrawn his account. As he faces a difficult assignment, he shrinks from it because he knows that according to all the laws of his own nature he will not have the strength to meet it. And then, when he gets to it, the strength flows into him. He has the strength, not according to any laws that he knew previously, but according to other laws which have been set in operation. It is as though there were an angel strengthening him.

So, there were these *two* influences at work in the case of the gate that opened of its own accord. Up from the earth came the stream of prayer. Sometimes think of that when you are in trouble; think of that constant stream of vitality rising up as if to touch the skies. And then, from the other direction, from the other world of mystery and power, coming down from above, was an angel of the Lord, like a flash of light. When those two things come together it is no wonder that something unusual happens, and that the gate opens of its own accord.

This is a story with a moral. In fact, there are two morals. The first is that nothing is impossible. That may sound exaggerated to you; it may sound like preacher's rhetoric. I know that if you pressed me logically to certain specific instances here, there, and everywhere, it could not always be proven; but by and large, I say that the moral and the lesson of this story, and one which we need so much to learn, is that nothing is impossible. We live in an unrestricted universe in which spiritual forces can master material situations. They do not always do it, granted. The

330

angel does not always come, and the gates do not always open. We are ready to grant that. But it can happen; *and it is more likely to happen when we believe that it can happen.*

Sometimes we look at the gates that lead to peace—world peace—and we say to ourselves, "They can never open. They are closed—they are closed by the laws by which human beings operate, namely, the law of self-centeredness, greed, aggressiveness, lust for power. Those laws are fixed, they will not change; and the gates to peace can never be opened."

Never say it! Those laws need not be violated, but new laws can be put into action, the law of self-contribution, the law of self-sacrifice, good-will, greater understanding—those, too, are laws of human nature; and they may be put into operation in such a way, as though something came down from above, that the gate to peace will open as if of its own accord.

Sometimes you feel like a hopeless individual. I know you do because some of you tell me that you do. At least, you feel as if you were in a hopeless situation. You look around and you see not one single opening or way out. You feel just as confined as Peter did in his cell, although you have the freedom of the city of Boston, or the whole countryside in which you live. You say to yourself, "I am a hopeless case. I know the laws that operate in my case, and I know that they cannot be changed. This is my fate and I will grit my teeth and bear it."

Never say it! There are no hopeless cases for no one knows when, without violating any of the laws that are operating now in your situation, some new law may be brought to bear from above that will completely change your situation and release you, liberate you, and set you free. It may be an angel in the shape of a man or a woman. It may be some new idea that gets possession of your mind and displaces the demonic ideas. But whatever it is, the possibility of it is there, and so long as the possibility of it is there, and so long as the possibility of change and improvement, escape, and release is there, never believe that it is hopeless.

As I said before, I am not prepared to say that miracles always happen, and the man who counts on them is bound to be disappointed. Sometimes people get into a jam, and they apparently stay there for a long time and nothing happens. But living in the kind of universe that we do, our task is to keep our minds open to the possibility that anything *may* happen, not counting on a miracle, but ready for it if it should happen; for when the streams of prayer begin to go up, and the flights of angels begin to come down, then you can expect a miracle.

The other moral is this. Nothing is so hard as you think it is going to be. That, I admit, may seem like whistling in the dark, and perhaps it is not true to your experience, but it is to mine. Nothing is so hard as you think it is going to be. We have a way—it is a habit of ours because we are human and have imagination, which is our blessing and sometimes our curse for our peace of mind—we have a way of looking into the future and, as we do, we can see all sorts of obstacles, tremendous hazards, things that we think we never can possibly meet or overcome.

Then we find that when we get there, they are not so bad as we thought. We stand looking at them and, as we do, we dread them. I am willing to confess that I, and I am sure you too, have wasted more energy in dreading the things that were ahead than doing any amount of work that I was called upon to do. As I thought about it, it reminded me of driving an automobile in the old days before all the hills and valleys were smoothed out of the highways. Do you remember as you drove down a steep hill and saw another hill ahead of you, it would look so steep that no car could possibly make it? Then when you got to the hill and began to go up, it didn't seem steep at all. There are burdens like that. As you look at them and weigh them in preparation, they seem so heavy that no human shoulder could ever carry them; but when you pick them up, they are not nearly so heavy as you thought they were going to be.

Think how much time you spend dreading the future. I am frank to say that I have even dreaded going to the dentist and when I got there, I found it not pleasant, but the way was open and the ordeal of no such magnitude as I had foolishly imagined it. I have had personal interviews to look forward to which I knew were going to be unpleasant for me and for the other person, and I have spent hours night and day dreading them. Then when I got there and sat down with the person, I will not say it was easy but the way was open and all I had to do was to go through. When you begin to shoulder the task, in shouldering it the weight is diminished.

So, when we get to these gates that seem to be so impenetrable and so thoroughly closed, they have a strange way of seeming to open of their own accord. Even the gates of death, I have learned, which seem to be so fastly closed and so terrible to anticipate, when you get to them they open as if to welcome a friend and you go through without any fear or any dread.

What I am asking you to do now is to face frankly the fact that there is something in your future that you dread. I wish I knew for my own satisfaction if there is anyone who has nothing in the future that he dreads. It may be disease or old age, embarrassment, failure, disappointment in love. Whatever it is, take that thing out and look at it and then say to yourself, in secret, in the presence of God, "I am never going to dread that again. I am going to do everything I can to prepare to meet it and then I am going to forget it, because I know that when I get there, the gate will open of its own accord." You can never force the gate open; it will not respond to the battering of impatient men. All you can do is to move steadily toward it.

If your mind works at all the way mine does, when you get in a state of panic in your dread of something that you are looking forward to, you might just close your eyes and say this to yourself: "I am going to remember the story about the iron gate." Picture it in your imagination, closed; then walk up to the gate, picturing yourself drawing closer and closer to it, and then, in your mind's eye, you see the gate quietly, slowly, easily open, and you go through.

As the curtain falls on this story of Peter and the gate, we see Peter going down the street after he has been released from prison; he goes just one block, and the angel leaves him. It is as though when we need strength to meet some great emergency in life, the strength comes, and when we go through the gate and are set free once more into the ordinary paths of life, the angel leaves us and lets us go on our own free way. But we go with the reassurance and the remembrance of the time when the going was hard, and the angel of the Lord visited us, and there was a light in the cell, and the gate opened of its own accord!

O most loving Father, who willest us to give thanks for all things, to dread nothing but the loss of thee, and to cast all our care on thee who carest for us, preserve us from faithless fears and worldly anxieties, and grant that no clouds of this mortal life may hide us from the light of that love which is immortal, which thou hast manifested unto us in thy Son Jesus Christ our Lord. Amen.

The Battle against Disease

❧

I AM GOING TO SPEAK to you tonight and on the next two Sundays about three major battles of everyday life. And the first is the battle against disease. From that battle there are no exemptions. Some people are drafted for lifelong struggles against chronic ailments, permanent handicaps, and native disabilities. Others, more fortunate, have occasional engagements with the enemy. All of us sooner or later in some form or other meet the enemy and we had better be prepared for that engagement. Our question is, what part does religion play in the battle against disease?

In answer to this question there are two extreme views. According to the first view, religion plays the whole part in the battle against disease, and the exponents of that view in our time are Christian Scientists, and many others who travel their way. They believe, as nearly as I can discover, that God is good, that disease is evil; therefore God cannot and did not make disease and disease has no part in His universe and hence no reality. *Man* makes disease, they believe, by his imperfect and impure thinking; and *man* can therefore destroy disease by correcting his thinking and purifying his belief. According to this view the doctor has no place at all, for disease is by its nature an invisible, spiritual thing and can be fought only with spiritual weapons.

On the other extreme, there are those who believe that religion plays no part in the battle against disease and my guess is, excepting the Christian Scientists, that most Christians in practice hold that point in view. They may pray when they are sick, and there are exceptional examples of Christians who depend upon spiritual reserves in time of illness, but by and large, you and I, tacitly at any rate, hold the view that religion plays no direct part in the battle against disease.

335

In our pattern of life, the doctor and the minister work, practically speaking, independently of each other. Each has his own sphere of influence. The minister's sphere is the soul of a man and the character that he can build, while the doctor's sphere is the body of a man and the health he can maintain. Those two men work along in parallel lines, often on friendly terms, but by and large their ways do not cross and one does not assume that the other has much to do with his part of a man's care.

There is, however, a third point of view—that which we find so clearly expressed in the New Testament that I wonder it has not been more of an embarrassment to us who have acted, at least, on the theory that religion plays no part in the battle against disease. That point of view is never expressed in a theoretical way because Jesus was not a theorizing person. It is expressed in action. Let me recall four facts describing the action of Jesus and you decide for yourself what his point of view was on this particular subject.

The first fact is that Jesus indisputably made sick people well. "And when the sun was setting, all they that had any sick brought them unto him; and he laid his hands on every one of them, and healed them." Second, he often made people *well* before he made them *good*. That, I think, is something of a shock to us with our moral emphasis upon all of life. "And whithersoever he entered, into villages, or cities, or country, they laid the sick in the streets, and as many as touched him were made whole." And that happened, apparently, even before he had had a chance to preach to them about the moral demands of God. Third, when he gave his credentials to those who came from John the Baptist to ask if he were the Messiah or not, notice the order in which he listed them. "The blind receive their sight, the lame walk, the lepers are cleansed, the deaf hear, and the poor have the Gospel preached unto them." Finally, when he sent out his disciples, he gave them orders to do the selfsame thing. According to Luke he sent them forth with this charge, "And he sent them out to preach the Kingdom of God, *and to heal the sick.*"

It is difficult to get around those facts, and if we put any confidence at all in the picture of Jesus as it comes from the Synoptic Gospels, it is the picture of a man who made his first impression upon the people of his own time as one who could and did make sick people well. He did not proceed, mark you, to theorize about it or philosophize about the nature of reality. He did not say that disease is unreal, or that it is always curable. *He did not cure everyone.* He accepted it as a fact and brought to bear upon the battle against the enemy all the spiritual energy that he could muster from the hand of Almighty God.

Current experience and practice confirms the New Testament point of view. The things that I shall say to elaborate this claim you all know. The difficult thing for a great many of us is to *know* something intellectually and also to *feel* it so that we can appropriate it to ourselves and apply it to our needs. One of the first things that current experience has discovered and developed is this: *man is all of a piece, not a collection of parts.* One of the results of our analytical study of man is that we have divided him into three parts, body, mind, and spirit. That is an accurate and useful analysis. But in these last analytical, scientific years we have often treated man as though he moved along in three parallel lines, body, mind, and spirit, rather than in mesh, as a unit; not a collection of parts, but as a trinity in unity.

It is hard to believe that we went so far off the track for the simplest experience shows us that these three parts of our nature are all tied up together. For instance, when you have a splitting headache, that is when your body suffers, you are not likely to think clearly, for it affects your mind. And when you are bearing a severe sinus pain, your disposition may not be as sweet as it would be otherwise, for your spirit is affected by your body. Likewise, you know as well as I do that when your mind is harassed by grave doubts, when you have to make decisions that are difficult, your body soon shows the strain and you complain to your family that you cannot sleep. Above all, when your spirit suffers, your body suffers. We all know the simple facts. When you are nervous your knees shake, an example of a spiritual disorder with a physical consequence. Likewise, when you are filled with anxiety, your mouth is dry. When you are enraged, your face is red. When you lose heart about life, you are likely to lose your appetite. And a pimple can be a sign of an upset conscience as well as of an upset stomach. In other words, man's tormented body is more than once a sign of his twisted spirit. For man

337

is a trinity of interrelated parts, body, mind, and spirit, these three. That is the first thing that current medical practice has confirmed.

But the greatest of these is spirit. The spirit has the upper hand in this trinity of parts. We have not always believed that. Most of us doubt it now when we come to a difficult place .We believe instinctively that we are defined and confined by our physical equipment; that we can go no further than our bodies will allow us; that in the long run, our bodies have the last word. None of the facts of life confirm that. Rather all experience of everyday life confirms the insight that in the long run, allowing the body its sphere of influence, a man's spirit has the upper hand, for the greatest of these is spirit.

For example, one of the classic stories that has been told over and over again to illustrate the power of spirit over body is the story of a boy who was being chased by a ferocious animal and in his fear, he scaled a fence which he not only had never been able to scale before but which even as a grown man he could never again scale. For the spiritual dynamics that were potential in him, once stirred, enhanced his physical equipment, and the spirit it was that had the upper hand.

We do not have to turn to people in books to find confirmations of this fact. How many of you have been called upon to exertions which seemed to you incredible and in anticipation you had asked yourself, Can I do it? you would have said, I cannot. And yet through those long periods of stress and strain, caring for someone whom you love through a long illness, the reserves of your physical equipment seem to be reinforced and replenished indefinitely, and in that emergency you know that your spirit has the upper hand. One of the illustrations that is classic is from the life of Clarence Day. He died in 1935. He was a cripple with arthritis the larger part of his life. He was on a bed of pain and from that bed he made the whole nation laugh. *Life with Father* was from that bed of pain produced.

> The foe that crippled his frame,
> That sought to stifle the flame,
> Itself was trapped in the frame,
> Singed by the flame—
> Stopped, surprised by a spirit

Which having no call to fear it
Counterattacked, pursued
With weapons shrewd—
Humor and fortitude.

Man, indeed, is a trinity—body, mind, and spirit, *but the greatest of these is spirit.*

The spirit, we go on to say in confirming what the New Testament so amazingly affirmed by insight twenty centuries ago, the spirit is like a river, not a reservoir. The spirit, that is the invisible, instinctive, emotional drives that compose your spirit and mine, when you think of that spirit, do you think of something that can be contained in a receptacle? Or do you more correctly think of it as something that flows through you as through a channel? It makes all the difference in the world, for if it is like a river, then like a river it must flow. When it ceases to flow, it becomes stagnant and when it becomes stagnant, it becomes poisoned. The spiritual life of a man, his instinctive, emotional drives that are the sources of his energy, are like a stream; they must flow. They cannot be contained; they can only be transmitted as through a channel. Therefore, as with a river, it must be open and flowing. If a river is blocked at the mouth it becomes stagnant; if it is blocked at the source, it soon dries up.

One of the reasons why you and I are as sick as we are many times is that we are blocked either at the mouth or the source. Some of us at times are blocked at the mouth, and instead of expending the energy that comes from God upon our fellowmen and letting this stream flow through us in self-forgetfulness, in a kind of self-abandon, so that the energy is moving all the time, we hold back our energies for fear that if we spend them fully, we will lose them. Our lives are dammed up and we are obsessed with ourselves, preoccupied with our own needs, and then we wonder why our bodies flag and are fatigued; we are fatigued not because we are exhausted but because we are stagnant! No one can have real health and at the same time have no interest outside himself.

Other people are blocked more seriously at the source. They do not really trust God. Nobody—and I am prepared to submit this as a proposition upon which you can experiment—nobody can be vigorously and vitally well physically who does not trust God. I do not care in what language you trust Him, or according to what rite or ceremony. By trusting Him I mean things like this: a man who trusts God does not fear the past once it is done, no matter how black it may be; he is not preoccupied with his own health and he can say to God, I am here to do thy will, sick or well, dead or alive; it makes not much difference what happens to me in the doing of it. He is able to say to himself, God will keep me through everything, not protecting me from all the strains and trials of life, not insuring me against all disaster and pain, for life is not like that, and the God of things as they are is not that kind of a God. But God will keep me; He will never let me go, just as my family keeps me always in their care, no matter where I am, and so long as I know that my God will keep me in sickness and in health, I know that I can go through all things and that I can master the enemy. There is nothing that can happen to me that I am afraid of.

Now when a man's life is open that way so that the spiritual energies can flow through it, then as the poisons that flow into a river do not corrupt it but are carried off in that great moving stream until they are washed out into the purities of the infinite sea, so the disease that threatens us every moment is overcome by the vitality and power of our lives. I am not promising you perfect health if you trust in God. What I, as a minister of religion, am promising you is this: that with that confidence in the eternal Source of Life, that openness toward Him which eliminates fear and frenzy, breaks through the barriers of distrust and doubt, and sets life in motion, you will have at your disposal His energy and His weapons and all the purity that comes from life to meet the enemy and to triumph over it.

If these things are true, what then is our course of action? I shall briefly set down three specific items. The first item in the course of action is this: Prevent sickness by preserving a healthy mind and spirit by daily associating with the power and the vitality of God. It is a poor policy to wait until we get sick and then pray violently that God will make us well. What we need to do is to relate our lives every day to Him who is the source of all life so that from day to day we grow in confidence, not cocksureness, but quiet and simple confidence that God will keep us. That is a daily procedure and it cannot be done at the last minute.

The second item is this: In case of sickness consult not only a doctor but a physician of the soul. Most ministers nowadays are trained in their seminaries to know something about the maladies that lurk in these treacherous, instinctive, impulsive emotions of man's nature and most of them can be a help to people who consult them personally. It cannot be done in congregations.

Finally, the last item in our prescription is this: When sickness cannot be prevented, and it cannot always, *accept* it as the raw material with which to build and set about under those conditions to do God's will. It always seems to me that the sign of a man's spiritual maturity is this, when he can take that which is his infirmity and say with St. Paul, "If I must glory I will glory in the things that concern mine infirmities," believing that even in those infirmities he will be able to do the will of God and show forth his glory. When Stephen Phillips was in such a position and had not been able to prevent soul-sickness, he wrote this, and I have said it many a time myself:

> Sustain me in that hour with thy left hand,
> And aid me, when I cease to soar, to stand!
> Make me thy athlete even in my bed,
> Thy girded runner though the course be sped.

This, then is the first major battle of everyday life, the battle against disease.

Loosen our spirits, O Lord, that our bodies may have the perfect liberty of health. Amen.

The Battle against Unhappiness

༜

THE SECOND MAJOR BATTLE of everyday life is the battle against unhappiness. Everybody wants to be happy; yet, how few there are who are really happy. It seems as though Henry Thoreau was exaggerating the facts when he wrote that the mass of men lead lives of "quiet desperation." And yet, a French Gallup poll taken on this question of happiness reveals the fact that of the people who answered the question forty-four percent said that they were moderately happy; forty percent, not very happy; eight percent, happy; and the other eight percent did not know whether they were or not. Eight out of a hundred happy! This, therefore, is a battle in which, like the battle against disease, we are all engaged. And this sermon stands against the background of two convictions; first, that happiness is not entirely a matter of disposition and temperament; it can be cultivated and won. Second, real happiness, that is, pure joy, and real Christianity go hand in hand, and we can even go further and say that you never have real Christianity without happiness.

Consider first two classic strategies that have been used over and over again in this battle against unhappiness. The first one is the strategy of *detachment*. It is a strategy of withdrawal, denial. It is quite obviously a strategy of defense. It is an attempt to eliminate from a man's life those things which might be the cause of unhappiness. It is a strategy as old as the hills.

Three hundred years before Christ a Greek philosopher named Pyrrho rebuked the terror of the passengers in a storm at sea by pointing to a little pig that kept on feeding throughout the commotion. "Such," he said, "ought to be the tranquility of the wise man." His gospel was the gospel of imperturbability achieved by reducing life to its lowest terms, and when the American philosopher Paul Elmer More commented on the story of the pig, he said, "There is an example of an affirmation, an affirmation of the *sty*."

Three hundred and fifty years later Epictetus was more explicit in the counsel that he gave. "When you fondle your wife or your child," he said, "say to yourself that you are fondling just a human being; so that, should they die, it will not affect you." It is the strategy of detachment. Do not become too involved in human emotions and then when those whom you love are taken away, you will be left in all the serenity of your imperturbability.

Perhaps you think that that is not characteristic of people in our own time. Listen to this, that one of the characters in Somerset Maugham's *Christmas Holiday* said to another character whom he claimed to think more of than anybody else in the world. "You are," he said, "the only person I have ever cared for in the world. I shall not rest until I know in my bones that if it were necessary to put you against a wall and shoot you with my own hands, I could do it without a moment's hesitation and without a moment's regret." That is the strategy of detachment applied to the battle against unhappiness.

We see many other expressions of it in our own time. A man, for instance, who has loved deeply and been hurt greatly by the one whom he loved says, "I have been burned once, but it will not happen again," and he proceeds to encase himself in a coat of mail lest his emotions ever again be tricked into that treachery. Or, a man has thrown in his lot with a great political cause and after he has spent everything in that cause, the party turns against him and betrays him. He says, "I have been hurt once but never again," and withdraws from active political life. It is expressed in the advice that the fond parent gives to the child who is desperately longing for something way beyond him and the parent says, "Don't set your heart upon it." Another person who is giving advice says, "Don't expect too much and you will never be disappointed." It is, in other words, a strategy of reducing life to its lowest terms and achieving a kind of absence of pain and daring to call it happiness.

The other classic strategy, at the opposite extreme, we might call the strategy of *attachment*. It is the strategy of attack, of annexation to our lives of the things which we believe we need to make us happy (and we certainly ought to admit the fact that there are things in life that it is hard to be happy without). Bertrand Russell has made a list of four things that a man needs in his life in order to be happy. Most of us, I think, would subscribe to that list. The first one is this, health and a certain amount of economic security. Most of us would find it hard to be happy if we should be stricken with paralysis tonight so that tomorrow and the day after we could not go about our way, and I know that I would find it difficult to be happy if I looked forward to a winter in which there was no fuel in the cellar, no heat in the house, and inadequate food in the cupboard. We need, in other words, the minimum of health and economic security.

The second thing that a man needs is work that is worth doing. A man must earn a living, but he must do something more than that for one of his characteristics is that he is made by God to share in God's creative enterprise, and no one is happy, basically happy, unless he is doing something that he recognizes is worth doing and that gives him an opportunity to express something at least of his own native talent and genius.

The third requirement is this, people to live with and love. Some of us like to have periods of solitude and seclusion, but most of us would find it hard to be happy without people around us whom we love and above all, a family that loves us. And fourth, Bertrand Russell lists interests that are worth cultivating, that is, a breadth of interest which gives a man a delight in many things. I remember that Emerson once said, "I like a man who likes to see a fine barn as well as a good tragedy." These four, then, we might say are the basic things, the necessities, that a man sets out to attach to himself in order to be happy.

But all those things are here today and gone tomorrow. Health is not constant; it flares up with all of its vibrant exuberance, and then fades into the ill health and weakness of old age. Money, wealth, security, comfort evaporate like the morning dew. People we love come and disappear in the twilight. And the interests that we delight in begin to shrink as we grow older. That makes us wonder about this strategy for happiness and we wonder even more when we go on to note the fact that there are some people who have all those things and yet are miserable, and others who have practically none of those things and yet about their lives there is a wondrous kind of radiance. So, while happiness is not entirely independent of external circumstances, and let none of us become so sentimental that we talk about happiness entirely in terms of our inner attitude, nevertheless, the secret of happiness, real happiness, is certainly not to be found in any of these stage properties of life.

There is, therefore, a *third* strategy suggested by the word that I have used a great many times to suggest other things, the word *commitment*. A commitment is a response to a recognized claim. You see at once the contrast between this strategy and the other two. In contrast with detachment this is positive, not negative, and in contrast with attachment, it is not possessive, but its desire is to be possessed by something good or someone great. The person who goes out to attach things to himself finds the center of gravity right here in himself, whereas the person who goes out to make a great commitment finds the center of gravity out there, toward which he is drawn by some irresistible power greater than himself, and it is that way that real happiness lies.

Let us take an example from a familiar situation in life in the realm of human relationships, and that, I think, is the realm in which most unhappiness grows. Imagine, if you can, three mothers. Each one has a son and each son marries a wife so that the mother becomes a mother-in-law. What we say of this personal situation is true of all human relations but perhaps it is more intense in this particular one. The first mother-in-law says to herself something like this: They will have to lead their own life and I will lead mine. My son has left me and my home, my care and my responsibility, and taken a wife and his own way of life. That is perfectly right. He should. I will go my way and they will go their way and we will never come into conflict. I will keep at a safe distance from my daughter-in-law and there will be no trouble. That is the strategy of detachment.

The second mother-in-law says, My son has not left me; he has brought to me another child and I will put my arms about her and include them both in my embrace. They will come to live with me, they will fill my life in my old age, they will make the pattern of life beautiful for me as I travel down the twilight path. They will live my way and think my thoughts and when they have children, their children will grow up in the pattern and tradition of their grandfather and their grandmother. That is the fatal strategy of attachment. In other words, it is the strategy of absorption. Ultimately, it leads to strangulation. It is my personal opinion that more lives are wrecked by parents who adopt this fatal strategy than by almost any other single cause.

The third mother-in-law says, Here is a new family beginning. They will go their way and develop along their own lines. I know that I can never have all of them. (I wish that we could realize that we can never have all of anyone.) I never can have all of their life. I don't expect them to spend all their time with me, or to do everything the way I have done it. I will not be hurt when they prefer the company of their contemporaries to mine; that is as it should be. Their life must go its own way and develop according to its own bent. Their life cannot be the way my life is, but I recognize their claim upon my affection, my care, and my love and I stand here committed to that family. Everything that I have is theirs if they want it, and if they don't want it, all that I am in love and affection is theirs. That is the strategy of commitment.

Perhaps we cannot see that particular strategy at its best unless we see it at its highest level in a person like Paul the Apostle. Paul ought to be an encouragement to some of you whose dispositions do not slope toward the southern exposure, for Paul was not a man with a sunny disposition. If his letters show us anything of what he was like in his early days, he was a man whose disposition might almost be described as sour. He had a great many fears, he was tied up in knots inside, he had a supersensitive conscience which gave him the sense of guilt that was sometimes unbearable. He was a fanatic; he persecuted and tried to kill Christians; and you can be sure that wherever you find a fanatic you have found a very unhappy person.

Paul did not try the way of detachment for that was entirely foreign to him; but he did try the strategy of attachment. He went at religion, he ate it up, so to speak, he tried to annex all the powers and the techniques, the rewards and the privileges of religion to himself by observing every last rule and regulation and law. And the harder he tried the more unhappy he was. It was like a tapeworm. The more religion he had, the more he wanted it. The more he tried to be good, the more conscious he was of falling short of the goal, and it was not until on one momentous day of his life that he made a commitment, a kind of in-trustment, a heroic surrender to a God whom he saw expressed visibly in Christ, that he found the way of happiness.

It was after that, that he could write a letter from prison to his friends in which the word that occurs most frequently is the word *rejoice*. And it was in that letter that he said this, which is the text of this sermon, "I have learned in whatever state I am to be content. I know how to be abased, and I know how to abound; in any and all circumstances I have learned the secret of facing plenty and hunger, abundance and want."

Let me put this in a parable. Suppose three passengers go aboard an ocean liner for a long cruise at sea. One of them, as he goes aboard makes a solemn promise to himself not to get involved in the life of the ship or the people on it. He has his meals sent to his room, he never takes a chair on deck. He walks on the deck but he walks rapidly and never stops to talk with anyone. His strategy is to keep himself free from all involvements. His one aim is to get where he is going with as little dis-turbance en route as possible. When a storm comes, at least there is no-body to bother him and nobody to tell him that he ought to be up and doing when he feels like doing exactly the reverse. He has a kind of happiness aboard ship.

The second man goes aboard with the intention of attaching the life of the ship to himself. He may want to attach a prospective mate, or he may be looking for "lions" which he can attach to himself, great names, famous people. He is anxious to meet the captain. He wants to bring to himself, to bend to himself, everything that is going on aboard the ship. Then when the storm comes and prevents him from making those at-tachments, he is full of resentment, unhappy, and miserable. His cruise is a complete failure.

The third man goes aboard with something like this in his mind: I am committing myself to the life of this ship. Everything that goes on I am interested in, all the variegated details of the ship's life; I am committed to that. Without trying to he gets to know the captain. The captain at night takes him up on the bridge and shows him all the silent majesty of the stars. And then, one day he takes him down into the boiler room and shows him the dynamics of the ship. He learns to trust the captain. He knows how his mind works and how much he cares for the ship, how good his judgment is, and how good a navigator he is. When the storm comes, he is not discouraged or resentful because he has committed himself to the life of the ship, and this is one of the major factors in the life of any ship—a storm at sea. He does not enjoy it, but he does not shrink from it in resentment. Neither is he afraid of it, because he trusts the captain and he knows that no matter how great the tempest may be the captain knows what he is doing and he will guide the ship into safe harbor.

Which of these three is happy? I leave that question with you, making only this comment. It seems to me that a Christian is a person who in this life of tragedy and triumph, with its mingled pain and pleasure, says, I commit myself to the life of the world, all of it, good and bad, light and shade, joy and grief. He can say with Paul the Apostle, "I have learned, whether at sea or on land, in storm or in sunshine, to be content. I know how to be abased and how to abound." In the battle against unhappiness, he is well on his way toward victory.

Send us into life, O God, with our banners flying and our arms outreaching with eagerness to all things that are good and great; grant that we may never be discouraged and never be afraid, knowing that thou art Captain of our ship and the Master of our souls; through Jesus Christ, our Lord. Amen.

The Battle against Sin

፠

T<small>HE THIRD AND LAST</small> major battle of everyday life is the battle against sin. In three specific ways the battle against sin is different from the other two battles against disease and against unhappiness. First, the issue in this battle is far greater. Important as it is to have men healthy and happy, how much more important it is that they be good, for healthy men and happy men who are evil can be beasts, and beasts can destroy the world. Second, it is different in that the ranks are smaller. Everybody fights for health and everybody fights for happiness, but not everyone fights for holiness. And the third, the battle against sin, unlike the other two, is almost always fought on foreign soil. When it comes to fighting for health and happiness, it is our own that we are fighting for, but when it comes to fighting for holiness it is usually someone else's holiness that we are fighting for. It is much easier to fight against sin in city politicians than it is to fight against sin in yourself.

The purpose, therefore, of this sermon is to spur you on to new efforts in this battle against sin with the understanding that the battle be fought on your own home ground. When we ourselves have made some steps toward growth in the good life, then perhaps we shall be in a position to make the mayors, the governors, and the leaders of the nation good.

Before we proceed we must make it clear what we mean by sin. It is a comment, I suppose, on the atmosphere of our time, that the word *sin* is by no means clear to many people, and we can say at the beginning that we do not mean by it what most of you think we mean by it. By sin we do not mean a series of taboos that are arbitrarily imposed upon us by an autocratic God who sits severely above us like a policeman with a big stick. We do not mean a series of restrictions and restraints imposed as upon little children by a parent who has no understanding of the child's life and whose restrictions and restraints the child has outgrown. We mean, rather, by sin what Paul the Apostle meant when he wrote his letter to the Romans. When he spoke of sin he used a Greek word which meant simply "to miss the mark." That is a non-theological definition, and is plain and simple. When St. Paul talked about sin (and you know he talked about it more than anyone else in the New Testament) he meant nearly always this: that to sin is to miss the mark. If we put it in our American slang (which I always hesitate to do but I have an idea that a little clean slang once in a while may do a sermon some good) we would say that to sin is "to miss the bus," and everybody knows what that means. (There is more to sin than this, but this is a good place to begin.)

The only time I ever saw Dick Shephard, that incredible vicar of St. Martin-in-the-Fields in London, I drove him from Grace Church to his hotel in uptown New York, and I can remember the anguish written across his face when he described the condition of the church in England in that postwar period, and he said to me, "You know, we've missed the bus." I knew exactly what he meant. If that is what sin means, then it includes us all and the battle is on. We have all missed the mark. Over and over again we have missed the mark in our personal relationships; in our families there has been friction where there ought to have been faith and confidence; there has been jealousy where there ought to have been trust; there has been misunderstanding and sometimes slander when there ought to have been sympathy. We have missed the mark in our own personal lives. We had potential possibilities of grandeur and over and over again we have thrown them away as though they were waste material.

There is an uneasiness and we know what one of the characters in Gene Fowler's novels meant when he cried out, "I'm a blunderer, Racey, forever stubbing my toes on the stairway to the stars." So we are ready to pick up that line in St. Paul's letter and take it for our own as a kind of springboard for this sermon on the battle against sin, "For all have missed the mark, and come short of the glory of God."

That definition implies that there is something to aim at. You cannot miss a mark unless there is a mark to miss. And before we go any further, we should make it perfectly clear what that mark is. Perhaps an illustration will help us. The musician, when he sits down to play a major work by one of the great composers, has something to aim at. Obviously, the first thing that he aims at is to play the right notes. He also aims at experiencing in himself a certain amount of pleasure that can come in no other way than in performing great music. But if he aims at nothing more than that he completely misses the point of the music. The intelligent pianist, when he sits down to perform the music of a great composer, aims above all at catching and interpreting the intention of the composer. He is not thinking about what *he* wants to play. His first desire is to understand what the composer means to be played. That does not submerge his personality; that is where the mystery lies, for the more completely the pianist surrenders himself to the will of the composer the more completely his own personality is expressed and realized. If a man can succeed in doing that, even though he may miss a few notes, he is spared by the critic because it is recognized that he has understood the intention of the composer, and has been faithful to that.

In this strange life that we live it is our faith and belief as Christians that God is the composer; we are the performers. We do not always act that way. We often act as though we were the composers and that what we wanted is what we expect to do and what we aim at. But if God is the composer, we have something to aim at. To be sure, like the musician who aims at playing the right notes, we have to live twenty-four hours a day; we have to aim at raising a family; we have to aim at making a living; but if we aim at nothing more than that we know that we will miss the mark. The Christian aim is to respond to the intention of God, for himself and for the whole of creation, so that when he sets upon any enterprise, big or small, his aim is to do what the Lord God wants him to do. He tries to work his daily life into the wondrously woven pattern of creation, and together with all others who are doing the will of the Most High produce something that is beautiful and good.

What, then, is the intention of God? You will never find it written in a book, and many people fall into a pitfall because they look in a book to find the will of God. If you are a parent, could you ever express your will for your children in a book of rules? You could not, because the rules would be different under different circumstances. Your will might one day be that your child *not* go in swimming; the water is too cold, too dangerous. But if his younger brother or sister were drowning, your will would be that he plunge in and attempt to rescue him. You cannot put a personal will in a book of rules because it is flexible; it is alive.

We are more likely to find the intention of God written in code in the events of history. Certainly, it seems to me that a man would be blind if he could look at current events in our time and not see the will of God made so clear that it is God's intention that we do away with might and power and all the destructive weapons that are slaughtering this human creation of his and live together in one world. That is pretty clear. Also the will of God, his intention, is reflected by our own conscience. We have that capacity within us; it is the department of our mind that makes moral judgments; it is like a shell that we pick up on the beach in which we catch the distant sound of the sea. So the conscience is that capacity in us which catches the distant, perhaps, yet eternally real values and standards of the moral kingdom of which God is the King.

But, of course, the intention of God for us is most explicit as it is acted out by Jesus. Jesus, one like us in many ways, made such a delicate and accurate response to the will of God that as we watch him respond to God's intention it is as though the will of God came right through him; and to see him, see how he behaved, and the decisions that he made, the things that he did and said, it is as though we were seeing acted out before us the intention of God; namely, that we live as His sons, that we trust Him as children trust their father, and that we treat other human beings as members of the same household. It sounds so simple when we say it, and yet we know how difficult it is and how many times we miss the mark.

If the mark is as clear as that, we say to ourselves, why do we miss it so many times? Why do you think you miss it so many times? As far as I can see there are only two reasons why people ever miss a mark, and the first is that they do not aim at it. You never hit a mark unless you aim at it. You may not hit it then, but you certainly will not hit it if you never aim in its direction. I am afraid some people do not aim at this mark because they assume in the beginning that they can never hit it anyway and so they set it aside in favor of something else. That kind of discouragement certainly is unworthy of us. You and I will never achieve the moral stature of our Lord Jesus Christ, but we move toward it with diligence so that we may somehow or other approach more closely to it. It is only a coward who ceases to aim at the goal set in Christ because he thinks that he will never hit it.

Some, of course, do not aim at it because they have never seen it. They look at it Sunday after Sunday in church perhaps, and it may sound strange to you for me to say it, but there are a great many people in our Christian churches who go through all the forms and the motions and have never yet seen the mystery, the beauty, and the power of the intention of God as it is made explicitly real in the heroic life and death of Jesus. They say they believe in love but they trust in force and power; they say they believe in God but they are afraid in the dark; they confirm their faith that they believe in the right of all human beings to exist as children of God but they treat them like dirt under their feet. They have never really seen the goal; hence they never aim at it; hence they never hit it.

Others, of course, have seen something else that they like better; other goals and ambitions and aims which have charmed them and they have never attempted to shoot at the goal we are setting before ourselves because they have been lured toward others that charmed them more.

The other reason why a great many of us do not hit the mark more often is that we do not aim accurately. Some of us, you know, when we are aiming a gun or a bow and arrow, find that we shake a little, or that our vision is not quite accurate. So, as we try to aim at this mark that Christ has set before us, there are many things that disturb the accuracy of our aim. First of all, we have inherited the failures of our ancestors. They are in our blood. That is what the church calls, in language that some people do not understand, original sin. We inherit all the blunders of our forefathers. We carry somehow in our bloodstream and in our bones all their failures to hit the mark. And then, of course, we are disturbed by social conditions. We live in a secular world in which people are not thinking much about the values and realities of the spirit and throw us off when we try to take our aim. Ask any parent how easy it is to bring up children today within the great traditions of our spiritual heritage when the other children around them are spending most of their time at the movies or beside a TV set.

Also, we have personal weaknesses within us which deflect us from the goal and the aim which we are trying to hit. Children who are stupid in school and seem to be indifferent in their work are examined by a doctor and many times it is discovered that the reason they seem to be stupid is the fact that their eyesight is defective and they are reading backward instead of forward. One of the reasons why so many people today miss the mark is that there are disturbances inside them which must be corrected before we can expect them to do anything in this Christian way of life. Most alcoholics, for instance, are not moral failures; they are physical failures, and it is not until we make allowance for those conditions that we will make any intelligent approach to this whole question of the battle against sin. A thief is likely to be compensating for something he missed in childhood, and a braggart is making up for some secret shortcoming. I have always liked the line of Baron von Hügel when he said that men are not primarily wicked, but primarily weak.

Those two reasons, then, account for the fact that we miss the mark so many times. Let me repeat them and direct them at you. We miss the mark because we are not aiming at it—are you? And because we do not aim accurately—how accurate is your aim?

We want, of course, before we leave this subject of the battle against sin to say something about how we can take a better aim, what we can do to come somewhere nearer the mark. I cannot presume to give you any cut-and-dried prescription. I do know this, though, that when you want to hit a golf ball you keep your eye on the ball. If, on the other hand, you want to hit a duck on the wing, you keep your eye not on the duck but ahead of it. Sin is like that. If you want to hit sin, don't keep your eye on sin. You have to keep your eye on something ahead of it, something shining, something wonderfully good.

I have said this before, and I say it once more because I think that sometimes personal witness helps more than propositions. When I am dealing with people who are difficult (and I know you will understand what I mean when I say that sometimes some of you are difficult) the only thing that can keep me anywhere near the mark is to ask myself again and again during the interview, How can I let the spirit of Christ speak through me? What would he think of this person? What would he say to this person who belongs to his God? And somehow as that simple technique is practiced day after day after day, you find that while you may never hit the mark squarely, you come perhaps a little closer to it than you have before. Don't try harder—that is fatal. Love harder. Love him more deeply and more realistically; let him speak through you and show his power through you, and then without your realizing it, people will point at you one day and say, Look at him. He hit the mark right on the head. He is on his way toward holiness. In these three battles we have come face to face with three of the by-products, or the fruits, of the Christian religion. They abide—health, happiness, and holiness, these three; but the greatest of these is holiness.

Help us, O God, as we fight against those things which hold us back from the goal. Purify our lives, clarify our thinking, and strengthen our wills, that as we love him who loved us we may grow to be more like him. Amen.

The Importance of Caring

In July 1957, the English people opened and dedicated what they call the House of Citizenship on its beautiful new premises and in its new building near Aylesbury. Lady Mountbatten made the dedicatory address, and in the course of it she said that if she had her choice of human qualities, these are the ones she would choose in order of priority: first, courage; second, loyalty; and third, tolerance.

A commentator in the English periodical *Time and Tide* objected to what Lady Mountbatten gave by way of advice to the young people in the audience. He pointed out quite rightly that all three of these virtues or qualities were secondary in the sense that any gangster might have all three. He might have incredible courage to do things he had no business to do, and inordinate loyalty to the gang who supported him, and he might also have a certain kind of tolerance toward a man who would rather be a monk than a gangster.

He wished that something better than that could have been offered to the young people in the audience, and therefore he raised this interesting question: What would be your choice of the most important virtue? I wish I could ask you and hear your answer. You might begin, if you are middle-aged, with the cardinal virtues which you learned in college: justice, prudence, temperance, fortitude. Or you might be so bold as to put humility first; possibly, chastity.

That is beside the point because we are interested at the moment in the commentator's answer. I confess it rather surprised me, which in itself is a commentary on our age. In answer to his question, he said, "I think I should put kindness first." That does surprise you a little, doesn't it? *Time and Tide* is not a theological or religious periodical, mind you, but a purely secular one, and yet this anonymous commentator protested against courage, loyalty, and tolerance as claiming the first place in a man's life, and suggested kindness in their place, although the same objection could be made to kindness that he made to the other three. A gangster can be kind.

I think I should put kindness first too, but I might like to change the word. *Kindness*, I am afraid, is too mild a word for what probably the commentator as well as I have in mind. You often use it with reference to something a "kindly old man" does, with the implication that he does it because he hasn't anything much more important to do. It means much more than that. *Compassion* is a better word. Even though it is made up of two words that come to us from another language, nevertheless it seems to me to come a little closer to what the writer had in mind and suggest some of the passion that is implied, a feeling with and for other people, a capacity to suffer with and for other people. On the whole, however, I think the much-used, little Anglo-Saxon word *care* is even better.

Care can mean anxiety, and as such, of course, all sane men and women shun it and try to root it out of their lives. But care on its other side, turned around the other way, can mean that deep concern of one person for another person, that amazing composite of a cultivated imagination and an insatiable desire to be part of life and to be of use. It means that capacity in human beings to get outside of themselves and to care about people who do not deserve to be cared about, and to care not only about people but about life because they think it is good, because they can affirm it, because in spite of all its inconsistencies and contradictions, in spite of all the shadows that darken their path, nevertheless they can approach life affirmatively and positively as they care about it and yield themselves to it. Whether it is to music, or sports, or work, or the rocks of their geological surveys, or the stars above them, or the sea around them, whatever it is, they care about it and they care about it deeply.

It can also be used to mean that care that a man has for the things that are beyond the world we live in, the care that a man has for the very Source of his existence, namely, God. Yes, I think that I should put *care* first in my list of so-called virtues.

When I read the article about Lady Mountbatten's address, it started

357

me thinking. I thought to myself that you might almost divide the people of the world, roughly of course, into two groups, those who care and those who don't. I realize that it is dangerous to make any such cut and dried division as that; people are too much of a mixture of things to do that, and there are people who at times would fall on one side and at other times on the other side. But it clarifies the picture for us if we make it with this qualification in mind.

I thought of it when I went once again to see Napoleon's tomb. I cannot tell you why I went. I had seen it before, years ago, and never had any desire to see it again, and Napoleon is not one of my heroes. But I had recently read a short life of Napoleon, and my interest in that strange man who kept Europe in a state of alarm for over twenty years was once again aroused, and I thought I would like to see his tomb again. I went, of course, to the place where thousands of visitors and tourists go every year, to the Chapel in the yard of the Hotel des Invalides, an elaborate, baroque, Renaissance building with a great Italian-style dome, directly under which, in the crypt, is the tomb of the Emperor. The base of the tomb is green granite from the Vosges mountains, the sarcophagus is red quartzite from Finland, and we are told by the best guidebooks that the body of Napoleon I, in the uniform of a Chasseur de la Garde, reposes within, protected by six coffins. I stooped down and looked at the remains of that strange little man, if I may dare to refer to him in that way, surrounded by so much splendor, the possessor of so much ability, some would say genius, and I thought to myself, This is the man who when his army occupied Syria ordered that twelve hundred prisoners of war be shot at once because they were an encumbrance. This is the man who wrote one time to Metternich, "A man like me doesn't care a damn for a million lives." I thought to myself, There is one who did *not* care.

A few weeks later I was in Westminster Abbey. It was on a Sunday after Evensong so that there were not too many tourists moving about in the Abbey and, as I went up the central aisle in the Nave, I stood still to look at something. Then I happened to look down at my feet and, to my amazement and wonderment, I found that I was standing over the remains of David Livingstone. This is what it said on the simple slab in the floor of the main aisle of the Abbey: *David Livingstone 1813–1873. For 30 years his life was spent in an unwearied effort to evangelize native races, to explore the undiscovered secrets, to abolish the desolating slave trade of central Africa.* Then this quotation from Livingstone himself: "All I can add in my solitude is, may heaven's rich blessing come down on every one, American, English, or Turk, who will help to heal this open sore of the world." I thought to myself, There is one who *did* care.

Those who care and those who do not care are not all great, distinguished persons you find in the history books, and they are not by any means all buried. You find them very much alive and almost everywhere. On the highways, for example, there are those who care even at the price of their own inconvenience for other people who are travelling the same highway, for the children who are riding bicycles along the side of the road, and the pedestrians who are bravely trying to cross it. They try to obey the laws that were made to protect other people on the highways. They care. And there are those who do not care. They go as fast as they want to go to get where they want to get. They drive under any conditions that suit them and, when they hit someone, they are just as likely to keep right on driving. One of my friends whose young nephew was killed last summer found to his amazement that the truck driver who hit him and knocked him off the road when he was driving at a very reasonable rate of speed never even stopped.

You find them in business. It is encouraging to me to realize how many people in business today are seriously interested in the welfare of the people who work for them. Employees are no longer at the mercy of employers. The courses that are given every year at the Harvard Business School are a witness to the fact that business people are caring more and more about the conditions under which their people live and work, what their wages are, what kind of schools their children go to, and what opportunities they have for recreation. And there are the people who do not care. They are the "hard-as-nails" variety who are willing to crush their competitors to get what they want, to squeeze the last drop of life out of the people who work for them. They go ahead without any hesitation to do their own will, not caring in the least about what happens to the people they fire.

There are both sorts of people in college. You will find the college student who, when he is appealed to on behalf of some issue, such as the right of a Negro or a Jew to join a fraternity, will respond by saying, "I couldn't care less." And you will also find those who care and care deeply, even at the risk of their reputation among their contemporaries, and sometimes even to the point of being expelled from the school.

These two groups of people you will find in life, those who care and those who don't. Sooner or later, every man and every woman has to decide where he wants to stand, in which group he would like his life to be lived. He knows ahead of time that he will often be divided in himself; nevertheless, he has to make the decision that in the long run he wants to throw his weight on the side of those who care, or on the side of those who don't.

Then I began to ask myself a question. My question was one that you may already be asking. It was this: Are the people who care getting anywhere? That is, if you should decide to live your life as well as you could with the group of people who care, would you have any reason to feel that you were on a winning team and not a losing one? Or, to put it in other words, is the world any better for the effort and work of those who care?

It is hard to say. After all, there are no statistics that we can use to answer such a question as this. The answer people give is bound to be influenced by their own personal experience and temperament. If you had lived in the vicinity of Dachau, you might find it hard to think that the people who cared were getting very far.

Again, something in Paris illustrated to me the difficulty of answering the question, and suggested some of the factors involved. It was the Place de la Concorde. In the center of it, you may remember, is an obelisk seventy-five feet high and three thousand years old, which once stood at the entrance of the Temple of Amon at Luxor in Egypt—a moving thing, when you think of it. More moving was it for me to remember that in the same place in 1793, not so very long ago, stood the scaffold from which swung Louis XVI, King of France, Marie Antoinette, Charlotte Corday, Danton, Robespierre, and many others.

You might say to yourself, See how the wave of compassion is gain-ing ground: 1793, a scaffold; 1957, a straight obelisk raised to the glory of light. Then you remember that in 1944, in the same square, took place the fiercest fighting which took place anywhere in Paris. Scores of people were killed and their names are recorded in a tablet on one of the buildings in the Rue de Rivoli. So you realize that this tide of caring and compassion comes in and goes out, and we can never be complacent about it. We can never preen ourselves and say, "Look at us; we have gone forward so much further than any of our predecessors. We have made a world in which a man's life is safe because we care so much about him." We dare not say that. We know not at what moment violence and cruelty will break out again.

Having said that, my own impression—and it is only my impression —is that there has been a real advance that we can recognize without pride, but with satisfaction. I shall suggest in a few sentences what I mean. I cannot prove it by statistics, but I think that at least in the Western world, which is the only world that I know anything about, a woman has a better chance to live her life fully and completely than she had two thousand years ago. I think that a child, no matter what the social and ecomonic background of his parents may be, has a better chance to be educated and thus fulfill the potentialities of his life than he had five hundred years ago. I think that a sick person in any part of the Western world has a better chance to get well and to be taken care of than he had two hundred years ago. And I think that a plain man without any particular qualifications for life has a better chance for a fair deal now than he had a hundred years ago. And all this is because more people care more about the lives of the people around them. In other words, I feel that we who try to care are on a winning team and that as man moves out of the jungle toward something better, namely, the place in life where he becomes a son of God, his movement is steady and sure. There are retrogressions, but there is advance. In other words, when man grows, he grows in the direction of greater caring.

You may have a question about all this and, coming from all sorts of ecclesiastical backgrounds and traditions as you do, your question may be this: What has all this to do with Christianity? After all, I haven't said a word about the church or the Bible. The word *care*, as a matter of fact, hardly appears in the Bible in the sense in which we have been using it. I have hardly mentioned God, said nothing about Christ, and not even referred to your salvation. What, then, has this to do with Christianity? My answer is that it has everything to do with Christianity. Indeed, this *is* Christianity. Not all of Christianity, to be sure, but it is so large a part of Christianity that I, for one, can say that it is Christianity.

Christians have no monopoly on care, never forget that. But Christians believe that God cares about the world, else He would not have made it, and He cares so much about it that one time He became human to save the world from its folly. That human life was the life of Jesus, and Jesus cared. He talked constantly about care—the father who cared about his wayward son, the shepherd who cared about the lost sheep, the Samaritan who cared about the man who was stripped and left for dead, and the God who cares about His children. He cared himself, especially for the people nobody else cared for, the people who had been left out in life, and he gave only one test to the people who were to follow him, and the test was this, that they care about their fellow men in trouble. He died because he cared so much, and he lives now in the people who care about him.

Christians go so far as to say that God *is* care, and a Christian might be described as a person committed to the importance of caring. St. John, in his first Epistle, put it in the most point-blank way he could. He wrote, "God is love." Baron von Hügel, at the end of his life of Christian devotion, put it even more emphatically, more plainly. He said, "Caring is everything. Nothing matters but caring."

If you have never thought about that before, think about it now. Try to see where you stand in life, whether you are with those who care or with those who don't.

O God, take that buried impulse to care for other people and make it grow until we care more and more about more and more people, so that through us thine own care is made real and thine own arms support those who are falling. Help us, O Lord, to care. Amen.

The Lost Child

LAST NIGHT at the midnight service I gave a brief address and began it by reading the first part of a letter that had come to me the day before from the Bishop of New Hampshire. For a great many years he has written to me on my birthday and in some way not understood by me, knowing the irregularities of the mails, he always manages to get the letter to me on the very day. Only once, I think, was it a day late. This year it didn't come all day and I went out for a birthday dinner with some friends. By the time I got back to the Rectory, I had forgotten about it. It was about quarter to eleven and in the mail slot was a Special Delivery letter. There it was! I shall read the first paragraph which tells, as he usually does in the first part of his letter, an anecdote or an experience from his own life or ministry. This year this is the way it began:

> Years ago—twenty-five at least—I clipped an AP newspaper article about a little child who was lost in one of those vast corn farms in Iowa. Family and friends searched a day and a night and did not find the child. Another day and night the search continued. On the third day one of the searching party said: "Let's join hands." Then a single column of hundreds of people, hand in hand, moved across the field. Later that day they found the child, dead. And a grieving mother said, "Why didn't we join hands sooner?"

Then the Bishop went on, "I retold this story last September in Hartford when I gave an address at the Annual Convention of the North American Conference on Alcoholism and Drugs. I tried to explain the church's mission in these areas of concern. After the address an older man in the audience came to the podium and said very quietly, 'I am a Lutheran minister. I was that family's pastor in Iowa. I searched with the others for 67 hours until at last we joined hands.' Suddenly," the Bishop wrote, "the story became very real, very personal."

Coming just before Christmas it made me think of things that I might not otherwise have thought of, and the first thing was, How many people there are in trouble every Christmas, various kinds of trouble, from trivial annoyance to dark tragedy. In a dramatic way it was revealed in a diary of a young woman in the *New York Times* on Friday. It was her diary for Christmas Day; she began it in 1962. The entry that year was all joy for it was the first Christmas after she was married to a man about to begin medical school, and the day was filled with the happiness of newlyweds. Then, the next Christmas: "So wonderful, our daughter born on Christmas Day." Then in 1964 and '65 came toys and the laughter of a little girl beginning to enjoy the day. Christmas 1966: "We swam on Christmas Day. My husband was doing an internship at Triple Army Hospital in Honolulu. My husband made his rounds that morning in the hospital—so many wounded men. The next month he volunteered for duty in Vietnam." 1967—"Explain to a child on her fourth birthday what 'missing in action' means. She reminds me, 'Daddy said he won't be home when I'm four, but he promised to get back when I get five.' I was carrying our second child. 1968—waiting. 1969, 1970—the beginnings of disillusionment. Public concern ineffective, Congress apathetic. The Sonta raid brought me to a low point. Some troops are being withdrawn, but my husband was not home. His agony was being used to prolong the war.

Finally, she comes to Christmas 1971. "I have been married for ten Christmases. This is the fifth year of separation. The words choke me. Our Christmas child does not make any predictions for her ninth birthday. Withdrawn. Winding-down. Vietnamization. Meaningless phrases. Must have an end to this war. I see no end. I cannot rejoice in the birth of the Son of God. My son has no father. This Christmas Day we celebrate the birth of a son to Mary. This Christmas Day some other mother's son will die in Vietnam. The death takes away all that was taught by Christ's birth."

It is a heart-rending story, all the more so because you know that there are thousands of other people in various ways going through similar things. But as I thought about the Son of Mary I remembered that Mary didn't have too easy a time of it, either. When Jesus was born, *her* son, there wasn't any place for them. They were "little" people being pushed around and they had to take the best they could get. When he was a boy, there was a generation gap. After they got home from Jerusalem, he couldn't understand why they didn't know where to find him: Didn't you know that I would be in my Father's house? Where else would I be? he asked them. "And they understood not the saying which he spake unto them." When he was a young man, he left home. There was a large family to support there. His mother thought at one point that he had lost his wits. And while he was still a young man they hung him on a tree.

It isn't a story of uninterrupted joy and gladness, and it reminds us that Christmas doesn't wipe away all the tears in life. It doesn't suddenly drain off all the trouble in the world. It doesn't take away life's "immemorial pain." Every Christmas there are wars being fought; if not world wars, then local wars; and if not wars on battlefields, wars going on in families, in political factions, in neighborhood feuds. There are always wards filled with the sick and the dying, always homes broken or breaking, always aches and pains that will never be recorded. There will never be a Christmas without the needy, the lonely, and the lost.

What Christmas does is this. It joins us together. We all have, some more than others, a tendency to go off in a corner by ourselves. There are times when we want to be alone, we want to be left alone, we need to be alone. If we are in trouble, we want to shed our own tears in private, nurse our own wounds by ourselves, be bitter if we want to be, be stony-faced against the world. We say to a well-meaning friend, You go your way and I'll go my way. That is part of our nature as an individual. There are times for that.

But you don't get very far alone, ever, not if you cut yourself off from the rest of the family. I mean not only your immediate family but the total human family. When you do that, the only way you are likely to go is *downward*. It is the only way I have ever seen people go when they cut themselves off from the rest of the family, withdraw into their own private world of trouble and pain.

If you haven't been well and you want to get well, you've got to join hands. You can't do it yourself. You join hands with the ones who can help you—a doctor, a nurse, a friend; you join hands with God. If you have lost your husband or your wife and you want to get out of that valley of the shadow of death, not to reject it, but to get out of it so that you can give something to other people, you have to join hands with other people who have been through the same thing, who know what it is all about, who can help you get through it and out into the light. And if you have lost your grip on life, as so many people have now, lost your confidence not only in yourself but in life, in the world, in the system by which we operate and which is getting creaky in so many places—if you have lost that confidence, you have to join hands with others if you want to do anything about it. You don't go into a corner and sulk in private or tear your heart out about it in public protest.

The fact is that at Christmas we begin, at least most people do, to reach out to others and others reach out to us. That is, messages come on cards, telephone calls, people we meet on the street we greet; and we feel a little freer communication between them and us. Even families reach out from one generation to another, children to the older ones in the family, fathers and mothers to the children. And, as you get older you reach backward through your memory to all the Christmases that have gone before. I can't help doing it now. I think of the Christmases thirty years ago in this very same church; how different they were, and yet how much the same. Of course, I'm different too! You are bound to be different as you get older, sometimes for better and sometimes for worse; but you change.

In other words, at a season like this we begin to join hands. We don't get back exactly what we lost, not often. We get something else. We get—at least what I get—is a new perspective on things. I see things from a broader view, a more inclusive one than I had before. We get a new vitality, energy, and at some point along the way we come to the conclusion that life isn't a joyride. When you are young, you are tempted to think it is, because it often is at the beginning. Mine was in many ways. But you come to the conclusion that life is not a joyride. It's a journey, and on that journey there are many rough spots and some smooth places, bright and dark, happy and sad, all kinds of things, and anything can happen, anything. We are not guaranteed protection or insurance against anything that can happen, whether it is physical, moral, economic, or spiritual; whatever it is it can happen, and you know it.

At Christmas we continue the same old journey, but a little better prepared to meet the vicissitudes that are bound to come simply because we have joined hands with a few other people. We have given up the idea that we can go it alone.

Why is this? Is it trumped up? Is it all a pose? Is it a fake? Is it a result of all the artificial sentimentality that is deliberately cultivated by various commercial interests at Christmas? I don't think so. This happens because we remember and give thanks that once upon a time God reached out to us, to this human family, this race to which we belong. He reached out in a Man very much like us, with many of the same trials and tribulations we have, with the same need to go off at times by himself and work it out alone, with the same moments of joy and ecstasy. And what he did when he came was—I have put it in various ways, but I think of it this way now—he reached out to everyone and said, Join hands with me; help me find the lost child.

Now, the lost child may be a grown man or woman who has lost his way, and there are scores of them; we don't need to go far to find them. We know them; we don't always succeed in helping them to find their way. But what I am thinking about more now is that it may be the lost child in you and in me, and in others. There are many things, of course, that a child can well afford to lose as he grows up, things he has to shed. But there are two things that he has when he's a child that he must recapture as an adult—his trust and his wonder. As a child he has them naturally. Then as he grows up he begins to lose that spontaneous trust.

He says, I've seen too much. And the wonder begins to rub off because he says, I've heard it all before. That lost trust and wonder he must find again.

That, I suspect, is what Jesus meant when he said that unless you become like a child you haven't a chance to see the Kingdom of God, to know what it's all about; you have to recover that natural innocence, having been through "the works," and you have to find again that trust and wonder after you have lost it, so that you trust not blindly as a child trusts, but knowingly as an adult trusts, and you wonder not because you know so little, but because you know how much there is you don't know.

We sometimes think we have seen too much. The truth is that we haven't seen enough; we haven't seen the broad sweep of things. Sometimes we see the clouds but not the stars, the pollution but not the purifiers, the warmakers of every description, but not the peacemakers, the wreckers but not the reconcilers.

So you want to find the lost child, that "first fine careless rapture," the excitement that you once had and have lost. Some of you still have it, I know. Every once in a while I lose it and I think that it may be gone for good; but it hasn't because it always comes back when someone else appears on the scene, comes into the picture, and takes me out of myself. You cannot do it by yourself. Not until you join hands will you ever find that lost child; and when you do find him, the child is not dead; he is alive.

Lord, as we meet together to remember and give thanks for the birth of Jesus, and as we remember what he was like when he once moved among men and what his Spirit can do now when he moves in a group of people or even in one of us, help us to be open and ready to receive him so that we may never be lost, never lose that trust and wonder without the possibility of regaining it once we join hands with at least a few other people who are looking for the same child. Amen.

(*This sermon was preached by the Reverend Theodore P. Ferris on the last Christmas Day of his life.*)

DATE DUE